OF THIS OUR COUNTRY

OF THIS OUR COUNTRY

Acclaimed Nigerian writers on the home,
identity and culture they know

THE BOROUGH PRESS

The Borough Press
An imprint of HarperCollins*Publishers* Ltd
1 London Bridge Street
London SE1 9GF

www.harpercollins.co.uk

HarperCollins*Publishers*
1st Floor, Watermarque Building, Ringsend Road
Dublin 4, Ireland

Published by HarperCollins*Publishers* 2021

3

MIX
Paper from
responsible sources
FSC™ C007454

Contents

Introduction   ix

Clarion Calls Ayọ̀bámi Adébáyọ̀   1

Home History Caleb Femi   11

Father's Land Umar Turaki   19

Of Country and Reverie Irenosen Okojie   29

A Brief History of Suya. Inua Ellams   37

Coming to Lagos Helon Habila   49

Still Becoming Chimamanda Ngozi Adichie   61

Elephants and Giraffes Oyinkan Akande   73

Against Enough J K Chukwu   83

Life is a Marketplace Chịkọdịlị Emelụmadụ   93

Rites of Passage Anietie Isong   103

Until We Meet Again Hafsa Zayyan   113

Nostalgia is an Extreme Sport Lola Shoneyin   123

Amaechina Chika Unigwe   133

*One Season, Many Decade*s, Abubakar Adam Ibrahim   145

War and Peace Okey Ndibe   157

A Banner Without Stain Ike Anya   169

Pride and Punishment Chigozie Obioma   183

Contradictions Bolu Babalola   193

Nulli Secundus Nels Abbey   205

Contents

#RepresentationMatters: The Oppressor in the Mirror   219
Yomi Adegoke
Education as Saviour Cheluchi Onyemelukwe   231
Renewal Sefi Atta   243
You Are Not Going Back Abi Daré   255
About the Authors   267
Acknowledgements   273

'If you want to know a country, read its writers.'
—Aminatta Forna, 'Survival instincts', *Guardian, April 24, 2009*

Introduction

In September 2020, while the world was locked inside, people were once again falling into other worlds, through podcasts, through films, through TV, through books. Books in particular became a new haven for those who found themselves lost during the pandemic. In the books they read, they discovered solace and escape among the stories created by different writers and visited different cities, cultures and histories on every page.

As avid readers ourselves, we couldn't help but notice how many of the stories being acquired, published and widely read were written by Nigerians, nor could we deny the exceptional quality of their work. From prizewinners to emerging talent, Nigerian writers were topping charts globally and making an impact not only within the publishing industry, but outside it too.

We realized that storytelling among Nigerians wasn't just a coincidence, but part of a national and cultural inheritance. We knew then that to bring so many of those writers together would be something special, and that in doing so, we – two Nigerian women – could enable readers to explore Nigeria through the memories and experiences of the phenomenal writers it has produced. After narrowing down an extensive list of incredible writers, we recognized that a cohesive collection would need a brief that anchored it to a single concept, while giving each writer the creative freedom to approach it in their own way:

The Brief

Form
- A personal essay

Content
- Reflections on the Nigeria that you know
- A memory or memories you have of Nigeria that is/are significant to you
- How and where you have experienced Nigeria, whether that be in the country itself, or in an aspect of its culture and traditions found elsewhere in the world

This collection – including the cover, also designed by a Nigerian – is a powerful and unforgettable response to that brief, a vital contribution to national conversations, and attests to the centrality of storytellers in any society.

Ore Agbaje-Williams & Nancy Adimora
The Editors, *Of This Our Country*

Clarion Calls

Ayọ̀bámi Adébáyọ̀

I

At one of the four primary schools I attend, I learn to sing the national anthem before I know the words. By the time I enrol in the third one, a Catholic school, I can gauge the interval between the anthem's notes and guide my voice through its rhythms. I sing with a mix of abandon and confidence that I will leave behind in childhood. My renditions are always part of a student body's, so my errors stay nestled in our chorus, unnoticed by anyone who can correct them. What I know in those early years I learn by osmosis, fumbling through gibberish to wrong words until I know the right ones.

Pledging allegiance to the country and singing its anthem is customary in educational institutions across Nigeria. Tertiary institutions often restrict this show of patriotism to formal ceremonies. In primary and secondary schools, though, days begin with routines that include both the anthem and the national pledge. In my Catholic school, we call this the morning assembly. It begins thirty minutes before classes are scheduled to start and is held on the large school lawn. A teacher prays, we sing a hymn, then there's a charge from scripture. Sometimes there is a Bible reading. Always, this part of the day seems guided towards dual climaxes: the anthem and the pledge.

We sing both stanzas of the national anthem if we are on time and settle for just the first if an earlier component of the morning assembly has lasted too long. We recite the pledge with our right palms pressed over our hearts. In all, this daily attempt to inculcate virtue in us before our minds are submitted to knowledge lasts about twenty minutes.

When they were schoolchildren, my parents' participation in this process of interpellation featured other anthems. My father was born five years before Independence and he probably sang 'God Save The Queen' a few times before he had to learn a new song of allegiance. In 1960, when colonial totems were superseded by newly minted national symbols, 'Nigeria We Hail Thee' replaced prayers for a coloniser and for eighteen more years, Nigerians pledged fealty with a song composed by Britons.

The anthem I butcher is the first to have been composed by Nigerians. Eventually, I discover its correct lyrics on the back of a notebook and realize that the third word in the song is 'compatriots'. This clarification comes after I have mastered the anthem's melody and felt transported by several earnest if meaningless moments of unisonance. For a while I'm embarrassed by the knowledge that I spent years bellowing *arise o compassions*, then I come to know that many of my peers did the same and shame recedes, making room for amusement.

Even when I know the right lyrics, I continue to sing the anthem mindlessly. Though the words I now use are correct, they remain opaque to me, revealing nothing of the ideas and imperatives they are meant to conjure. Nigeria, compatriots, and arising to obey a country's call are abstractions to me until the day my father sticks branches in front of his car so he can get me to school.

This incidence happens after the 1993 elections are annulled. I know the annulment is some grave injustice from listening to my parents and their friends rage about it. Clusters of protesters have been gathering in the streets, increasing in number daily. My parents have stocked the pantry with food, matches and salt. When she's not nursing my weeks-old sister, my mother thinks about safe ways to store extra gas cylinders. She reminds my father to replenish the first-aid box. She makes lists of what we might need in an emergency and checks in on her ageing parents. Clouds are gathering but the sky has not darkened yet. Certain the downpour is still days or weeks away, my father ferries me to school as he has always done. On this morning though, our route has been totally blocked. There are old tyres in the middle of the road. Logs of wood and metal drums have been arranged into a makeshift obstacle course. Behind those, the clusters of the last few days have congregated into a crowd that blocks our access.

My father parks the car and goes to look for a tree. Other motorists have done the same, leaving their vehicles to go scout any form of vegetation within sight. In this situation, any branch would do as an olive branch, but some marker of solidarity is required before a vehicle is let through. I watch the protesters through the windshield of my father's blue Santana and have the sense that these people are the ones I have been singing about all this time. These people who have taken over the road are compatriots arising to obey a call I could not quite piece together from listening to my parents' complaints about the military regime. As I watch them wave placards and sing protest songs I have never heard before, I become sure of two things. Not only have these men and women somehow eavesdropped on the angry complaints my parents share with each other and their friends, they understand every word and are going to do something about each discontent.

I am transfixed by the crowd ahead and don't notice how much time passes before my father returns with several branches. He sticks them all in front of the car and begins to drive again, inching the Santana forward until I can see those protesting up close. Suddenly, the national anthem's abstractions have crystallised into something I could touch if I try. They wave my father through when they see I am wearing a school uniform and I am deflated as we leave them behind. It is the first time Nigeria means anything tangible to me, the first time I feel a surge of affection towards this thing I've claimed as mine daily on the school lawn: *I pledge to Nigeria my country* . . . Yet what I imagine to be the full state of being Nigerian is still amorphous. To my primary school self, it becomes something enacted collectively by all those people who are shrinking to dots in the Santana's rear-view mirror.

II

I learn about the National Youth Service Corps from Aunty Y. She comes visiting halfway through her service year, bearing donkwa balls that are better than any I've tasted before, and dried leaves that she boils to make my first cup of zobo. My aunt's travels seem more exciting because I have not been on many journeys since my father died. Our last family trip beyond the south-west had been to Maiduguri, to visit my paternal grandmother who had settled there when my father was a child. My mother is not as adventurous as he was. There have been no recent impromptu trips to waterfalls or beaches.

My aunt shows me pictures as she tells stories about serving Nigeria in Jos. She pulls the photos from an A4 envelope in envy-inducing sequence. Here, she is atop a mountain, arms spread wide as though to embrace the world. There she is mid-march, hands balled into fists, right foot stretched out so. Finally, here she is, decked in the khaki imitation of military fatigues, hair covered with an emblazoned face cap. My imagination is briefly channelled towards a future in which I recreate these images. I do not understand or care about what a service year would entail, but I desperately want my own version of my aunt's cool face cap and jungle boots.

My father's friend, Uncle P, calls me on the day I am to discover where I will serve Nigeria. A decade has passed since Aunty Y's visit, and time has hardened my eagerness about the Youth Service scheme into resentment. I can tell that Uncle P is upset with me because I have not given him the details he needs to influence my posting to a state in the south-west. He believes it is his duty as a good friend to make sure I serve in Lagos; he is sure my father would not have wanted me to spend the service year in a strange city. I do not know what my father would have wanted for me – I will never know, neither will my father. Uncle P uses the present tense when he talks about his friend. I have not found the tense to speak about my father, so I keep quiet and listen.

Later, at my university's division of student affairs, I am surrounded by people from all the faculties on campus. As we wait to receive the call-up letters that will let us know which end of the country we will be heading to within a few days, the chatter around me mirrors my discontent. All of us have spent five years or more in frustration as our graduation dates shifted further into the horizon, out of our reach or control, trapped in endless cycles of strikes and counter-strikes. A year spent ostensibly serving Nigeria sounded like another opportunity to waste our time. It was inescapable though; we could not get jobs or start postgraduate studies without a certificate that proved we had served our country for a year. Singing the national anthem thousands of times before any of us turned 18 has not prevented us from feeling wearied by the university education that has qualified us for national service.

During our first year, lecture halls were so overcrowded, many students could only attend 101 classes if they sat on the floor. The only alternative, if you could not grab a proper seat long before a lecture began, was to stand outside the class with your nose pressed against louvre blades while you balanced your notebook on one hand and took notes with the other. Those of us in the humanities had it better – friends in the sciences routinely spent the night in lecture halls so they could secure a seat for the next day's class. Only a few lecturers made allowances for the difficult circumstances. After a few evaluations we knew papers were graded the same whether you got a seat in the classroom or had to use your knees as a desk while you wrote your test in the sports centre. Some professors believed that all this suffering would make us resilient, even exceptional. They insisted that if we could succeed under terrible circumstances, we would be ready for the 'real world'. This always sounded ominous to me, as though university education was preparation for citizenship in a country that demanded your soul and gave little in return.

My resentment lifts and a measure of excitement is restored when I get my call-up letter. I have been posted to Plateau State. The first three weeks of my service year will be spent at the orientation camp in Bukuru, which is close to Jos. I do not want to stay in the south-west. If I am to participate in a scheme I have no interest in, I might as well see more of the country.

I arrive in Bukuru hours after the orientation camp is open. The camp is a government secondary school that has been modified to serve the National Youth Service Corps' purposes for three weeks. As I settle in, I realize that I have been gravely mistaken. I have assumed that this public school would have similar facilities to the private one I attended. Perhaps Uncle P is right and I don't know what I am doing.

The dormitory that has been set aside for women is a long, unpainted hall. In place of windows, a few gashes in the wall have been covered with transparent tarp. I feel both lucky and miserable when I get a lower bunk close to the gashes. I discover that there is no bathroom, only an outhouse lined with pit latrines. Someone explains that we are expected to shower inside the maggot-ridden space, but after dark, I notice that the women I share the dormitory with are bathing right outside. I join them. When I speak to friends in other camps across the country, only those in Lagos and Nasarawa appear to be in much better situations.

The next day, military officers in the camp enforce attendance at the morning assembly by threatening to burst into our dormitory. The assembly feels like a return to the rituals of primary and secondary school but there are a few key variations. Here we are corpers, not pupils. This assembly begins at 5 a.m. Prayers are rotated between Muslims and Christians and admonitions could be drawn from the Bible or the Quran. We line up according to the platoons we've been sectioned into and military officers patrol the gaps between our lines. There is another anthem we must now memorize: *Youth obey the clarion call . . .* We sing it right after the national anthem.

Orientation takes the form of seminar-like programmes about subjects someone in the Service Corps' bureaucracy has decided we need. Breakfast is usually followed by lectures that stretch until we take the lunch break. The speakers talk to us in what must be the school hall. They come from known and obscure government parastatals. While most stick to telling us about what their agencies do for the country, many are intent on cajoling or scolding us into patriotism. We are made to sing anthems again and again. We are reminded that we're invaluable to Nigeria, although the condition of the space we're being sequestered in makes this less convincing – that officers routinely slap or push corpers makes this hilarious. There are language classes and skill acquisition programmes on offer. If you want, you could learn how to make beads, bake meat pies or braid hair.

7

Within days, I see why my aunts and uncles are nostalgic when they speak about these weeks. I become fast friends with T, who was my classmate throughout university, although we've never really spoken to each other until now. We're in the same platoon but she's more involved in its various activities. She acts in a drama and represents the platoon in a dance competition. I'm there to cheer her on in the evenings when much of the socialising happens as platoons put on shows or engage in competitions. When we are bored, T and I get a drink and pepper soup at the mammy market with other new friends we've made. After a day of following time-tables, the unstructured evenings are languorous and it all begins to feel idyllic, if not fun.

We are warned repeatedly during the morning assembly to stop showering outside. No one takes this seriously. I'm nauseous when I consider what the camp commandant suggests, using the designated area meant bathing while maggots crawled around your feet in a space so malodorous you could hardly breathe. The rebukes seem pointless when there is no real alternative. I continue to get up around 3 a.m. so I can take a quick shower long before dawn. I'm in the middle of one when military officers attempt to attack us. The corridor is full of bathing women when someone notices that the men in the distance are advancing upon us. Already they are cursing at us, brandishing their torchlights as we've seen them brandish whips. It is clear they're intent on catching a scapegoat and everyone begins to run back into the room. I am one of those who slips and falls but I make it inside before the officers get to the corridor. Fortunately, everyone manages to rush inside in time. While the officers parade the corridor outside, spewing insults and curses towards the dormitory, I take stock as I limp back to my bunk. My naked body is still soaped up. I've lost my towel in the scramble and my bucket is still outside. There is a cut on my knee.

The cut is bleeding. Most of the dormitory is now awake, and in hushed tones people wonder if the officers will get tired of pacing the corridor and come inside. There is no door to shut behind us and they could walk in if they wanted. Eventually, their footsteps recede and their voices fade, but my knee won't stop bleeding. This could be because I am trying to staunch the flow with paper towels. It could be because my hands won't stop shaking.

Some corpers gather around me, murmuring, 'sorry o', 'inin', 'pele dear', 'ndo'. Across the dormitory, similar clusters form around the shaken, injured or weeping women who were outside with me. My bunkmate examines my wound. She fetches a pack of beauty wipes and bottle of facial cleanser and sits beside me so she can clean my knee. Someone drapes a wrapper around me. Another asks if I'm all right, if any of those stupid men touched me. I have never felt more cared for by my people. Yes and no, I say to the woman who asked the questions. Even though the answer to both questions is no. Someone places a curse on the officers. Another makes a joke about them and we all laugh to push back our fear.

Home History

Caleb Femi

When I was born my mum panicked because she thought she had given birth to an alien. Her words, not mine. Truth is, I was born with my amniotic sac still intact, an occurrence widely known as an 'en caul' birth or 'veiled' birth. According to my mum, she saw the hands of the doctor and midwives holding a gooey bubble of a thing and she screamed, *what is that, where's the baby?* Most midwives go through their entire careers not witnessing an 'en caul' birth, such is the rarity of the occurrence, but a Hausa midwife in attendance, having witnessed it before, quelled my mum's hysterics, reassuring her that it was a 'mergia'; there was nothing to fear. In fact, she said, this was a rare blessing. When a child is born like this, it is because they remember their previous life, how harsh the world can be – so they re-enter it, bringing with them all the protection of the womb. They re-enter wiser and more cautious. I love musing on cultural myths and superstitions. I love the humility it grants me to see the world beyond my own perspective. Such things birth questions that colour my imagination: if I *have* been in this world before, what was my experience of Nigeria like? What happened that left an impression so deep in my soul that it followed me into my next life? Was it political? Was I a chief or a politician witnessing the nation's independence? Was I a herdsman, a shoemaker or one of the numerous wives of a rich man? Was it personal? Like a brutal heart-break? A thought worth entertaining seeing as my due date was Valentine's Day and I did all I could to avoid meeting it.

Of all of them, my favourite en-caul myth is the one that states that babies born en caul can never drown. I was 5 years old when I was taken to the beach for the first time. The ocean was a magnificent thing to behold, I remember my feet softly ensconced in the sand and the horizon of water looking like the edge of the world. The salt in the air and water magnetised and pulled my body forward. There was no resistance, simply a curiosity that entranced me. I was already neck-deep in the water by the time I came to my senses. The panic. The attempt to scream choked by saltwater. The pull of the waves. The pull. The fading of a life I had briefly known. Then a tree trunk of an arm grabbed my torso and plucked me out of the sea: *Idiot, you no get sense, you dey enter wata and no fi swim, where your mama?* My saviour scolded me as he carried me back to my uncle for my second scolding. Turns out, in a roundabout way, the myth could be true. Though now I'm a strong swimmer, I'm not willing to test its credibility again.

I find that the contemplation of en-caul myths keeps me rooted to Nigeria – even now as a grown man who no longer lives in his home country. They keep me thinking about the many incarnations of Nigeria, past and present. I think about the region of my birthplace before and after it was colonially known as Kano. I think about Jos, the city I grew up in. Specifically the street that held the large compound my siblings, grandmother, uncle and I shared with numerous other families. The compound was two stories high, with a large square at its centre. Our home was a one-bedroom apartment on the ground floor which was backlit by the sunrise and served as a platform from which my boyish sensibilities perceived the rest of Nigeria.

Our neighbours came from all over Nigeria. We had Igbo neighbours, Yoruba, Hausa, Calabar, Edo. Our community was very close – I remember the normality of walking into my neighbours' homes unannounced and being welcomed. We would celebrate together: Christmas, Eid, birthdays. And we would mourn together, the funerals and other bad news that required commemorating. We would share compound duties: a rota told each neighbour which day they'd have to wake up at the crack of dawn to sweep the compound square. I've only recently been able to forgive myself for forgetting the song my grandmother would sing as she rhythmically swept with the igbale she used specifically for that activity. I didn't know how fond she was of that particular igbale until the day it was spirited away and she made me a messenger of her wrath, sending me from neighbour to neighbour to state that *our* household will opt out of sweeping duty until *that* igbale, and not any other, was returned to her.

In the compound, there were a few absolute truths about my grandmother. One was her skin's radiance, how ethereal it was, how void of blemishes, how breathtaking it was in the sun. Another was her resolve. Her spirit was known to be ironclad: if she threatened that she would do something and she sealed it with *wallahi tallahi*, you'd have more success trying to stop the sun from rising than getting her to change her mind. And so my grandmother woke up on the dawn of our sweep day to sit on her stool outside our door and do nothing but sing her song. By the third week, her igbale was returned.

*

I was 3 years old when I moved to the compound and by the age of 6, I was fluent in English, Hausa, Yoruba and my Igbo was conversational. But truly my first language had no words: it was Nigeria.

It was my dialogue with the space it contained, the interaction with the ground, the touch of the breeze, the kitchen sink I'd climb into to cool down, the skin of mango I'd suck on, the sounds, colours, shapes, patterns, the people. All the things that I conversed with through my senses before I could assign words to them. Truly, my first language was Nigeria. I like to think that my incentive to pick up the other four spoken languages was play. I wanted to play with any other kid I came into contact with inside and outside the compound, and not only participate in their games but win them. But in order to win, I knew that the way to access the hidden tactics and tricks that guaranteed an advantage was buried in the language of that circle. Shout out to the social battery of children because I really yearned to be invited into every circle of laughing children (nowadays , I'd need at least a week to muster up the energy to attend a social gathering). Knowing four languages meant there was never a part of Nigeria that felt alien to me. No matter where I ended up, at least one of the languages in my repertoire would act as a tool to forge a bond with my people.

I left Nigeria at 7 years old to join my parents and siblings in London. When I returned for a holiday at the age of 10, my limbs were longer and my eyes could see clearer. The buildings I once knew had shrunk and the distance between places didn't seem as far apart. I had grown into the physical expanse of Nigeria, I could see the spirit of the land in its entirety: the cracks, more variation in the shades of its colour. It became apparent that I didn't know my home country as well as I thought. Nostalgia is a wicked thing, isn't? My childhood memories of living in the compound might make you think the country was a utopian fairy tale. But memories made with juvenile sensibilities are easily manipulated by nostalgia. Turns out I had taken with me to London the effulgent memories of Nigeria and left behind those that were darker. And in the dark is where I'll leave

14

those memories; why add more traumatic imagery to the brimming well of violence and sorrow that make up much of the collective memory of many Nigerians?

My return to Nigeria sparked my interest in the country's history and politics, and upon returning to London, I had questions. Who was Abacha? Who was Obasanjo? What was the Biafran War? Why were we living in London? It took years to really piece together the answers to all of my questions. My mother, bless her heart, indulged me by telling me child-friendly versions of Nigeria under the regime of past presidents. It wasn't until I employed stealth tactics, by silently creeping down the stairs after my bedtime to perch outside the living room door, and eavesdropped on my parents – who talked on the phone or with visitors – that I was able to learn about my intimate connections with Nigeria's historical events. When I asked about the Biafran War, my mother gave me a matter-of-fact answer: she told me about the sides involved, their respective motivations and the outcome of the war. But in dimly-lit pockets of the hallway where I avoided creaking floorboards, I strained my ears and heard my mother, an Ukwuani child at the time, talk of the famine created by the Federal Military Government's blockade during the war. I heard her talk about the starvation she and her family endured which, by the end, had claimed the life of her younger sister. When I returned to my bed later that night, my grief ushered away sleep until the small light of the following day ebbed through the heavy curtains.

My mother had never told me she had a sibling other than my uncle, so for an aunty to be given and taken away from me in the same breath was tough to process. It was the thought of my mother, who would have been younger than I was at the time, dealing with such unspeakable grief that broke my heart. Something shifted in me after that night: there was a new understanding when she spoke to me or my siblings, layers of meaning in her instructions I hadn't perceived before. Much of my childish complaints, like why she'd always served my siblings and I excessively large portions of food, had quelled. It's one thing to know the history of your home country. It's another thing to know your home's history of your home country.

As the years went by, my understanding of Nigeria and Nigerians deepened. I understood more of the tensions between tribes as well as the role Britain had and continues to play in the governance of the country. I saw that Nigeria was a mapped land birthed from colonial pillaging, from greed gift wrapped as a business deal. And, perhaps most importantly, that the spirit of its people thrived in spite of its colonial contamination and its corruption. The more I dove into my family history, the more it drew parallels to the history of Nigeria. The most poignant parallel was discovering that my parents' respective families vehemently opposed their marriage. My father is a solemn man, when his heart is set on something there is no changing it. A trait he inherited from his mother, who raised me in the compound in Jos. When he was a young man running the streets like young men do, his friend took him to the training camp of the Nigeria women's national basketball team to sit and watch a training session. Turns out, his friend was seeing a player on the team and wanted my father to accompany him, later that day, on a double date with the best friend of the woman he was dating. This is how my father and mother met. From that day on, my father was set on marrying her. A year or so later, the two made their union official despite the strong opposition of family and friends who were against intertribal marriages. Forty years later, in a marriage that – according to some – should not have been, my parents have built a good life for themselves with five happy children. The union of my parents and the union of the territories in the Niger area are by no means politically or contextually the same. For me, the parallel is in the fruits of happiness and hope that were born from the respective unions. The Nigerian people, like my siblings and me, are beautiful children of a conflicted union.

*

In 2016, I was appointed the Young People's Laureate for London, a role in which I would use poetry to be of service to the social and welfare needs of young people in the city (and by extension, the country and the rest of the world). The appointment was reported in national newspapers as anticipated (embargoed interviews and PR campaigns), but I was pleasantly surprised to see it appear in Nigerian publications. After decades of no longer living in the country, it's easy to feel like word of your achievements is contained within British shores, but I felt a loving embrace by Nigeria, like a son proud to be recognized by a mother(land).

A year later, my role would then take me back to Nigeria to participate in a literary festival. When I landed in Abuja, it occurred to me that I had not known Nigeria as an adult. I had never navigated its landscape without the guidance of someone senior and I was there in the airport alone and even unable to draw from my repertoire of languages that allowed me to move easily between tribal circles as a child in Jos because I no longer spoke Hausa, Igbo and my Yoruba was barely conversational. I was back in Nigeria, lacking in confidence and wavering between a space of familiarity and unfamiliarity of cultural and social cues. This disorientation later grew into a heavy angst as I worried about how the *Nigerianness* of my work would be received in the literary festival. Nowadays, I look back at myself and laugh at the dramatics of this angst. One that came from a limited scope of how my identity underpinned my work, coupled with a sense of inadequacy – even shame – at the fact that I didn't know Nigeria anymore. But once I was able to move past it, my time at the festival was edifying for my spirit as a Nigerian and my development as a writer. For three days, I read stories and heard poetry by Nigerian writers covering a multitude of lived experiences and fantasies. It seemed that, in a roundabout way, every piece of literature written by a Nigerian offers an answer to the question, *who* is Nigeria? And in the ever-changing and infinite faces of this land, both past, present and of those to come, who of us can say they truly know this country? No one does, at least not objectively speaking. The only Nigeria a Nigerian can be certain of is the one they knew in their own homes. The Nigeria seen through the windows of bedrooms, through the skin of family and friends, through the local landscape that forged their sense of body and spirit, through their language(s), spoken and felt.

Father's Land

Umar Turaki

The land where Father is born. It is my land too. Father says so and teaches me so. With his choices and his living and his working. Even with his dying. Father works for the land, in a manner of saying so. But also in a concrete sense, because Father works with concrete and the kinds of things that go into concrete: sand, gravel. Father also knows a lot about the land. He knows about rocks and minerals and metals. He also knows the deep stuff, like ores and tectonic plates and fault lines. There's a picture of him as a younger man in an underground mine. He's wearing heavy-duty overalls and a yellow helmet with a headlight. I can't recall if he's holding a pickaxe or not, but it is an image that hurries forth whenever I think about Father and his work. On a fishing trip once somewhere in Rayfield, back when it is just the back of town and not the swathe of real estate that gouges you penniless if you don't take time, I see a hillside made of kaolin and stop to pick up a few lumps as a birthday gift for Father, knowing he loves rocks. I am 10 years old.

Father is around a lot until they take him far away and put him in the place of iron, right next to the place of steel. The place of steel is a project that many have called a white elephant. Then he comes and goes. The place where they put him is the place that becomes his end. But at first, it looks like a promotion. There's a white house with a swimming pool, and five bedrooms, and three living rooms, and a water fountain that never works. Holidays are spent there, memories of gold are spun until there's nothing left to spin. Father has a stunning Peugeot 504 Bestline, and an orderly who sits in the front of the car. White elephants. By the time they are done with him in the place of iron, Father is without a job, let alone a promotion, back home in this city, back home in his private room, typing away on his Dell, typing his revenge. He's around more often – until he isn't around at all.

It is about this time one of the house staff tells me to tell Father to send me to school in London, 'London' being a euphemism for anywhere overseas. Actually, all of the house staff. I don't remember what prompts this happening, or maybe I have never known. They congregate around me in the washing area. Their words are now lost forever – as are most of them – but the hardness of the day, the concreteness of the moment, is there in the water splashing on the cement floor and the clammy smell of NASCO Plus soap and the bite of the cold mountain air on all of our beautiful, sun-soaked skins. By this age, I have joined most adults in the understanding that Father's land is a place to aspire to leave. Every cell of my 10-year-old body becomes alive with the idea that I can be packed up and shipped off to some London where everything is better. There is a shared feeling, gleaned from the very air we breathe, that something is fundamentally wrong with this place, with this land. By extension, I accept that something is fundamentally wrong with me and my skin and all the other ways I inhabit the world. By this age, I have already memorized and envied Elijah Wood in *The Good Son* and Joseph Mazzello in *Jurassic Park*: I have memorized their comeliness, their straightness of hair – I have memorized what I do not understand to be their whiteness. By this age, I have asked another long-lost grown-up from those years whether it is possible to wash your skin so clean that it stops being black.

I wait until nightfall to ambush Father. He is eating dinner, slowly, meticulously. Mother is there too. They both look at me after I speak, and I realize the ambush has already backfired. I panic as I find myself cornered and peppered with questions. Who have you been talking to? Did someone put this idea in your head? Why do you suddenly want to go abroad? It doesn't make any sense, are you sure nobody put you up to this?

Gently, Father asphyxiates the idea with his quiet, succinct words. I feel it withering away inside as he speaks. By the time he has finished, it has stopped moving altogether. Memory can be the most useless thing in the world when it chooses to be. The Hausa words spoken in that room are also lost forever, with only their import left, the same import that anvils my shoulders as I walk away: this place is my home whether I like it or not. I feel powerless and raw, as if he has just removed his belt and taken it to my insides. I also feel like my feet have been encased in concrete.

*

If eating is an art form, then Father is an artist. He holds his fork and knife aloft, his paintbrush and scalpel. He chews silently and slowly. The crockery clinks with the softness of his touch. It doesn't matter what is on his plate, it will receive the same dignified treatment. Tuwon semo da miyan kuka* is sliced and diced and dunked. Yam and stew is sliced and diced and dunked. Rice is heaped on a fork and hemmed in with a knife. Pancake and kidney sauce is sliced and folded. I remember Sunday breakfasts of fried liver coated in flour. And golden, hairy yam balls, the way they fall open and steam when Father cuts. White spaghetti and stew and boiled chicken.

---

* Hausa for 'swallow' made from semolina and eaten with baobab-leaf soup.

Curry sauce and white rice. Couscous. Steamed vegetables: carrots, cauliflower, broccoli and peas. The table is sometimes our meeting place, particularly on weekends. Father has diabetes, so no sugar allowed. He suggests I try my oatmeal with honey. To my surprise, I enjoy it. For some time after that, I eat oatmeal with honey. When Father passes away, I commit to it. It becomes my way of remembering him, honouring him. I stop chewing gum for some time too, remembering him, honouring him (he asks what nutritional benefit there is to bubble gum, though I suspect he simply hated the sight of the human mouth moving for no essential reason).

My remembering and honouring gradually billow into more consequential things. I wear his designer shirts and gold watches around like badges of honour. I keep his PhD thesis on my bookshelf, though I don't know what a word of it means. I read his old books where his name is inscribed in his physician's scrawl and the date of purchase rendered in Roman numerals (that's how I also start writing into new books the names of cities where I discover the books). After four years of chasing my bachelor's degree around Africa and Europe, and finally bagging it in America, while at the same time satisfying an intense wanderlust, the next logical step is to return home. I want to come back to replant my feet into the concrete of Father's land. There's no place like home and I'm feeling like Father's son.

The first inanimate thing that truly welcomes me home is the taste of fried eggs. The spicy, decadent, glorious, rich taste of fried eggs. I don't remember who made it. There is too much oil, and the onions look like they're competing for attention, but they hardly steal the show. It tastes so, so *sweet*. It *bangs*. It really *slaps*. Thinking about it now, it strikes me how given to excess the people of Father's land are. We like our soups rich with oil and meat. It isn't food if there isn't MSG for every grain, for every drop. It doesn't end with food. Visiting Father's land for the very first time, Cameroonian-

Gabonese Brother-in-law is struck, of all things, by the size of the buildings that accompany the filling stations. We travel across three states and nothing draws his attention and his ire more.

They're like mansions, he says. Why do they need so much space?

I never thought about it. I am the fish in David Foster Wallace's proverbial water. I have become so steeped in the water of this land that I no longer see it. The way we are all steeped in the water of our lives. The water is all over our skins, a second skin. It coats our eyeballs with its wetness, becoming its own lens. How can we see our own lives when it is all we see? This is why we all need a crash course in astral projection. In stepping outside of ourselves and taking a good look at ourselves. Annie Dillard is a good teacher. She writes about finding workable compromises between the sublimity of our ideas and the absurdity of the fact of us as the primary business of being human.*

I like that she gives hope to this impossible struggle between our divine souls and the annoying, biotic functionality of our bodies. It gives me my own kind of hope. After honouring Father with my return to the homeland, I begin to sense a familiar itch. I gave in to it for four years, chasing that degree, packing up and moving on from campus to campus, until I grew tired of the fact that my life had become a thoroughfare through which a constant flow of new friends passed.

A year after my return to Father's land, I apply for a Master's programme in London, giving in to the wanderlust once again. But I am rejected and forced to remain in Father's land. I try to make the most of it. I try to take pride in it. This is home, a concrete foundation on which to build my dreams. I set up an office and go about the business of living and dreaming in this land. I try to make

---

* Annie Dillard, 'An Expedition to The Pole', *The Annie Dillard Reader* (1995): 30.

a film in Ngas, in Mother's village. I fail to raise the required funds but shoot it anyway. It is an unqualified mess. I try to salvage what I can from it and try to raise more funds. I use a rubber string to hold my phone together because I have no money to buy a new one. The 'idea' of my artistic dreams and the 'absurdity of the fact' of myself are never more incongruous. One day, I have barely enough cash to get home from the office and have to walk halfway. When I ask for food without pepper, there is laughter because it barely exists. There is pepper in jollof rice, fried rice, rice and stew, yam pottage, bitterleaf soup, okra soup, and egusi* soup. Excess. I try to speak Pidgin but only attract more laughter: I lack the energy, that bubbling, buoyant, poised edge. In other words, I have no effizy.† It is the lingua franca of the young people of Father's land. They revel in it and are united in it. I am meant to be one of them but find myself outside the circle instead. I struggle to find workable compromises in this, struggle to sit with the liminality that seems to follow me around, touching everything I do or try to become. It's hard, like everything else: hard as concrete. Still, I am proud to be planted in Father's land, a land where a fuel tanker can crash through your television screen and into your living room; a land where, too often, death is a way of life. I feel like Father's son.

Mayonnaise and mwir pet‡ prove to be effective antidotes to the excess of pepper. And the food, always and forever, remains a joy. It isn't only our own brand of eggs I have missed. I have missed the thick, mealy texture of lightly salted yams. The warm fluffiness of semolina. The rich bodiliness of kunun zaki§ as it glides down my

---

* Pumpkin seeds.
† Pidgin: an evocative word that can loosely be translated as 'charm' or 'charisma'.
‡ Ngas: a dark oil extracted from atili (Hausa) or African pear (often confused with olives).
§ Hausa: a sweet, non-alcoholic brew made from guinea corn or other grains.

throat. I discover a profound affection for rice and beans with stew, in that specific combination. And, of course, miyan wake*– it is the pinnacle of the culinary heritage that Father has inadvertently gifted me. And now that I think of it, miyan wake with the customary tuwon shinkafa† is something I never got to share with Father.

*

Father's land is stitched up along ethnic seams, and those fault lines run through my own body. They cleave me into two equal halves. On one side, Father's Nupe. On the other, Mother's Ngas. And if they are fault lines, then it should be their destiny to go off like dynamite sticks arranged neatly in a row. Still, why does my body feel like one body? Why does it feel so normal? My seams aren't unravelling. Peace lives here inside this casket of flesh and bones. This is true even though voices have trailed me through my life, accusing me of abandoning Father because Father is gone. Remember that you're a man, the voices say. The words of Father's tongue have evaporated from my lips, I can't taste them at all.

Rather, because of a chance of life and destiny, it is Mother's tongue that has come the closest to filling my mouth. It is her words and her ways that have filled my voids for the simple reason that she outlived Father, and that her ways were always within reach. My Ngas vocabulary isn't completely hopeless. At any given moment, I can pause and translate random words in my head, relishing that sensation of freedom that language can provide: Nana, mother; yil, land; posin, night; zing, truth; mbise, food. Still, I wish the words flowed like water out of me in a steady stream of essence and identity. But

---

* Hausa: a soup made from beans, a flagship dish of the Nupe people.
† Hausa: a 'swallow' made from rice.

again those sweet voices, demanding to know why I haven't learned a word of Father's tongue, as if a complete embrace of Mother's culture is a complete rebuff of Father's heritage. Besides, I already feel guilty – because I want it all: everything Father gave me, everything Mother gave me. I want them all swimming inside me, mixing, stewing and being served up. To miss any one part would feel like a piece of myself going into extinction. It would feel like nothing less than failure. This begs the question whether it is possible for a human being to live in harmony with their many selves. If the answer is yes, can the same be expected of a nation? Even a varied and splintered and wounded land, like Father's?

Annie Dillard hints at a whisper of hope in the task of carving out an existence in the push and pull between two opposites. Whether we are speaking of metaphysical ways of being, cultural ways of being, or geographical ways of being. You could call it paradox. For instance, Father's land attracts and repels me at the same time. No sooner do I settle in and try to go about the business of living and I am yearning for the open horizon of the world, longing for God-knows-what, feeling that familiar itch. It is tempting to blame it on the dysfunction of the land. But if all was well and beautiful and lovely, I suspect that dissatisfaction would still be there. At the same time, no sooner am I in some other place that isn't Father's land and I find myself pierced by a sense of failure, a sense of longing to return to it. It is tempting to blame *that* on my village people.*

For the first time, I consider how Father and the ways he chose to live have funnelled into my choices and the person I have become. Does the fact that he was well-travelled – over thirty countries visited before death took him – feed into my desire to see the world? Does my feeling that when I am away from Father's land, I don't feel like

---

* Don't ask.

Father's son, stem from his refusal to be planted anywhere other than in this land? I see now how paradox trailed Father in his life, and into his death. Knowing that he and his body and his brilliance would have thrived like a wild bush in some other, less dysfunctional place, smarts. But he chose to live for this land, and, whether by choice or not, he died for it. Instinctively, I have honoured this by trying to make my life mirror his in this regard, proud when I feel like I've pulled it off, afraid that the similarities may stray beyond life and into death. This brings me up against yet more difficulty, more paradox: the thought that you can die for something and be killed by it at the same time, even though the two should be separate; the irony of honouring a dead man by shoring up loyalty for a land that took his life. But there's hope, Annie says. Workable compromise. For in the scheme of things, all of mankind deals with the same problem. After all, humanity is an impossible state of being – yet we manage.

*

Daughter's little body is split three ways, and she doesn't know it yet. Three separate ethnic bloodlines collide in her veins. She doesn't know that her mother's Mwaghavul side is the largest single piece of her. If her ancestry were mapped across the land, she would be the product of four villages, three local government areas and two states. One day, she will have to decide what to do with that knowledge. But what can she do with it, given a few facts? Her mother's Mwaghavul is all but stillborn on her tongue. Her father barely speaks Ngas and no Nupe at all. He still wonders whether to bother teaching her Hausa. He is looking for workable compromises in the knowledge that there is more to Father's land than three 'major' ethnic groups, even though the ubiquitous Hausa provides an easy, accessible distinction that sets one apart from the standard-issue English. Her father worries that when he is gone and none of the many, many sounds of Father's land fill her mouth, his failure will be certified. He worries that she may become a rootless, yearning thing, lost in the bigness of the world. But when he holds her and tells her how complete, how enough she is, he also wants to tell her that, one day when she is faced with all the pieces of herself, choice will be a valid tool in that affair, and whatever she chooses will be enough. Because identity isn't made of concrete; and if you insist that it is, then it can become a dead weight – or a white elephant. At the same time, he wants to tell her that, secretly, he will pray she chooses to find ways, great or small, to keep all those parts of herself alive.

Daughter only knows her mother's milk for now. Will she like puk luluk* or miyan wake or puk fori?† Will her palate be epicurean or rustic? Time will speak to all things. For now, there is an undying light in her eyes, and each day, her father looks for her grin and the chatter of her voice so that it fills the house with nonsensical words. It's the most precious language to his ears. He will tell her that this is her land too. But he will also say that, no matter what choices she makes, no matter what land she sinks her roots into, she will always be her father's daughter.

---

* Mwaghavul: a pungent soup made from dried locust beans, a customary dish of the Mwaghavul people.
† Ngas: a soup made from sorrel leaves and thickened with groundnut, a customary dish of the Ngas people.

Check Out Receipt

Tuesday, July 5, 2022 10:48:40 AM
05865

Item: 31183206864032
Title: Of this our country : acclaimed Nigerian
writers on the home, identity and culture they k
ow.
Call no.: 966.9 O
ue: 7/26/2022

Total items: 1

You just saved $26.99 by using your
library today.

EE TO BE ALL IN

of July 1, 2021, late fees no
nger assessed for overdue items!
us for details or visit bcpl.info

Of Country and Reverie

Irenosen Okojie

At Murtala Muhammed Airport, the memory of my father, and I, as a little girl, dancing to Tina Turner on our old veranda in Lagos, rises to the fore. A moment of pure, unfiltered joy forever embedded in me on a cellular level, it makes an occasional appearance like an old guest wanting to stretch its legs. Only the record needle glinting suspiciously is no longer scratching that circular black disk but intercepting the swirl of activities, keen to mark this latest milestone between us.

I am exhausted yet excited. There is a humming in my brain that feels like a static assembling, masking the disembodied parts of scenes that are yet to come. I am in Nigeria for Aké Literature Festival but will combine the trip with seeing family.

My eyes swim a little from the flurries of movement and the volume of noise around me at the Arrivals hall. My feet have not touched Nigerian soil for several years, and like a woman hungry for my motherland, I inhale the sights before me, the airport acting as a microcosm of what is to come. Pidgin English swells then dwindles in my ears, pockets of people with suitcases piled in precarious constructs spilling from their trolleys rush to embrace loved ones. The feeling in me is akin to a levee within breaking,

29

threatening to leak its contents on the floor and infiltrate the lives of others.

I have not seen my father for a few years. Our sole form of communication has been phone calls where his voice still maintains the same clarity and inflections; his robust laughter is still irrepressible, infectious. I picture him before I arrived in his and my mother's life, a highly intelligent, unorthodox man riding his motorcycle to Abuja, then Port Harcourt, casually smoking a cigarette at pit stops, daring the quiet forces at work to deter him from a future path in politics. I want to know how these trips shaped him. I want to discover if he was always gregarious, unpredictable, mercurial and quick-tempered during times one would expect certainty. A cluster of flies hover near me. I need to tell my father I have brought insects I built with my own hands during nights of insomnia; they are in my pockets waiting to be finite soldiers dispersed in the heat. I want to tell him that I wield the debris from past wreckages in my life I trace every so often as though it is a comfort.

The record needle shrinks between Black bodies moving like slip-streams. It will find its way back to the memory bank that sits between Lagos, Benin and East London, slowly encroaching in either direction when I need it to. The static temporarily disintegrates. I know they are in collusion, combining their strengths to create elements of the unknown on this trip.

I feel conspicuous waiting in my English clothes, surrounded by people in regal traditional wear, somehow transparently caught between two identities, two cultures – but then I spot my father making his way towards me through a throng of people with his usual happy disposition. He smiles broadly. His dark skin has a sheen to it. He is older. His hair shot with grey, his stomach a little rounder. But he is still handsome, possessing the same indefinable charismatic quality that propelled him into Nigeria's political sphere as a young man. He embraces me warmly, saying, 'Hello, daughter. So you came to see the old man in his habitat?'

A weight falls off my shoulders. A tension in me eases. A feeling of relief spreads. It feels like home being near my father again. As if a part of a puzzle is slotted into place. There is so much to say, I picture all our lost conversations as pieces dented by time waiting on the baggage carousel. We do not stop chattering as we make our way through the airport. I tell him that I have been dreaming of my favourite childhood snack – suya – for days, that the first thing we have to do is buy suya from a street vendor. As if on cue for a disruption, a one-armed man offers to assist us with our luggage for a fee.

My father and I spend the next two weeks staying at my uncle's house in Victoria Island, Lagos, in a well-to-do neighbourhood with colourful, dynamically designed houses. We discuss his ecology projects to help his local community in Uromi. We have meals together in a dining room bearing the faint buzz of an air conditioner, sleek leather upholstered chairs and satellite TV beaming down diets of CNN news and endless streams of world disasters. We eat pounded yam and black soup, yams with stew, goat pepper soup. I savour these meals with relish. It is communion with my father.

Here, there is a cook, a houseboy or housegirl to do chores, a driver. I have forgotten these class disparities. It is part of the culture yet I feel a niggling discomfort. I listen to highlife music making my own bed, washing dishes, tidying the downstairs rooms. It is a kind of defiance. I accompany my father to meetings where he introduces me as his 'daughter from London', as though it has a certain cache. In a way this amuses me. I am reminded of being a little girl when my father would take me along to business meetings and the men would smile ruefully while I watched them from the sidelines.

Now, the memory bank is spilling bloodied shards of glass. I am rushing towards those shards, back into a long-buried scene. I am 7 years old. My brother and I are playing hide and seek outside my father's office. He chases me. I run like there is a wind in my veins urging me to outrun it, so much so, the double glass doors of the office look like air to me. In the moment, I feel invincible. My body hurtles through the glass. Everything slows down in an intense heat. I am standing beneath the sun's glare, now a tree with branches made of glass and blood. My father runs towards me with a look of horror on his face. My brother's expression collapses in terror. Our childhood experiences of my father are different. There is no time for this old guilt to surface. He shrinks back. Somebody flags down a car. Next, my father is holding my bloodied body in a yellow taxi, screaming at the driver through the traffic. I do not know it yet but those first injuries will attempt to migrate towards my father's hands again over the years.

My father and I drive from Lagos to Benin in a reliable black Mercedes van that sputters over bumps on treacherous roads. It is just the two of us, him at the wheel and me as his copilot. I buy agege bread, water and groundnuts from young girls balancing snacks for sale on their heads. It is a long journey, and the only road trip I have made with him since I was a girl. Along the way, we break at rest stops for meals and respite. He tells me he read my novel with great pride and interest. He comments on the use of language, the character arcs and the sex scenes with custom frankness. I know in that instance it is possible to miss someone while sitting next to them. I am negotiating love, resentment and a dampened anger simultaneously. I wish he had been there to pull me back from the edges I leapt off that neither of us saw coming. Our road trip is the freest I feel in a long while. I cry a little inside knowing how much of each other we lost over the years. In Benin, he takes me to his father's house, his grandfather's land. We walk around it, discussing the Benin kingdom while the dust settles. It feels like a holy grail, a path back to my ancestors.

Two weeks later in Abeokuta, the hotel is a stone's throw away from the literature festival venue. Living in England since the age of eight, I am acutely aware of how Black bodies learn to police themselves there. The contrast in Africa is liberating. The freedom, this lack of inhibition, a certain buoyancy of expression is evident all around me. I see it in the bright, bustling markets where the stall-holders shift from quick humour to cheeky persuasion to sell their wares, in the children playing with their friends sipping from bottles of Coca-Cola and Fanta, running amok in the afternoon heat. I see it in the hotel staff once you establish a rapport with them. Here, our bodies aren't held to ransom in the same way they are in the West. It is a revelation so transparent yet so deep, I find myself ruminating on it, on and off, during one day.

In the festival bookshop, surrounded by a symphony of African literary voices and intellectual dexterity, I almost start to weep at the thought. I tell my father this in a conversation over the phone. Nightly calls have become our ritual since I arrived in Abeokuta. I confess how easily I slip from English to pidgin again, that I have harboured it in me for so long, it needed to be released, that I am waiting for the other inheritances my body has carried to reveal themselves when I least expect it. My father laughs in delight; I picture him angling his head to the side as if posing a question: 'Africa is the richest continent beyond monetary value. Nigeria is at the forefront of that. You must maintain your connection to your culture. You should always cultivate the ties with your homeland. It will reward you in ways you cannot begin to imagine.' I think on how I clung to aspects of my culture over the years. It was an anchor if I felt adrift; actively listening to my mother speak her native tongue when visitors came, digesting it so it settled like an internal lining, watching Nollywood movies during my university years to absorb the physicality, the rhythms of expression, dressing up in traditional attire to attend parties organised by African hosts.

I end the call on a high, the line still crackling in my ears. The night expands with the promise of future possibilities. I feel closer to my father than I have in ages. His decision to live in Nigeria while his children studied abroad in the UK had had reverberations over the years. It meant a physical gulf that was hard to bridge through time as well as complicated relationships with each of my siblings that grew more nuanced as we reached adulthood.

The memory bank produces a hand-carved wooden flute. It is the flute my father bought for me in Festac as a girl. The first instrument I attempted to master before he paid for piano lessons for me and violin lessons for my sister in London. The flute hovers above my restless fingers. It presses its eye against mine for a shared tear while its sound mutates in the distance.

And later:

The memory bank releases a dog. It is a precocious Alsatian that belonged to my brother at our house in Festac, along with his parrot and monkey who stole from the local markets. I cannot remember what happened to the dog in the end. But I recall cutting my forehead on the aluminium roof of its cage while it leapt at the latch, barking as if communicating to other dogs in the neighbourhood about a rescue mission. I prod my father on this dog. He does not recall what happened to it either. The dog is gaunt now, sporting a replica of my forehead scar, a caterpillar stopped in its tracks. My brother's arm appears in the frame, older now, trying to put a leash

34

*on the dog's neck but it dodges it each time, lapping at his arm
affectionately instead.*

The memory bank retreats in a dazed state.

My father does not tell me, but overnight, he drives all the way from
Benin to Abeokuta to surprise me at the festival. I am deeply moved
by this. It is these trips that he and I make to each other that feel
like home to me. From London to Lagos, Lagos to Benin, from
Benin to Uromi. Seeing my father in Nigeria, this country he loves
so passionately is witnessing the best version of him. It seeps into
me, this desire to unearth the strongest iteration of myself too. He
is always imbuing in me a love of my Nigerian ancestry. We are
connected because of this shared passion for our ancestral lands. I
realize then on the evening of his arrival that my father is so intrin-
sically linked to my favourite experiences of Nigeria, woven into it
like a dazzling thread in the fabric of my time there; I cannot imagine
coming home without him present.

A Brief History of Suya.

Inua Ellams

It began this way. A long time ago, in the land before the country, on an afternoon in which the sun stood static and thankless in the sky, it grew angry. Such was its fury at that thanklessness that it stuffed the breeze back down the gullets of wind tunnels, roared at crippled remnants of rain, boiled the breath of the land to slow ooze of air, and maintained a steady and solid beating down on the desert ground.

Such was its fervour that the scorpions found it too unbearable to move, meerkats had altogether stopped playing, the ostriches had shrugged off their feathers, all the cacti had shrivelled up, camels had gone on strike – beaching themselves on the shores of dunes – and even the snakes had shed down to their thinnest skins. In a nearby cave, two thieves, hiding from the travelling Tuaregs they had stolen from, were baking in the thick, voiceless dark, famished and desperately parched.

They waited for dusk to settle then crept out with their dry lips cracked and thin rivulets of blood seeping like tiny springs. They licked these wounds, hissing at the sharp pain, their tongues like sandpaper. Across the dunes they could see an encampment, an archipelago of campfires where flames flickered like dancing beacons. They could hear the lull of a lute, a red pipe's floating lilt and a kettledrum mingling with laughter and dancing feet. They moved to satiate their hunger, creeping close and closer, their bodies never more than an inch off the shifting sands, their eyes like four low-lying moons, luminous in the night.

One had a stone knife, its obsidian blade tucked into an antler-bone handle, the other a length of rope woven from palm fronds – tools of their nefarious trade. They slid past the kitchen quarters, the cleric's sprawling tent, the courtesans' caravans, and came to the clearing that held the cattle. There, they rose to their feet and stared.

*

My earliest memory of storytelling also happened at night – centuries after these thieves, decades after the land had become the country, and thousands of miles further south, in the breakneck speedy city of Lagos. By then the country had wrestled itself away from those who had 'invented' it. It had survived a civil war, begun to trade in oil, persevered through several coups, and from these close shaves with destruction and desertion had spun new stories of ingenuity and resilience in the face of impossible odds. These thematic strands were woven into the fabric of the Nigerian spirit, and that night, my father and his friends were deep in its folds.

They had gathered in the living room of our house in Ebute Metta and they had been talking for hours. They had drunk enough beer to sink a dwarf whale, and you could tell by how richly they laughed at thin jokes, how completely they emptied themselves of all reservations, cackling into the briefest silences or cascading with thunderous joys, that they were completely at ease in their company, that they could end and begin each other's sentences; they were that close, so intimately known to each other. On the table before them was a mountain of suya and around them, fist-sized newspaper parcels of extra red pepper, groundnuts and thinly sliced raw onions.

The mountain of meat was Everest to me, and I wanted to eat its summit. My eyes were levelled at its topmost slice, the aroma moving my mouth to water. My father, knowing his son, warned, 'This boy, you didn't learn your lesson from last time eh?' and the friends erupted into laughter. 'Like father, like son!' one chimed, and the bouts of laughter strengthened anew.

*

The thieves were a perfect duo. The knife-wielder cunning and the rope-bearer strong. Among the cattle, they stood far apart and opposite each other with their arms spread out and walked forward, getting closer and closer until they had cornered a small goat. The rope-bearer swiftly bound its mouth – to keep it from bleating – then its legs, and the knife-bearer slid a thin wooden pole he'd broken from the fence under the knots. They found the trough filled with water for the cattle, gulped down as much as they could, and crawled back to the bound-up animal. They crouched down, lifted one end of the pole onto a shoulder each and looked around to ensure no job-obsessed goatherd, wandering guests, no young couple or drunken reveller, no one was tottering towards them, then rose up and fled back across the dunes, the night eating up the dust raised by their feet.

They came to rest in a rocky ravine. They collapsed panting, looking over their shoulders and about them, ensuring they were not being followed. The sun, just beginning its rise, was low on the horizon. It would hide the glow of their fire. Soon it would be safe to roast. The knife-bearer stood watch over the goat as the rope-bearer looked for firewood.

As he built the fire, the knife-bearer dug a hole in the hard ground, said a prayer that Allah might bless the beast, and slit its throat. The blood pooled into the hole and by the time he had swept the sand back into it, to soak and stiffen the blood, leaving the ground spotless, the fire was raging and the sun was at its highest.

Hours later, the fire was out and the sun was dipping its toes towards the land. The wood had turned to ash and the ash was thick with animal fat. The goat's head lay meters away from its licked-clean pile of bones, and its skin lay draped across a boulder, drying. Their stomachs had swelled past the point of satisfaction; the duo had eaten themselves to stupor and from there, had fallen into deepest and soundest sleep.

They were roused by sharp kicks to their torsos. The knife-bearer jerked awake and discovered that he no longer bore his knife, and neither did the rope-bearer bear his rope, for this was indeed the very coil wrapped around their chest, arms and legs. They lay there, like dwarf whales, like beached camels. Opposite them sat a young woman with the knife in her hand. She stood up, walked forward and brought the blade right up to their necks, where it caught and shimmered with the sun's fire and mirrored the quick flash of heat, the temper and intention in her eyes. 'The meat . . .' she asked '. . . where is the rest?'

*

The first time I saw suya, it was a smaller hill around which my father and a smaller group of his friends were sat, feasting, sweating and guzzling water noisily. I reached for the piece in my father's hand and he jerked back, warning me I could not handle the spices. I frowned, slipped away from him and walked towards the hill. Yet again I was denied one of the steaming juicy morsels of meat until

I broke into a scream that humbled the protective instincts of all the adults. I broke free, selected the largest piece I could find, which happened to be shaki – the elastic cut from a goat's stomach. I clamped my teeth around it and tried to tear off a piece.

My father says from the onset he knew I'd lose the battle. It was tough. The piece of meat was tougher than he knew I knew meat could be, and as I furrowed my brow, gripped and pulled with my small fists, my tiny fingers like blades of brown grass, my father says he saw what occurred unfold in slow motion. The meat drew out, as if Muhammad Ali in his prime, leaning far back against the ropes, away from his opponent's fists, then quick as a flash, leaned in, slipped through my fingers and – snap – landed squarely in the eyes.

It took hours for the pain to subside, for the blend of lava-like spices to be washed out, for the redness to fade from my eyes, for my tongue too cool down to its languidity, and for sleep to finally claim me.

*

The young woman looked wild. Her hair was a raging black bushfire crowning a hard face and tough mouth, her clothes were stitched of sackcloth and hung misshapen off her thin shoulders. She kicked the men again: 'Where's the rest of the meat?' 'We ate everything,' the knife-man replied. 'Liar! That is impossible! Tell me where it is?' 'You can't steal from us! Stealing is haram!' the rope-man responded. 'Haram? You stole the goat from the cleric! From an actual servant of God!' she said. 'That doesn't make what you are doing just. Only Allah decides what is just, stealing is stealing!' spat the rope-man. 'Perhaps I am Allah's instrument of justice. Did you think of that?' she asked, pushing the knife harder against his neck. 'Where. Is. The. Meat?' The knife-man sighed and pointed towards a pile of stones.

She walked over, unearthed the leftovers, thin strips of meat wrapped in goatskin. She shook her head angrily, 'What am I to do with this?' 'We weren't expecting guests,' the rope-man replied, which sent the knife-man spiralling into laughter, only to cease abruptly as the ropes cut deeper into his ribs. She walked a little away from them and began to build a fire.

She lifted each strip of meat to the sun, inspecting it thoroughly before conceding . . . 'This will not taste well. It needs . . .' she sighed again, and ruffled through the tiny bag she had tied to her waist. She poured out its contents: a handful of peanuts, dried pepper and ginger. It wasn't perfect. It wasn't even enough, but it would do. These were the basics for the more elaborate dishes her master could make. She had purchased them at the last market she had visited days before she fled. From the scarifications on her body, the men knew she had once been enslaved. They correctly guessed she had run away, but dared not ask from which rich family she had fled. Instead, they fell to silence, hypnotised by her works as she began to crush her ingredients into powder and smear them across the strips of meat, her hands like restless butterflies. The men shifted their positions, taking keener interest, sitting up as she worked.

'What are you doing?' The knife-man eventually asked. 'You are destroying the meat! No . . . don't . . . ahh!' He moaned as if her actions were causing him physical pain. 'Wait . . . wait! Save the last strip at least! Eat that pure! We worked hard to get that, I don't want to see it wasted.' But the louder he chastised her, the harder she pretended she could not hear a word, until the rope-man said, 'We should give her the salt.' She froze. 'Why?' asked the knife-man. 'We can't do anything with it now. She will leave us like this, we will die and when we do so, we will become the salt of the earth. We won't need more salt. It is useless to us. And, Allah may look kindly on our souls for this last generous deed.' The knife-man nodded thoughtfully. 'Fine. It is among our clothes. Over there,' he added, pointing with his chin.

When she took the first bite, the flavours in her mouth brought a satisfaction she could not have imagined. She sat back from the joy of it. It unleashed something she had never known she knew. The purity of her feeling was intense and further magnified by the empty sky, humbling yet growing within her. 'Mashallah,' she whispered, reaching for another piece. The aroma had been tormenting the men for so long that their necks hurt from the strain of leaning closer and closer to her. They saw her reaction and begged for a bite, their swollen bellies making space. 'For Allah's sake, I cannot begrudge you a last supper.' She walked over to them with small morsels she had stuck on the end of the thinnest sticks she could find and fed them at arm's length.

The men chewed, slowly, deeply savouring each scrap of meat, licking the insides of their mouths, picking their teeth clean, so focused were they that the ropes around their aching joints and bodies melted away under the spell and gave way to a dream, a future, from which the knife-man spoke: 'I have a business proposal. Will you listen?'

*

'You didn't learn your lesson from last time eh?' 'Like father, like son.' 'Look at his face, so focused!' The louder they spoke, the harder I pretended I could not hear their words, but this time I searched for a piece of meat that was proportional to my size, of a thickness weaker than the strength of my grip. I felt their eyes on me as I bit down, tore off a piece and chewed carefully, then thoroughly, savouring the flavour, the warmth in my mouth. I swallowed, reached for some groundnuts, which I washed down with chilled water, and reached for another piece of meat. I was determined not to be another story they would tell to each other. Instead, I thought, I want to be among their number, to tell stories too, to laugh like they do, to discover the secret to their community and communion, for this is what brought them together. The meat was just an excuse, an addition, the proverbial icing on the cake. What lay beneath was pure earth magic.

Nigeria has always been magical to me, a concept more than a country, a conundrum more than a complex, a being beyond comprehension, consistently mystifying even as it tried to demystify itself. When I was born, it was 24 years old and swaggered as 24-year-olds do, but it knew it was older than time. Old enough to know better but young enough not to care, it could shrug off its age like snakeskin and drape it back on like a coat of ostrich feathers. It could be weighed down by its chequered history, yet reinvent itself with a turn of a phrase. There were 500 ethnicities and languages and dialects, 500 parts to its body. Each part had a mouth and each mouth was telling its own story.

When we'd travel from Edo State to the Bendel region, from Jos to Lagos, from Ogun State to Kano, I'd strain to understand each story, and though I'd always fail, I'd be hypnotised by the attempt to understand, straining my ears, eyes closed, as my parents spoke to the locals. I'd lose myself in each tongue we'd encounter, marvelling at how from village to village – often just a few kilometres apart – language would change, the mouths would dazzle into other stories, the rhythm would tilt into something new, which like a spell, would hold me.

Stories are spells we tell each other and there is a rhythm to each. They are born out of necessity, built on collective memory and intertextual understandings, bejewelled with cultural and contextual specificity. They help us understand who we are and hint at who we might yet become. Nigeria is but a wide collection of stories. Sometimes they are cathartic, often they are lies, and though we know they are, we tell them in the guise of truth that they might speak to a greater truth. We welcome these spells, we dance them on our tongues, we turn them to music.

My father and his friends would swell with spells. Taking turns, they would rise to their feet and recount details of escaping bandits on treacherous roads, swindling swindlers out of money, standing up to abuses of power, quelling vast family disagreements with a turn of phrase, tales of mischievous youth, and in the small hours of the morning, the beer's grip loosening, they would tell of those who had passed away, conjuring them back to life as spells are said to do. Stories are spells, and watching my father speak was to witness at work the sorcerer supreme.

*

The trio trekked past a huddle of beautiful houses, the magnificent mosque, the factory district, the steaming pits where the Tuaregs dyed their lengths of fabric blue, and on to the market, where the knife- and rope-men disappeared to trade with whatever goodwill they had left in the little city. One went north, the other south as the young lady walked on. The knife-man spoke to his mother and father's people – the Nasarawa and Maguzawa – and the rope-man to his – the Kamberawa and the Bunjawa. Both switched from language to language, pleading deeply in their ancestral tongues. Only later, as they walked back to the market, did they revert to speaking Hausa. They returned with slabs of meat and the ingredients she had demanded they memorize. She had added a couple of other things her people had always cooked with: groundnuts, dried red pepper, salt, ginger, nutmeg, cloves and cinnamon. She crushed and mixed these into a fine powder as the rope-man stoked the fire beside her worktable and the knife-man cut the meat to strips, which he threaded with thin sticks as she had done days before.

The gentle breeze did most of the work. The aroma surreptitiously settled among the shoppers, who had only come to purchase clothes and tools. They found a longing unlocked within them; a longing altogether new but deeply familial and familiar. Their nostrils would flare, their mouths would pool with water, they'd follow primal instincts for nourishment and weave through the heaving market to the spot where the trio worked. There, they'd reach for their pouches. The shoppers gathered in groups as they chewed and tried to guess at the blend of spices. They all thought they knew; the flavours spoke to dishes they cooked themselves, but somehow the exact truth was beyond them. The rope-man ran back and forth with pouches of cowrie shells, buying as much meat as he could, burrowing and laying out benches as queues formed and lengthened around them.

By nightfall, they had requests for more portions, visitors promising to return the following day, and enough cowrie shells to purchase rooms in nearby lodgings. There, the trio bathed and slept soundly, as stars rose above them, twinkling like answered prayers.

Weeks later, they'd call the dish 'tsire', which in the Hausa tongue simply meant 'prepared meat'. The visiting foreigners from the south, from neighbouring towns, their mouths full, would mispronounce it 'sooya' and months later, after they had established a restaurant, after they had been asked a thousand times how they had met and arrived at this blend of flavours, this way of meat-making, the trio would establish a routine.

They would take it in turns and tell altogether different stories to the audience sat before them. Each would secretly laugh at the various ways the other would tell their version of what happened, from their point of view, with wild and specific references, straying far, far from the truth, yet somehow accurate and no less true, laughing at each other's brilliance, as if an in-joke, a secret language between them: they had grown so close you see, so intimately known to each other.

Their stories would spread far and wide and back down south with those visitors – who remade the dish, adding local spices to appease local tongues – and all would pass into legend, from legend to myth, and from myth to the thin wisps I have spun into this story.

*

In the final years of my youth in Lagos, my sorcerer supreme would take special pleasure from Sadaka, the aspect of the Festival of Eid where Muslims are required to be benevolent and charitable. My father, my uncles and I would have fattened a goat for weeks. We would then divide and distribute large portions of it to our neighbours, and in the evening, we'd make our own suya, soak and dry the goatskin, which would come to carpet the part of the living room I'd sit on.

Decades have passed since and though I've strayed far from home, as many Nigerians have – our footprints are found across the world, our voices in many non-native tongues – much remains the same. The country still swaggers, perhaps with an even wider stride, and notes as it strides that there are more mouths in its body, which grow only more tumultuous. Perhaps the only thing we the mouths can agree on, is that it is even more impossible to understand us at once. Instead, we'd ask the visitors to listen to the closest voice, to grasp what is possible, and weave from it a truth.

My truth is this: I am still that little boy in the living room. The goatskins are flatscreens now, but just as I was then, my fingers are greased with spices. I am imagining an audience, conjuring stories, making myth.

Coming to Lagos

Helon Habila

If you lived in the north of the country, going to Lagos was an epic performance; it was nothing short of a rite of passage. At 14, I felt like I was the only one amongst my friends who hadn't been to Lagos. They always returned with fantastic stories of the big city: countless bridges, impossibly tall buildings, labyrinthine roads that wove and disappeared into each other like puzzles for drivers to solve. My best friend had been to Lagos and returned with a swagger, walking with a slant to his right shoulder that he maintained to this day. He talked of thrilling encounters with dangerous Lagos denizens, Area Boys, with the air of a survivor who had laughed in the face of danger. The Area Boys, he said, would rob you in broad daylight, asking you to hand over your wallet, as if they were in a hurry and you were holding them up. He talked of street fights, bus touts exchanging blows and sometimes tearing off each other's clothes, right there on the streets. A scary place. It made us all the more eager to see and experience it. Thieves were set alight in public, right there and then: a rubber tyre around their neck, a little kerosene to get things going, a match, and the crowd cheering and urging it on. It was a savage place, one that my small-town imagination could not encompass. And the women, ah, Lagos women, sisi eko, here my friend wouldn't say more, hinting that he had not only seen these women, but had known them personally. Among the many things that my friend returned with was a Yoruba nickname, Alaiye Baba: King of the World.

That year I launched a campaign to wear down my mother's resistance. If my mother said yes, my father would agree – it was always that way. And one day, she said yes. I was going to Lagos. It was 1983, summer vacation – or the 'long vacation' as we called it.

There are different ways to travel to Lagos. If you lived in Gombe, like I did, you had to first get to Jos, by road, or to Kaduna – from there you take the 'Luxurious' bus, which was anything but, and from there you embark on the most reckless, the most dangerous ride of your life. There were rumours that the drivers took stimulants to help them stay awake – for some reason they always travelled by night. The roads were dark and narrow and full of potholes, and of course there were no speed limits. As for arrival date, there wasn't one. Two to three days was the usual estimate, but in reality, you got there when you got there. Because buses would break down on the way, in the middle of some god-awful forest far away from the nearest town or village, and the driver, under the pretext of going to look for a mechanic, would sneak away, never to be seen again, leaving his hapless conductor to deal with the irate passengers. Passengers had been known to wait for days, camped there by the roadside like refugees, before the bus was fixed. More experienced passengers who knew the drill would simply grab their bags and stop whatever passing vehicle they could to take them to the nearest town where they could catch another bus to their destination. If the bus didn't break down, there were armed robbers to contend with, lurking in the dark, waiting for cars or buses to crash into the huge boulders they had piled in the middle of the road, so they could rob the wounded and confused passengers at leisure.

Perhaps that was why my mother decided that I should go by train instead of by bus. I was going to visit my eldest sister, Ruth. Looking back, I am surprised that my mother actually allowed me to travel to Lagos on a train by myself at 14. I look at my 14-year-old son now, and there is no way I'd let him take that kind of trip by himself. But then, in my mother's defence, the world, Nigeria, was a much safer place than it is now. In 1983 the whole country was like a sleeping giant, slowly beginning to come awake. There were crimes and highway robberies, but they were very rare – they were not things that happened to you or your neighbours, you read about them in the papers with shock and surprise. Those were the days when armed robbers were shot in public executions at the beach in Lagos and in football stadiums in other cities – a spectacle to serve as a deterrent to aspiring robbers.

And, despite my young age, I was already something of a veteran traveller – though I had never been anywhere as far away as Lagos. My mother was one of those moms who love to send their children to visit relatives during the vacations; perhaps she was trying, through me, to fulfil a secret wish for travel which she now, as a wife and a mother, never could. She loved to listen to my vacation stories whenever I came back, every detail, about how her brothers and sisters lived, how their children behaved. Before I was 12, I had been to Zaria, Bauchi, Jos, Kaduna. I had caught the travel bug and come every vacation, my bag would be packed, ready for yet another trip, ready to see somewhere new; travelling was like putting together pieces of a map of the unknown world – each time I came back, a new piece of the puzzle fell into place. Slowly, this vast, diverse country was revealing itself to my young imagination. These imaginary places I had read about in my history and geography books were becoming actual places: now I could, with first-hand authority, talk about the temperate weather in the Jos plateau, which was unlike any other in the country; I had seen and touched the famous city walls of Zaria and Bauchi and walked the streets of Kaduna. I was like a man in a shuttered room who has found the window and is slowly opening it to reveal, inch by inch, the ineffable scenery outside.

*

I set out for Lagos from the Bauchi Railway Station. I came to Bauchi with my uncle Ezekiel in his brand-new Volkswagen; my uncle, always in a rush, left me at the entrance of the huge station building and waved goodbye. Now I was alone on the long, concrete platform and it would be hours before the Lagos train arrived. Next to me was my duffel bag, which contained a few changes of clothes and my toiletries. Now that I was here, and the trip was actually about to happen, my excitement had turned to trepidation. For one, I had never been on a train before.

Twice I had been to the train station in Gombe with my family to see my older brother off when he was going to Lagos to visit my sister. A fascinating place, the railway station, with its cavernous departure hall filled with passengers and their families, pulling their luggage behind them as they waited in line to buy their tickets. The anxiety and excitement etched on their faces as they kept looking at the huge clock over the door and then back at the single ticketing window that seemed so far away from them. Out on the single platform were little hills of boxes and portmanteaus and rucksacks over which stood their owners, already ticketed, their eyes fixed on the long stretch of narrow rail tracks gleaming dully under the floodlights and disappearing into the dark and humid night. And then finally came the distant, piercing horn of the approaching train accompanied by the clanking of its metal wheels on the tracks. We could see its lights now just outside the platform lights' perimeter, waiting for the all-clear sign. When finally the long length of engines and coaches pulled into the station, the sight of its gleaming metallic mass and the driver in his peak cap and passengers peeping out and waving through the windows stirred the waiting passengers like wind over a field of grass; the waft of wind from the train's air brakes sent bits of paper and dust into the night. The travellers surged at the opening doors, throwing themselves at it, forcing back the disembarking passengers. It was like a feeding frenzy; the men and women were piranhas snapping at their victim. A man threw a bag through an open window and then threw himself after it. A fat, breathless man picked up a terrified child and hurled it over the heads blocking the doorway into receiving hands, and then he pushed his way after it, dragging behind him another child. A woman was stuck halfway in a narrow window, kicking and pushing till a hand shoved at her rump and she fell inside, and more bodies followed her, stretching and contorting their bodies to fit between the window bars. Then suddenly it was over. Everyone was in, the platform became astonishingly calm and deserted, except for small groups of families waving at sons and daughters and uncles and aunts and friends going off to Lokoja and Kaduna and Enugu and Ibadan and Port Harcourt, and Lagos.

*

I was amazed at how quiet the station at Bauchi was. Only a few passengers had appeared on the platform in the couple of hours I had been there; some of them were now standing in groups, gazing without much enthusiasm in the direction the train would arrive. A large woman was sleeping on a bench facing the rail tracks, her legs sprawled out in front of her. When the train finally came in, around 6 p.m., it stopped for less than thirty minutes and was gone. I was surprised to see the carriage was full of people, for some reason I thought it would be as empty as the platform had been.

All the seats appeared to be taken. Some of the seats had top and bottom bunks – iron benches welded to the floor, with plastic foams covering the surface. I stood with my bag in hand, hanging onto a rail as the train gathered speed. I didn't know it was going to be so dark inside. Shadowy shapes sat pressed against each other, with children crying in discomfort; some were eating with their fingers from bowls held in their laps. The coach smelled of food and bodies and underneath that there was the smell of urine coming from the open toilets at each end of the coach. There was no air conditioning and the only fresh air came from the narrow windows placed at intervals along the length of the coach. When my eyes grew accustomed to the gloom, I noticed a young lady seated directly opposite me; she was pointing at the narrow space next to her. I sat down, smiling my thanks.

Her name, she told me when we got talking, was Ruth.

'Oh, that is my sister's name. I am going to visit her,' I said.

'Where?'

'Lagos.'

'That's where I am going too.'

She was about my age, maybe a year older. She spoke in fluent Hausa with a slight Yoruba accent. She was a student of the Federal Government Girls College in Yola and she was going home for the vacation. She must have travelled this route many times, I guessed, from the way she stoically turned her face away when a large woman suddenly squatted in the middle of the coach and began to pee noisily into a plastic bowl. I, on the other hand, couldn't turn away. I watched, shocked and surprised, till the woman finished and calmly threw the contents of the bowl out of the window. I turned to see Ruth looking at me, amused at my expression. She advised me not to go into the toilets, no matter what.

'Why?'

'It's not clean. Wait till we get to Lokoja. We'll be there in a few hours.'

*

We were in Lokoja for over five hours. We pulled into the station after midnight. It was dark and quiet in the coach, but out in the station it looked like day: lights blazed out of the huge terminal building, a high-life song played from speakers hanging from a pole in front of the building, children chased each other under the lights. Lokoja was one of the most important rail terminals in the country: here, the rail lines from the south-east and the south-west converged after crossing the Niger Bridge at Jebba, giving rise to a complex network of veins and arteries. In the colonial days and before the trains ground to a halt, this was where most of the traffic met, conveying their freight – groundnut and cattle and grains from the North, and palm oil and yam and cassava from the South – to be further conveyed by road to remote reaches of the country. Here, trains pulled in and out at all times of the day and night, and on the platforms and beside rail tracks, hawkers waited with their merchandise on trays and tables and bowls and basins, pushing their faces into the dark coaches, the bold ones jumping inside, calling out their wares to the sleepy and exhausted passengers.

Ruth stood up and pointed at her bag. 'I'll be back.'

I stood at the door and watched her cut through the mill of bodies getting on and off the train till she disappeared into the night. She was back in about thirty minutes, just when I was beginning to grow restless, wondering if she was returning. She looked refreshed, as if she had taken a bath; she had changed into a fresh blouse, the old one was folded in a plastic bag in her hand. She must have been on the train for as much as twenty-four hours, I calculated, travelling from Yola, with all the unscheduled stops on the way. Now it was her turn to look after the bags as I got off the train.

I bought a bottle of Coke and a loaf of bread and wolfed everything down, all the time keeping my gaze on the train, scared of being left behind. When I finished, I looked around for a toilet, and finding none, decided to go into the bushes. Trains stood like giant worms in the night, some looked dark and abandoned, others had lights moving about in them and passengers getting on and off. Old steam engines stood side by side with diesel engines. There were broken-down engines undergoing repairs. The Indian and local engineers went about purposefully with toolboxes, shining torches and lamps into the engines and clanking metal against metal. Away from the lights I saw people squatting casually not far from the trains, urinating or shitting, some squatting over the rail tracks, behind the coaches, some under trees. Men and women and children. And now I could smell the stink. I looked down, careful not to step in someone's faeces, as I joined them.

*

From Lokoja we turned southwards; in the other direction the rail ran all the way to Kano, 700 miles away from Lagos. The rest of the trip was a blur; the night turned to day, and day turned to night; lamps shone into the coach as the train stopped in yet another village and the hawkers came in with akara and roast groundnuts and moi moi and bananas and mangoes on trays, calling out in strange languages. In the kaleidoscopic crush of images and events I remember one stands out – crossing the River Niger at Jebba, about 306 miles to Lagos. We all rushed to the windows to watch the long and dark body of water below. I was excited by the symbolism of it: crossing the Niger meant stepping into what Northerners call generally 'South'.

I was in southern Nigeria, which for all practical purposes was like stepping into another country, for even the earth smelled differently from the sometimes dry, sometimes musky smell of the savannah I grew up with. From here, the trees got taller, the woods thicker, and the air denser with humidity and the smell of rotting vegetation. I realized how big and various the country was, and how far away from home I had come.

Ruth gave me a tired smile. This was our second night sitting side by side – often, for no reason, and with no warning, the train had stopped, and then the hawkers would emerge as if by magic out of the darkness, and the engineers would bang on the metal of the train engine with their tools; sometimes we remained stationary for hours and passengers would step outside to stretch their legs, at other times we stopped for only a few minutes before the train started moving again. I had slept only in fits and starts since I came on; my joints ached and my feet looked swollen. I watched the grime on the floor and on the handrails grow thicker. All open spaces were now packed with luggage as more passengers climbed in, all faces looked exhausted, smudged with grime. We tolerated each other's foul smells because we knew we also stank. Ruth told me that down the corridor, many coaches forward, was the first-class section; her voice was wistful. They had beds and showers and air conditioning and the cafeteria was clean and sold good food and drinks. The third-class cafeteria had been converted into a sleeping area – the caterers had long since abandoned it – and the only place to buy food was from the hawkers at the stations.

'Ibadan,' Ruth announced. She mostly sat in silence, looking out through the window when she was not sleeping. But now she looked lively, standing up to peek into the station. 'We will be in Lagos before morning.' Ibadan to Lagos was only 126 miles, but the train remained in Ibadan till morning, perhaps undergoing more repairs.

Some said it was because nobody wanted to enter Lagos at night. It was too dangerous, people had been known to get mugged by thugs, their bags snatched at knife-point. Ruth went out and came back with a bottle of Coke, which she handed to me. When I shook my head, she insisted, pushing it into my hands firmly.

'What do you look forward to seeing the most in Lagos?' she asked.

I did not hesitate. 'The sea.'

I had never seen the sea. I couldn't imagine a body of water stretching as far as the eye could see, rising up to meet the sky in the horizon. Towards morning, when the train slowly rolled out of the station amidst engine smoke and loud honks, Ruth took out a hairbrush and ran it over her cornrows before tying on a colourful headscarf. She soaked a handkerchief in water out of a bottle and used it to gently wipe her face and neck. When she finished, she looked so fresh and pretty I became doubly conscious of how grimy I looked. I had been in the same clothes and underwear for three days. My mouth felt so foul, I was afraid to speak. Soon, I told myself, it would be over soon. Ruth had given me directions for how to get to Mahyoung Barracks in Yaba. I was to jump off when the train got to Yaba, there was no point going all the way to the final stop at Iddo Terminus.

'You just jump off when the train slows down.'

When I looked doubtful, she laughed and said, 'It is easy. You don't have much luggage.'

It was easy. I was emboldened by the sight of others brushing past me and jumping off. The train was at an intersection next to the Yaba Market. It had come to a standstill, waiting for the intersection gates to be opened. I grabbed my bag and waved to Ruth, then I jumped down as the train started to roll forward. I stood in the gravel next to the rails, waving after the moving train. Ruth waved back, her head out of the train window, her red and yellow scarf shaking in the wind.

I turned, taking stock of where I was. I stood in the middle of a network of rail tracks; to my right was the bustling Yaba Market and the tracks ran right in front of the market. This was Lagos. I wasn't as excited and overwhelmed as I thought I would be, only tired and hungry, and a bit anxious. The excitement, I knew, would come later after I had rested. I took a deep breath, trying to see if I could smell the sea from here. I got a taxi and told the driver to take me to Mahyoung Barracks and to drop me at the Yaba Tech entrance.

Still Becoming

Chimamanda Ngozi Adichie

Lagos will not court you. It is a city that is what it is. I have lived part-time in Lagos for ten years and I complain about it each time I return from my home in the US – its allergy to order, its stultifying traffic, its power cuts. I like, though, that nothing about Lagos was crafted for the tourist, nothing done to appeal to the visitor. Tourism has its uses, but it can mangle a city, especially a developing city, and flatten it into a permanent shape of service: the city's default becomes a simpering bow, and its people turn the greyest parts of themselves into colourful props. In this sense, Lagos has a certain authenticity because it is indifferent to ingratiating itself; it will treat your love with an embrace, and your hate with a shrug. What you see in Lagos is what Lagos truly is.

And what do you see? A city in a state of shifting impermanence. A place still becoming. In newer Lagos, houses sprout up on land reclaimed from the sea, and in older Lagos, buildings are knocked down so that ambitious new ones might live. A street last seen six months ago is different today, sometimes imperceptibly so – a tiny store has appeared at a corner – and sometimes baldly so, with a structure gone, or shuttered, or expanded. Shops come and go. Today, a boutique's slender mannequin in a tightly pinned dress; tomorrow, a home accessories shop with gilt-edged furniture on display.

Admiralty Road is cluttered, pulsing, optimistic. It is the business heart of Lekki, in the highbrow part of Lagos called The Island. Twenty years ago, Lekki was swampland and today the houses in its estates cost millions of dollars. It was supposed to be mostly residential but now it is undecided, as though partly trying to fend off the relentless encroachment of commerce, and partly revelling in its ever-growing restaurants, nightclubs and shops.

I live in Lekki, but not in its most expensive centre, Phase 1. My house is farther away, close to the behemoth that is the oil company Chevron's headquarters. A modest house, by Lekki standards. 'It will be under water in thirty years,' a European acquaintance, a diplomat in Lagos, said sourly when I told him, years ago, that I was building a house there. He hated Lagos, and spoke of Lagosians with the resentment of a person who disliked the popular kids in the playground but still wanted to be their friend. I half-shared his apocalyptic vision; he was speaking to something unheeding in Lagos's development. Something almost reckless.

So forward-looking is Lagos, headlong, rushing, dissatisfied in its own frenzy, that in its haste it might very well sacrifice long-term planning or the possibility of permanence. Or the faith of its citizens. One wonders always: have things been done properly? Eko Atlantic City, the new ultra-expensive slice of land reclaimed from the Atlantic Ocean, has already been mostly sold to developers, and promises Dubai-like infrastructures, but my reaction remains one of scepticism. I cannot stop imagining the ocean one day re-taking its own.

My house had required some arcane engineering, sand-filling, levelling, to prevent the possibility of sinking. And during the construction, my relatives stopped by often to check on things. If you're building a house you must be present, otherwise the builders will slap-dash your tiling and roughen your finishing. This is a city in a rush and corners must be cut.

Lagos has an estimated population of 23.5 million – estimated because Nigeria has not had a proper census in decades. Population numbers determine how much resource states receive from the federal government, and census-taking is always contested and politicised. Lagos is expected to become, in the next ten years, one of the world's mega-cities, a term that conceals in its almost triumphant preface the chaos of overpopulation. Nigeria is Africa's most populous country – one in five Africans is Nigerian – and Lagos is Nigeria's commercial centre, its cultural centre, the aspirational axis where dreams will live or die.

And so people come. From other parts of Nigeria, from other West African countries, from other African countries, they come. Skilled workers come from countries as far away as South Africa while less-skilled workers are more likely to come from the countries that share a border with Nigeria. My gate man, Abdul, who has worked with me for six years, is a striking young Muslim from the Republic of Niger, Nigeria's northern neighbour. In his small ancestral village, Lagos was seen as the city of shining lights. He longed to leave and find work in Lagos. To live in Lagos and return twice a year with the sparkle of Lagos on his skin. Nigeria is to Africa what the United States is to the Americas: it dominates Africa's cultural imagination in a mix of admiration, resentment, affection and distrust. And the best of Nigeria's contemporary culture – music, film, fashion, literature and art – is tied in some way to Lagos.

If Lagos has a theme it is the hustle – the striving and trying. The working class does the impossible to scrape a living. The middle class has a side hustle. The banker sews clothes. The telecommunications analyst sells nappies. The school teacher organises private home lessons. Commerce rules. Enterprising people scrawl their advertisements on public walls, in chalk: 'Call for affordable generator'. 'I am buying condemned inverter'. 'Need a washerman?'

63

Perhaps this is why corporations are not viewed with the knowing suspicion so common in the West. 'Branding' is a word entirely free of irony, and people use it to refer even to themselves. 'I want to become a big brand,' young people brazenly say. Big companies adopt state schools and refurbish them, they organise de-worming exercises in poor areas, they award prizes to journalists. Even the too-few green spaces in public areas are branded, a burst of beautiful shrubs and plants defaced with the logo of whatever bank or telecommunications company is paying for its upkeep.

This is a city of blurred boundaries. Religion and commerce are intertwined. Lagos has a Muslim population but, like all of southern Nigeria, it is a predominantly Christian city. Drive past a gleaming modern building and it might be a bank or a church. Huge signboards advertise church programmes with photos of nicely dressed pastors, and on Sundays the city is as close as it can get to being traffic-free, because Lagosians are at rest, back home from morning service. Pentecostal Christianity is fashionable, prayers are held before corporate board meetings, and 'We thank God' is an appropriate response to a compliment, or even merely to the question, 'How are you?'

This Christianity is selectively conservative, it glances away from government corruption, preaches prosperity, casts ostentatious wealth as a blessing, and disapproves of socially progressive norms. Women are to submit to their husbands. Hierarchies matter. God wants you to be rich. But it also unites Lagosians; people who attend the same church become surrogate families, and together they attend large vigil services more exciting than music concerts, where urbane men and glamorous women sing praise-songs deep into the night and in the morning return to their well-paid jobs in the high rises of The Island.

In Lagos, ethnicity both matters and doesn't matter. Lagos is ancestral Yoruba land and Yoruba is spoken widely, but it is also

Nigeria's polyglot centre, and the dream-seekers who have come from all parts of the country communicate by Nigeria's official language of English and unofficial lingua franca of Pidgin English.

Some areas are known as ethnic – the Hausa sector where working-class Northern Muslims live, the areas with large markets run by people from my own south-eastern Igbo ethnic group – but none of them are affluent. With wealth, overt appeals to ethnicity retreat.

My cousin lives in a lower middle-class area, heavily populated by Igbo traders. Once, on my way to visit her, the car stuck in traffic, a hawker pressed his packs of chewing gum against my window. Gabriel, my driver of ten years, said to me, 'Ma, your bag.' A simple reminder. I swiftly moved my handbag from the back seat to the floor, pushed it under my seat.

My cousin was robbed in traffic on her way home from work, a gun to her head, her bag and phone taken, and beside her people kept slow-driving, face-forward. And now she has a fake bag and a fake phone that she leaves on display in her front seat whenever she drives home, because robbers target women driving alone, and if she has nothing to give them they might shoot her.

My brother-in-law was also robbed not far from here. He was in traffic on a bright afternoon, his windows down, and someone shouted from the outside, something about his car, and he looked out of the window and back to the road and in that brief sliver of time a hand slid through the other window and his phone was gone. He told the story, later, with a tinge of admiring defeat.

He, a real Lagosian who had lived in Lagos for forty years and knew its wiles and its corners, and yet they had managed to fool him. He had fallen for the seamless ingenuity of Lagos's thieves. To live in Lagos is to live on distrust. You assume you will be cheated, and what matters is that you avert it, that you will not be taken in by it. Lagosians will speak of this with something close to pride, as though their survival is a testament to their fortitude, because Lagos is Lagos. It does not have the tame amiability of Accra. It is not like Nairobi, where flowers are sold in traffic.

In other parts of Lagos, especially the wealthy areas on The Island, I wouldn't hide my handbag in traffic, because I would assume myself to be safe. Here, security is status. Lagos is a city of estates; groups of houses, each individually walled off, are enclosed in yet another walled fence, with a central gate and a level of security proportional to the residents' privilege. The estates not blessed with wealth lock their gates before midnight, to keep out armed robbers. Nightclub-goers living there know not to return home until 5 a.m. when the gates are opened. Expensive estates have elaborate set ups at their entrances: you park your car and wait for the security guards to call whomever you're visiting, or you are given a visitor's card as identification, or you are asked to open your boot, or a jaunty guard walks around your car with a mirror lest you have a bomb strapped underneath.

In a city like Mumbai, which is as complicated as Lagos, it is easy to understand why the expensive parts are expensive just by driving through them, but in Lagos one might be confused. Mansions sit Buddha-like behind high gates but the streets still have potholes, and are still half-sunken in puddles during the rainy season and still have the ramshackle kiosk in a corner where drivers buy their lunch. High-end estates still have about them an air of the unfinished. Next to a perfectly landscaped compound with ornate gates might sit an empty lot, astonishingly expensive, and overgrown with weeds and grass.

I live in Lekki and dream of Old Ikoyi. British colonial government officers lived in Old Ikoyi starting in the Twenties, a time of mild apartheid when Africans could not live there and could not go to the 'white' hospital, and could not apply for high-profile jobs. Today,

Old Ikoyi has about it that stubborn, undeniable beauty that is the troubled legacy of injustice. With its leafy grounds, and trees leaning across the streets, it reminds me a little of my childhood in the small university town of Nsukka, an eight-hour drive from Lagos: quiet, restful, frangipani trees dotting the compound, purple bougainvillea climbing the walls.

And so I find myself wishing I lived in Old Ikoyi and mourning its slow disappearance. Gracious columned houses are being knocked down for tall apartment buildings and large homes with unintentionally baroque facades. 'Beware of Lagos', I heard often while growing up on the other side of Nigeria. Lagos was said to be a city of shallowness and phony people. There were many shimmering, mythical examples of this, stories repeated in various permutations, with the characters from different ethnic groups, and small details changed: the suave man who drives a Range Rover but is penniless and lives on the couches of friends; the beautiful woman who parades herself as an accomplished business person but is really a con artist. And who would blame them, those self-reinventors so firmly invested in their own burnished surfaces?

Here, appearance matters. You can talk your way into almost any space in Lagos if you look the part and drive the right car. In many estates, the guards fling open the gates when the latest model of a particular brand of car drives up, the questions they have been trained to ask promptly forgotten. But approach in an old Toyota and they will unleash their petty power.

Snobbery here is unsubtle. Western designer logos are so common among elite Lagosians that style journalists write of Gucci and Chanel as though they were easily affordable by a majority of the people. Still, style is democratic. Young working-class women are the most original: they shop in open markets, a mass of second-hand clothes spread on the ground under umbrellas, and they emerge in the perfect pair of skinny jeans, the right flattering dresses. Young working-class men are not left behind, in their long-sleeved tucked-in shirts, their crisp traditional matching tunics and trousers. And so Lagos intimidates with its materialism, its insolence, its beautiful people.

A young woman told me that when she was considering entering the Miss Nigeria beauty pageant she decided not to try out in Lagos, even though she lived there. 'Too many fine babes in Lagos,' she said. And so she went to Enugu, her ancestral hometown, where she believed her chances were better.

Young people complain of the dating scene. Nobody is honest, they say. Men and women perform. Everyone is looking for what is shinier and better. 'Why do you choose to live in Lagos, then?' I once asked a young woman. Every time I ask this of a young person dissatisfied with Lagos, they invariably look puzzled to be asked, as though they assumed it to be obvious they would never consider leaving. Everybody complains about Lagos but nobody wants to leave. And why do I live here? Why didn't I build my house in Enugu, for example, a slow, clean, appealing city in the south-east, close to where I grew up?

It is clichéd to speak of the 'energy' of Lagos, and it can sometimes sound like a defensive retort in the face of the city's many infrastructural challenges. But Lagos does have a quality for which 'energy' is the most honest description. A dynamism. An absence of pallor. You can feel it in the uncomfortable humid air – the talent, the ingenuity, the bursting multi-ness of everything, the self-confidence of a city that knows it matters.

The only real functioning Nigerian port is in Lagos, and business people from all over the country have no choice but to import their goods through there. Nigerian business is headquartered in Lagos; not only the banks, and the telecommunications and oil and advertising companies, but also the emerging creative industries. Art galleries have frequent exhibitions of Nigeria's best artists. Fashion Week is here. The concerts are the biggest and noisiest. Nollywood stars might not shoot their films in Lagos – it's too expensive – but they premiere them in Lagos. The production of culture works in service to Lagos's unassailable cool.

There are some things of conventional touristic appeal. The last gasp of Brazilian architecture in the oldest parts of Lagos, houses built by formerly enslaved Africans who, starting in the 1830s, returned from Brazil and settled in Lagos. The Lekki Market, where beautiful sculptures and ornaments blend with kitsch, and where the sellers speak that brand of English reserved for foreigners. The National Museum with its carefully tended flowers outside the building and inside an air of exquisite abandon. The Lekki Conservation Centre, a small nature reserve, with bounteous greenery and some small animals. The first time I visited, with a friend, I asked the ticketing person what we might hope to see. 'No lions or elephants,' she said archly. The highlights are the gorgeous birds, and the monkeys, and the sheer surprise of an oasis of nature in the middle of Lagos's bustle. The nearby beaches are dirty and overcrowded but the beaches one reaches by taking a speedboat across the waters are clean, dotted with beach houses, and flanked by palms.

The restaurants in Lagos are owned by a Lebanese 'mafia', a friend once told me, only half-joking. Nigeria has a significant Lebanese presence. They very rarely inter-marry with Nigerians, and I sense in some Lebanese employers a unique scorn for their Nigerian staff, but their roots in Nigeria are firm. They are Lebanese Nigerians. And they own many restaurants, and their mark is obvious in the ubiquity of the shawarma. Young people go out for a shawarma. Kids ask for shawarmas as treats.

There are, of course, Nigerian-owned restaurants. The chains with basic, not untasty food, the mid-level restaurants that dispense with frills and serve the jollof rice one might have cooked at home, and the high-end restaurants that labour under the weight of their own pretensions. There are quirky shops that cater mostly to a new Lagos tribe, the returnees: young people who have returned from schooling in the US or Europe with new ideas, and might for example suggest that a thing being 'handmade' were remarkable, as though hand-making things were not the Nigerian norm. They represent a new globalised Nigerian, situated in Nigeria, au fait about the world.

It is the breathing human architecture of Lagos that thrills me most. For a novelist, no city is better for observing human beings. On Sundays, when the roads are not clogged up, I like to be driven around Lagos, headed nowhere, watching the city.

Past bus stops full of people with earphones stuck in their ears. A roadside market with colourful bras swinging from a balcony, wheel-barrows filled with carrots, a table laid out with wigs. Fat, glorious watermelons piled high. Hawkers selling onions, eggs, bread. In gutters clogged with sludgy, green water and cans and plastic bags, I imagine the possibility of a clean city. Lagos is full of notices. 'This house is not for sale' is the most common, scrawled on walls, a warning to those who might be duped by real estate shysters. Near a mosque, where a fashionable young woman in jeans and a headscarf walks past, is this in green letters: 'Chief Imam of Lagos Says No Parking Here'. From a bridge, I look across at shirtless men fishing on flimsy canoes. The second-hand books spread on low tables have curled covers, copies of *Mastering Mathematics* beside *How to Win Friends and Influence People*.

On these drives, I think of how quickly fights and friendships are formed in Lagos. A yellow danfo bus has hit another and both conductors have leapt out for a swift fight. People make friends while queuing – at banks, airports, bus stops – and they unite over obvious jokes and shared complaints.

At night, there are swathes of Lagos that are a gloomy grey from power cuts, lit only by a few generator-borne lights, and there are areas that are bright and glittering. And in both one sees the promise of this city: that you will find your kin, where you fit, that there is a space somewhere in Lagos for you.

Elephants and Giraffes

Oyinkan Akande

The first wedding I remember going to is my aunt's. I was only about 6 at the time, so it is a surprise how much I remember. What I recall most vividly is that both the bride and groom were missing. My aunt was the second child of my grandparents to get married and, like my mother before her, she chose a simple civil ceremony. My grandparents, frustrated by the insolence of their children choosing to get married without pomp and pageantry, decided that the presence of a couple at their own wedding was merely a technicality.

It is true that a traditional Yoruba wedding is more for the families than for the couple. The parents and older family members have the biggest role to play, greeting and welcoming each other with a fanfare that could absorb hours of the ceremony before the bride and groom even appear. Two women, called alagas,* charismatically lead the events and dictate the terms of the day. Next, the would-be husband arrives, flanked by an entourage of male friends. At the discretion of the alagas, he is made to jump through hoops, a sort of test performed in front of both families and their guests. Before he is allowed to sit, he must answer a series of

---

* Alaga – traditional master of ceremonies (usually female) at a traditional Yoruba wedding (igbeyawo). A wedding will typically have two, who play off each other.

questions satisfactorily. He and his friends must prostrate them-selves, lying entirely flat on the ground, in front of the family of the bride as a sign of respect and humility. Only after the union has been formally announced and accepted does the bride arrive, dancing in veiled and surrounded by her female friends to perform the crossing over from her family to her husband's. The bride crowns her husband with a fila* and takes her place next to him, typically on ornamented chairs placed in full view of the room, where they can be admired.

At my aunt's wedding, the bride and groom were substituted by two A3-sized portraits printed on thick wooden boards, each propped up against raffia peacock chairs and placed at the front of the cere-mony so that they could overlook the festivities. The human versions of the bride and groom were, by the time of the wedding-in-absentia, already married in a quiet North Carolina registry and were thousands of miles across the world.

I remember that it rained the whole day. The ground turned to brown sludge and before all the guests had arrived, we had to decamp – shifting the chairs out of the rain and attempting to squeeze the guests under an inadequate-sized marquee. By 'we', I mean the bedlam of people running around in my memory, most of whom are faceless, but one is my mother. I remember spotting her in the rain after she had been forced to change out of her aso ebi† so she could rescue the coolers of food and drink that were swishing about in the mud. Perhaps she was being punished for her role in all of it – her own audacious choice to get married in a court. She still laments the shoes she wore to her sister's wedding and how she lost them to the rain.

---

* Fila – Yoruba word for a cap, traditionally worn by men.

† Aso ebi – Yoruba word referring to the Nigerian tradition of wearing a specific fabric to social events, like weddings, birthdays and funerals, to designate your relationship to the celebrants or solidarity with a larger group.

They ended the day caked so that the two – shoe and mud – had become one.

I suspect my grandmother didn't mind the rain so much. She likes to say that if it rains on your birthday it is a sign of blessings for the year ahead – all the better for those of us whose birthdays fall within the rainy season. How much better is it then if it rains on your wedding day? Except, of course, this wasn't really my aunt's wedding. It was my grandparents'. Whenever my grandmother starts to talk about rain, she is sure to marvel at how hard it is falling and joke that it is not raining cats and dogs, but elephants and giraffes. It rained elephants and giraffes that day, but I doubt it bothered her – so long as the wedding continued.

My grandmother does recall how that morning a friend of my grandfather came to her, asking that she pay the local babalawos* at Ota, where the wedding was to be held, an exorbitant amount so that they could stop the approaching rain. A devout Christian and decidedly complacent with how sunny it was that morning, she was insulted. She sent the friend away with the words, 'Let it rain. Why should I pay them?' And so, rain it did and not before the hour was up. She also remembers the shoes she'd gone all the way to London to buy and how they didn't survive the mud either.

At this point, you might be wondering why they continued with the ceremony. *Why not give up?* To understand the reasoning behind their carrying on, you must first understand the culture of gbedu.†️ There is very little on the list of things that can stop a party in Nigeria. People near bankruptcy for the sake of extravagant events. Others throw parties despite already being in the red. If ever I attend

---

* Babalawo – Yoruba word literally meaning 'father of the mysteries'. It is a title for a spiritual priest.
†️ Gbedu – Yoruba word literally meaning 'beat'. Recently, it is adapted refer to a good vibe.

a Nigerian wedding that is called off, I expect the guests to turn up nonetheless and ask to be pointed in the direction of the jollof rice. You may deal with your matrimonial woes, of course, but you had better first make sure the DJ knows to continue playing. There are certain things that a Nigerian feels entitled to. And, first and foremost is enjoyment – by now not just a word, but an entire ethos.

'It's easy to love Nigeria in December o!' friends told me the first Christmas I came home. It had been ten years since I'd been back and just about then I was wondering why I'd stayed away so long. I was loving the endless slew of parties, concerts, weddings and beach days. Christmas in Nigeria is a particular fever of excitement, less about the 25th of December itself and more about the lead-up to it. In Lagos, the entire season is very much a mad scramble to do as much as you can before the year is out. Festivities abound so that, regardless of where you do choose to go, you're likely to suffer from fear of missing out on the event you didn't attend. Lagos, already an exhilarating cacophony of a city, has an unquantifiable spirit in December that could make an insomniac of many people and a pittance out of their bank accounts. Worried that I might decide to move back based on my experience of Detty December* alone, my friends were quick to warn me: 'Lagos is not like this the rest of the year.'

They were right. My experience that month would have left me ill-prepared for the realities of full-time life in Lagos. Still, the liveliness of the city in December is, to me, more than just a response to the arrival of the Christmas returnees, more than a simple coincidence of a calendar month. Rather, both these things were simply the hook on which we had chosen to hang our excuses to party. I've

* 'Detty December' is used to refer Nigerians spending December in a vivacious way.

seen Nigerians party just as hard at a child's naming ceremony. The mother was still weak from the birth so her family simply danced around her as she held her baby in her arms, not minding how the noise might upset her or the newborn.

There is something to be said for the wider politics of joy in Nigeria. There is a stubborn sense of a wrong in the air if one has reason to celebrate and does not do so. As my great grandmother turned 90, my family felt moved to celebrate her long, well-lived life without reservation. This meant bringing together as many friends, family and strangers as we could gather to join us in giving thanks for her. At the core of enjoyment is the desire to take – and create – any opportunity for joy and gratefulness. The value of enjoyment is as a palpable signifier of happiness. In a sort of ritualised thanksgiving, celebrating means publicly announcing your state of being, and it is a performative act of both flaunting and defiance.

Flaunting is the most evident aspect of a Nigerian's joy, based on a simple premise: it is not enough to be happy, people must be able to see how you celebrate being happy. So, if you are dancing, you must call people to watch you dance. It is an unsurprising fact that Nollywood's highest-grossing film at the time of writing is about a wedding and the obstacles that threaten it. *The Wedding Party* both demonstrates and satirises some of the typical rituals of a Nigerian wedding, including some of the customs around flaunting. In one of the early scenes, the mother of the bride, played by Sola Sobowale, becomes enraged when she discovers that her name is not mentioned in the wedding announcement in a society paper alongside her husband's and the names of the groom's parents. And, though this has no material significance for her daughter's wedding day, she feels slighted by her lack of visibility as one of the celebrants of the day. The mechanics of flaunting requires an audience. It is a performance where the gaze serves to encourage and nourish the gazed upon. So, it fails if visibility is obscured, interrupted or denied.

The mother of the bride is somewhat appeased when her husband shares news of the important men who have confirmed they will be at the wedding. And this, too, is an opportunity to flaunt. A typical wedding programme will include time for announcements recognizing any dignitaries and important people present, usually at the request of the parents and to the frustration of the bride and groom. The announcement presents you with an opportunity to flaunt your connections, however tenuous or incidental they may be. The point, again, is visibility. Flaunting does not require you to be the reason for the occasion, either. One can display happiness through dress, dance and food. Yes, even eating can be a sign of enjoyment if you do it with enough flourish and enthusiasm. Sobowale's character reclaims visibility later on, when she dances into the wedding reception with her husband and entourage, a spirited entrance where she performs her joy with a fever that not only riles up the guests, but also outshines the mother of the groom.

Ultimately, a Nigerian party is about finding ways to put yourself at the centre. It is an inherently self-serving exercise and those paying for the party have the upper hand. How else do you explain hosting a wedding with neither bride nor groom present? Or throwing a huge, lavish party for a child's first birthday and scheduling it to start just before the child is to be put to bed? All this might suggest that the Nigerian party culture is a vicious terrain of ego and rivalry. And, yes, there is an element of that. But, really, gbedu comprises the most fertile ground for joy to exist and thrive. There is, perhaps, no more unifying source of happiness than a place where everyone is committed to the vibe and doing the most. The fact is, it is contagious, this gbedu thing. As it is irresistible. Smiles are multiplied by other smiles. Laughter catches easily across the room. Eating together seems to make the food taste better. The lyrics of Burna Boy's '*Gbona*' mention how gbedu enters your body and causes you to dance. A formless, intangible thing, it compels nonetheless. Seeing others break out and shaku, it is hard not to join in – even for those of us who have *still* not quite mastered this step. And, so, flaunting is essentially both a challenge and an invitation for others to join you.

Understand that I recognize our folly as a people. Understand, also, that I am proud of it, too.

Yet, enjoyment is also about resilience. The more subtle reality of enjoyment is that, even amidst the jolly, Nigerians are always grafting. Lagos, in particular, is not for the faint-hearted. Whenever I am there, I find myself equally in danger of too much fun and too much stress. And, to live here is to know what your joy is in defiance of. Trust me when I say that after a day of exhausting car journeys punctuated by the niggling stop-start of traffic, electricity interrupted time and again, the scorch of a sun that waylays your day and chases you back inside, making it to the party is worth celebrating. When your reality means carving sense out of a city of hapless commerce, grossly inadequate governance and bureaucratic inefficiencies, then does one know what it means to 'turn up'? Something about it feels sweeter when it is hard-won, like the reward of the Twelve Labours of Hercules.

My aunt's wedding-in-absentia gained new significance for me as an act of resilience when I realized that it took place within the year following my grandfather's release from prison, a three-year stint that only ended due to the death of the military head of state who had put him there. Defiance, in the context of enjoyment, urges you to dance for every time you were unable and smile for all the times you had no reason. Would my grandfather truly be Nigerian if he had not come out of his imprisonment ready to party? If you had asked him then, I suspect he would have said that he had no other choice but to celebrate – even if he had to hijack his daughter's nuptials to do so. In this way, actually, enjoyment is quite odd. It treats any adversity as an investment in future joy. Conversely, the more hardship you have endured, the harder you might celebrate when the occasions present themselves.

Still, defiance means nothing if it is not dallying a little with hope. A man once came up to my grandmother while she was at a friend's birthday and told her that he had come all the way from Abeokuta because he heard she would be at the party. He wanted her help and had no doubt gate-crashed. He told her that he'd spent the last of his money getting there and didn't even have enough to get back home. He was certain that as long as he made it to the party, everything would be fine. There are many prudent things this man could have done with the last of his Naira and I think most would agree that attending a party is not among them. But, under the philosophy of my countrymen, where others have joy, there may be a little left over for you to have as well. The theory is that if you don't have food, you will find some at the party. You could also find your sponsor, your husband, wife, money or work. This is why owambe* parties are the ultimate enjoyment experience. Translating from Yoruba as 'it is there', the clamber and excitement around these parties speak to a belief that abundance and opportunity are couched in the course of these events. At the very least, you will dance. Defiance means joy-stepping in spite of your circumstances and in hope of a better one.

My grandmother tells me about my aunt's wedding-in-absentia, as she remembers it: 'Even as it rained, people came in spades. They didn't mind.' At the gate to the house, fights broke out among security, guests and gate-crashers. Seeing how soaked they all were as it started to rain, my grandmother instructed that everyone be let in

---

* Owambe – Yoruba word referring to parties and ceremonies with the predominant characteristic being that there is a lot of food, drink and music.

immediately. As usual, the food ran out, but not before some people had had three servings and others had packed away bags-full to take home. Seats ran out too, and drama erupted over who should be seated and who should be made to stand. The groom's family came dancing in full regalia, adorned in flamboyant wine-coloured lace and carrying what my grandmother calls a 'bounty'. One might assume that, with the absence of bride and groom, the ceremony would have been cut short, but they drew it out. The wedding went on past evening when the rain stopped. The clothes that were wet from the downpour dried on the bodies that wore them and it all seemed worth it. 'It turned into a great festival,' my grandmother says, smiling widely from reminiscing.

Against Enough

J K Chukwu

It's New Year's Eve, and time hinges my father and I's thoughts. As we sit adjacent to one another, magenta and silver balloons float above us. The inflated numbers of 21 float and flip from $^1\,_2$ $_1\,^2$ then $^2\,_1$ then again and again. Their strings divide the muted recap of 2020 that the television plays. Though pandemic days spin like a record, my father's and my position in the family room never changes. He stares. I watch. He talks. I listen. He remembers. I wait.

Tired of overhearing my sisters debate who is the true owner of a newly discovered Juvia's Place Palette (spoiler alert, it's me), I play 'It's Not Easy' by Ofege. My father's and my feet tap. Our heads nod. Our fingers are curled against plastic champagne glasses filled with Aldi's best. 'We had no money during the war. But when they came to play, we scraped together what we had,' my father says as he remembers the joy of musicians who came and fed them with the music during the Nigerian Civil War. We are both caught in his smile and his widened eyes as his mind traces his tucked memories from his first home. The moments where my father drifts to his past are infrequent – so infrequent that it wasn't until after college I realized that he, too, was once a child and matured into the father who proclaims that he is our house's chief, who watches my sisters, mother and me over his square glasses as he waits for the next Liverpool match to begin.

*

After college, without classes directing what my mind should become, I obsessed over how it should work. I believed that if I knew, then I could control the bouts of depression that haunted me, no matter which city I fled to. The obsession that became desperation to learn how I should be led me to attempt to trace myself in my father. After all, there had to be something. I knew that my humour, beauty and dyslexia, I received from my mother. But my mind's inheritance from my father, always the constant curiosity.

Throughout the years as I jumped between Chicago, Michigan, New York, Chicago, Michigan, Rhode Island, Michigan, Chicago, whenever I landed in Michigan, I asked my father incessant questions of, 'What subjects did you hate in school?', 'Were you bad?', 'What did you do for fun?' out of hopes that they would send him into his compound of quietly kept memories.

Most questions failed to retrieve the answer I crave. My father remains tight-lipped until he asks, 'Why do you want to know?'

'Because I do,' I respond.

We wait each other out and during this stalemate as we watch soccer players dart across the field, I wonder whether our next words will be truth or sarcasm. God oh god of gods, the wondering continues. My mind delves into created worlds of worries. The constant landscape of said worlds, my father is hushed because he sees me as unworthy of knowing his history. The shared cores, my inner child who picks and squeezes every shame-filled pustule of 'I' never being enough.

As I sink into these worlds, moving closer to my inner child, my mother, the nurse who is always vigilant to the slightest pain, attempts to catch me with her stories. Her tales – of my grandmother asking her children for their dream numbers to play in the lotto, of her sweet-sixteen party where *No Brothers!* were allowed, of Diana Ross blaring on the stereo and the hip switch runway walk that made the church crowd ask, *Beverly Johnson, who's that?*, and of us being from a lineage of women who always found a way – try to keep me above my most hated self.

And yes, for a moment, after the stories end, I am back. My mother's history helps pause my mind's submersion into the belief that I will never be enough *of* or *for* my family. For a moment and perhaps even two, I try believing that coded within my DNA is my every ancestor who has no shame inhabiting my mind despite its every flaw. But eventually, always eventually, my curiosity continues. It amalgamates, creating enough lives to populate another world of worries that blocks any light my mother's love provides. I return to my desperation, following it as I search for the answers to where my Nigerian identity resides outside of the blood rivering my veins.

Despite my father's proclamation that we are Igbo, despite custom suit jackets and dresses made of Ankara and lace, despite the love of Nigerian women who created atmospheres of support and life during 2020, the year of isolation and death, despite all this and the promise that even if I begin believing in marriage again, I will never relinquish my last name of Chukwu, a name that reminds me of the gods that created and cared before the whites destroyed, despite all this, I still struggle to call myself Igbo. As I contemplate how to be Nigerian enough so that my identity can become a home I can enter without discomfort, I pray for an answer. It never arrives, and I am left to weave together one from dregs of thoughts once abandoned. Thoughts being, if I marry, if I make money, if I get a Nigerian passport, then I will be enough. Enough, enough, that word haunting all of us. Us, those of two disparate worlds who attempt to understand the partitioning of ourselves as we desperately attempt to define then validate our identities.

While in pursuit of validation for Nigerian identity, my desperation defined the first understanding of myself – a child who had to prove that she was worth seeing. While growing up, when aunts and uncles – who were strangers to my wellbeing – made themselves at home in my identity, kicking their feet upon my heart and commenting on my lack of Nigerianness, I thought there were lessons from their cruelty. I took in every remark of bigotry as an entryway into a better, more Nigerian self. If I could earn straight *A*'s in the worthy subjects of math and science while also planning to study law, if I could starve myself into a hip-and-waist ratio of hourglass so to catch the attention of idle eyes at Yam festivals and graduation parties, then when it was time for them to gossip over abandoned cans of pop and stew-splattered tablecloths, my aunts and uncles could say, 'Eh, eh, Kelechi, she is a good one, oh.'

But throughout those years, all I learned were the ways of hatred. I continued hating myself as I tried to bludgeon my identity into a form recognizable to others, but unrecognizable to myself. Constructing and then living in this refractive identity dependent on outside validation, carved scars that, even after years of self-healing, still indent my mind. As I feel these indentations, remembering they are evidence of healing, remembering all the self-harm from self-love lost, I sit in silence and attempt to understand how I became a vampire in my identities as I waited, then begged for permission to enter myself.

I've spent years that will turn into decades unweaving through the partition of I against enough. While the material unravels and its strings tangle my hands, I see that this divide was never mine, nor yours, nor ours to begin with. If not mine, yours, or ours, then who does it belong to, and who does it benefit? God oh god of gods, the answer is a lesson that has destroyed nations and built empires.

History, from sea to shining sea, shows us that when the dominating cultures of colonialism, white supremacy and white terrorism are given the opportunity, they will use forms of violence to subjugate any and all entities they encounter. Their haunting violence that destroys and divides is never-ending. Even after the present violence and destruction of an individual or a nation ends, even after sovereignty or freedom is granted, and even if the dominating individuals are no longer the colonisers or the white terrorists, their ideology still remains, decomposing all of us that they made 'other'.

These haunting horrors of past subjugation leave the once conquered with two options. The first, either we unlearn all physical, spiritual and mental values attached to the previously dominating culture, typically the culture from whiteness, its terrorism and its impulse to colonise. The second, use the previously dominant culture to establish values, power and control. Simply, become like them. Bleach your skin, pray only to white Jesus, love and display affection in ways that mimic white heteronormativity, steal and hoard your wealth like their richest museums. Do anything and everything to show that you can be trusted. You and your culture are not a threat because you can be good like them. Yes, you can be good like them, but if and only if, you can learn to replicate the forms of hate, violence and destruction, which their culture has normalised, inside of yourself.

From this inner destruction, we live the lesson that has built empires – if we are able to become like them, and out of a sense of emptiness, lack and disrespect, go and plunder, copy and steal, and even kill ourselves towards a new self or home, then we will receive the honour of being enough. A false honour achieved by our destruction becomes so insurmountable that we now believe that we are ordained by the gods we have constructed to show others, who have not learned to hate their truest selves, how to abandon themselves to attain a false sense of enoughness, and ultimately place them on a path where there is no end or salvation in sight. Simply, as we are is not enough. While we are developing the consciousness that allows us to be the freest, there will always be a thing to attain. These things, as long as they match with the dominant culture, will make us 'right' and remove the shame of being other.

This lesson papers history books and threads together every experience of inaudible horror. This lesson deconstructs living into an evolution of varying degrees of embodied trauma. This lesson teaches me that as a descendant of those who survived imperialism and enslavement, parts of my Nigerian and Black American identity remain threaded with bloody imperialist and supremacist footprints that never dried. This lesson, this lesson, this lesson leaves me to unravel my histories and search for the threads that can be used to stitch me into the self I have created. This unravelling is necessary, especially after 2020 – the year, that year of wearing masks while the world's masks have fallen. The year, that year when we lived through death and terror, exhaustion and confusion, which all queued into each other like a playlist we never wanted. After that year of so many silences finally heard, unravelling becomes an act of coping, then of survival.

As I mourn the lives and hope lost from the BLM protests and the Lekki massacres, I unravel. As I wait for the next act of violence from white terrorists and debate whether trump who rots with hatred, whose murderous hands are dyed red from his ignorance, in truth, is the most American president since Andrew Jackson, I unravel. I unravel, I unravel.

Though necessary, the unravelling is exhausting and never-ending. When our minds sore from unbraiding all the threads, where is the comfort? Where is the moment that will allow the unthreading to feel a little less exhausting and more of joy inhabit the scattered parts?

As with my father, these questions, if I am determined to gain a certain answer, will fail to deliver any answer I initially desired. As I rest with these unanswerable questions, and time continues to spin, I see that it has a way of showing me what is necessary. I need the unanswerable questions and unravelled thoughts because they induce the memories and sensations that connect me to my freest consciousness. When I am connected, my thoughts deconstruct the worlds and worries to then use the dismantled pieces to build the realities I want to inhabit.

My friends, my unravellers, in this world of violence and of unravelling to survive any division inside yourself, I search for those before me who have survived the unhinging of every thread that separated them from themselves. Throughout my search, I return to artists, the practitioners of healing. With the artists and the lives that they have manifested in their artwork, my consciousness is constantly comforted. When I worry, and yes, I still worry, that I am too disharmonious to inhabit myself, I pour my red, red wine, and turn on my Nigerian Psychedelic Rock playlist, and let the music stay close to me.

Nigerian Psych Rock music emerged out of the horrors of the Nigerian Civil War, and decades later, it is still alive with disorientation and experimentation. Embodied in every note are memories, then questions of those who survived. And in these haunted and bleeding beats, 'guitars screeched like low-flying fighter jets, basslines thrummed like trundling tank tracks. This was new music filled with funk, fuzzy, and fury'.* While Nigeria wished to move through the past, out of hopes of creating a unified present then future, the musicians, like many of the Civil War's survivors, could not simply move past the horrors.

---

*   Eothen Alapatt and Uchenna Ikonne, 'Rock in the Wake of War' in *Wake Up You! The Rise and Fall of Nigerian Rock* (Now-Again, Los Angeles, 2016), 4.

The musicians' intertwining of their artistries and recent histories created music that not only birthed a new genre where they could process and mourn the war's horrors, but manifested a new manner of listening, wherein the music connected the listeners to the divine within them. And god, oh god of gods, this music with its construction of notes and half-notes, drums and voices, chords and tempos conjures a symphony of spirituality that extends beyond the immediate act of listening to entangle the audience in their synapses. While entangled, the connections between the present, their histories and their unanswerable questions are ignited with a fury akin to the music.

As I listen to Nigerian Psych Rock, I fall into the staff lines and flux with every beat. I oscillate between tempos and hear the calls, then chants, the harmonies and dissonance. The music twists my thoughts to unanswerable questions and those unanswerable questions to thoughts again and again. I am connected. I am unravelled. I am connected. I am unravelled, and as I am undone, I have no fear of my thoughts' terrain.

*

As I live in this world and learn that questions will fail to retrieve the answers I first craved, art portals me to the truth I needed. And so, if Kuti's 'Zombie' plays and my father is transported in the beat, he will tell the story of his childhood – a time of starvation and inhumanity, of hope for Biafra, a country that was. A time of slain soldiers and lost innocence, now restless ghosts wandering in the early morning. A time of prayer and family being the only way to survive a pogrom. Despite these remembered horrors, my father still smiles as he tells his stories of how he survived. Between us as the music plays, his hand rubs his stubbled chin and he reminisces, 'That music had power,' before returning to the present.

It is during these moments, where my father is a griot and I am his daughter and his student, where we are sitting in the truth of our histories, and I learn more about the haunting in storytelling, the strength in survival and the power of art of the once silenced, that I feel the most Igbo.

Still, there are days where shame rebuilds the divide between I and enough, and during those days, I stay with music, my spiritual practice. As the song plays, I feel Nigeria and my Nigerian identity tapping on my shoulder, waiting for me to turn and see. When I look, I see it is my Igbo father, my Detroitian mother, and my sisters. It is my southern great-grandfather sitting next to my great-grandmother, whose tribal tattoos sleeve her arm.

It is the ancestors who survived enslavement. It is the Igbo ancestors who drowned themselves before their ships reached the shores. It is the ancestors who died while enslaved. It is the ancestors who lived and then transitioned to watch over their descendants. It is all of us sitting in a compound, sipping palm wine and swapping parts of our soul's history, and it will always be enough.

Life is a Marketplace

Chịkọdịlị Emelụmadụ

I hate markets.

Perhaps this sentence should be in the past tense: hated. I hated markets. For most people, a trip to the market is a weekly or monthly experience worthy of precision planning and execution: lists, monies, mental mapping to hit all the required stalls in the shortest time possible, parking close enough to ferry packages without paying through the nose for barrow boys, shelling out to touts for vehicular protection against illegal parking attendants and thieves. If one did not own a car, it involved getting the right transport home, drivers known for taking care over potholes, polite conductors and cargo packed Tetris-tight into groaning buses, boots hanging open, fastened with twine or rubber strips cut out of tyre tubes.

For my family, living on Court Road opposite the major market in the capital of Anambra State, trips were a regular occurrence. We fetched Eke Awka Market like water. The slightest thing was an excuse for my mother to send us off, sometimes more than once a day. This is not to say that the planned monthly trips did not occur, they did, and were rightfully fraught with anxiety, but it was those daily jaunts that affected me the most.

The din, the smells, the jostling. Calves slashed open by rusty wheelbarrows, flip-flops trodden on and broken. Nigeria is no place

93

to be small, unless one is bolshy to boot and in the market arena, I was not. My courage shone in school plays, recitations and debates; events held in predictable, timetabled spaces. The market was an alien planet with a basic rule at its heart – survival of the fittest. The loudest trader got noticed, the strongest smells led the nose. On market days, Eke in this case, the arena drew people from all over and human traffic flowed fast. You moved of your own volition or the crowd moved you – to the ground if necessary, where you were trampled into the dirt. The market is no respecter of the vanquished.

The one exception to this rule is the Igbo woman, of course. For her, size does not matter. The market being a largely matriarchal domain, the expectation is that every female should not only feel at ease within, but command it. My mother, as the epitome of professional and domestic womanhood, existed confidently in this world, exchanging greetings on the go, the 'I-am-coming' promises to return which never arrive, recalling details from conversations held weeks prior. Her regulars were mostly persons from church (Catholic Women's Organisation, Young Christians, or her mentees from New Catechumen) or patients, or both. I stumbled along behind her, tripping over my feet or other people's, drawing her ire. She chastised me for everything: lagging, walking too fast, staring, not taking a heavy bag from her even if I could barely heft it myself, paying attention to public conversations, not paying attention to public conversations, trying to talk to her or falling silent, giving up the pretence of conversation altogether and letting my mind wander. The contradictions were myriad and exhausting.

The language of the market was not always verbal, and its minefields confounded me. I know how to speak Igbo, but the expressions of the marketplace were self-assured, confident, adult and rapid. There was the dance of 'How much?' and 'Eh, HOW MUCH?!' The theatre that is pretending to walk off, the dramatic pleading to stay, both seller and buyer matching step for step, 'Come now, Aunty, small thing you're vexing,' and 'Fine, haggle with me then,' followed by fast mental maths, working out what increments in price stop short of insulting both goods and trader, feeling with hands, reading your rival's every expression, a suppressed hiss or sigh, a downturned mouth, how chatty or taciturn. Was your face bad for market or was it 'just how they did'? An overly cheerful expression could disclose a trader's disposition or could conceal faulty wares, the desire to offload quickly. Finally, 'How much, last (price)?' before everything is settled, still watching the hands to make sure there is no last-minute switch, or dented measuring cup, and money is exchanged, examined for wear and tear before it goes in its place, mainly the end of a wrapper, tucked into the waist. On to the next.

The aim of the interaction for both parties however is not just the one contact but repeat custom. In the market, the ideal trader and the buyer are treated equally to the ultimate endearment of 'customer'.

Goods are gendered: men sell food crops like yam and cassava tubers, portions of beef, bloody and buzzing with flies, livestock, leather goods, frozen fish and hulks of iced bird parts like turkey thighs and chicken drumsticks. Women do dried fish and crayfish, grains and legumes, stew, and soup ingredients like tatashe, onions, vegetables and cooking oils. One would be forgiven for assuming that women would be in charge of beauty products, but their jurisdiction in beauty is mostly limited to baby soaps and lotions, clothing and accessories. Men surprisingly own the beauty and jewellery sections. All genders are responsible for rolls of cloth, but once it becomes contemporary clothing like denim trousers, t-shirts and handbags favoured by the young adult and university students, the arrow points towards the menfolk again. Second-hand clothing and lingerie, women.

My dislike for markets was not helped by the fact that we rarely visited the 'fun' parts: the baking-supply shops where my schoolmates said one could earn pinches of raisins from shopkeepers for greeting properly, keeping schtum and not fidgeting so they could try to take most of our mothers' money. Unless there was a special occasion, shopping with my mother, Obiageli, comprised bulk buys and uniforms: stockfish, tomatoes for blending and boiling down into crimson pastes ready to magic into stew, chequered blue cloth by the yard and white socks, retailed by women who bore their children's names as their own, prefixed proudly by the 'Mama' title. At Christmas, my mother might visit the 'Ready Made' quarters with shiny manmade fabric and netting conjured into puffy dresses with matching fabric wrist bags, or, 'Cosmetics', suffused with perfumed mists and floral chemical scents. These shops are packed, manned by beautiful, bleached boys with *guy names* like Edu-Brazil and Chisco and Inọ, short for 'Innocent'. As a child, I wondered why this, the holiest of female holies, remained the domain of fine boys. Are not all the unguents and potions supposed to be ours? These boys had soft hands and skin, they received manicures and pedicures at their stalls regularly, wore wavy, faded haircuts and trinkets. I have since concluded that despite the Igbo cultural celebration of beauty in all its forms, a woman preening and carrying on the way cosmetics boys did would be considered vain and therefore unwholesome, even if she had to maintain an even complexion and a toned physique as an advertisement of her own products. Despite the traditional association with matriarchy in the market, the deck seemed stacked against women in beauty, unless they owned boutiques or were based outside the main grounds, which, while being a component of general commerce, is apart from the stalls and does not count.

As I approached teenage years, the cosmetics boys grew in prominence and my mother's contradictory instructions came to the fore. I had to learn how to see without directly looking, to occupy space and yet be contained. I learned how to focus my smile on my mouth and take it away from my eyes, how to banter on the go with everyone. The Beauty Boys gave the best deals to those they favoured, and one had to be friendly enough to get the new products first, but not overly pleasant as to come across as flirtatious. As a part of the unspoken agreement, they did not grab at us as other young apprentices and traders did. Cosmetics was a refuge from the sort of terror which awaited young girls in most other parts of the market. This simultaneous duality is quite a skill: snatch your wrist away too harshly and you could do yourself an injury, not to mention the catcalls turning swiftly into jeers and boos. Traders will read you for filth every time, zeroing in on insecurities with the expertise of psychologists and broadcasting it to the whole marketplace, 'See her neck like tolotolo', etcetera. But let your wrist linger in their grasp and you might as well have raised your skirt and flashed them your pants.

The market may be a battleground, but it is not entirely without order. Every line has a leader, or captain, in keeping with the military analogy. These report to the heads of sections, who in turn report to the chairman. Chairmen wield the sort of power for which most politicians would barter their mothers. Nothing happens in the market without their say-so or knowledge and so, all the grabbing is merely considered the lifeblood of the market. Were a trader to go beyond this into assault, his punishment would be worse than if the police got involved in the first place (grabbing an arm would not count as assault, but stripping a person naked would, as would a slap on the bum or grabbing a breast on purpose). Markets are sacred places, holy grounds governed by the day god who lends the market their name (Eke, Olie, Afọ or Nkwọ) and any broken taboo or alụ could bring down punishment on all the traders in the form of unsuccessful sales, ruined goods, fires or flooding – a 'bad market'. The only people who might command the respect of marketplace rulers would be priests and vicars (and dibias), traditional rulers and medical personnel. Awka is the sort of place where people openly support their own, so, the Catholic traders would only visit Catholic doctors and Anglican and Pentecostals would only use hospitals owned by Protestants. Which is where my family benefited greatly: my mother was staunchly Catholic and my father was a knight in the Anglican Church. Their hospital got the goodwill of patients from both sides of this invisible divide. Sometimes, this meant protection from grabbing in the market. Someone would say something like 'That's an Emelumadu o!', which seemed to do it, and other times, that statement alone would spark a brazenness from the offender to dare, and a retort would ring out 'And so? They are also girls.' I became adept at sensing when I was about to be touched. Intent had a certain energy to it or maybe it was just the same culprits over and over. I would growl, spit, 'Leave me alone, will you!' in English. As a lot of traders quit school early to apprentice, they often attract the ridicule of the more educated of society. Using English in this manner temporarily disrupted the flow of the market and reversed its hierarchy, placing the educated firmly at the top and educated women particularly, out of reach.

Naturally, the market found a way around this. There are a good number of university graduates, especially young medical women who are married to largely illiterate – but not ignorant – traders. This distinction is crucial because the substitution of one word for another has led to one of the most amusing phenomena in recent times and has bred rivalry between university boys and traders. It was not uncommon for a girl to have a university boyfriend, a sort of 'parlour husband' if you will, whom she took to weddings, picnics, hanging out with friends and so on, but her life and allowance – with which, let us face it, she sponsored her boyfriend – could only happen because of her trader boyfriend or 'onye ime ụnọ' aka 'the person inside the house'. Traders were generous with their gifts. I had classmates who were presented with cars and phones and flats while I was yet living with my parents and attending university from home. Given the harsh employment landscape in Nigeria, and the ease with which said girl had glided through university life thus far, not having to focus on such petty concerns as fetching water or worrying about rent or whether she had transport money, it would be frankly ridiculous to expect her to wait for Uni Boy to catch up (and if you deny this, you are deceiving yourself and there is no truth in you). To go from her own air-conditioned car to jumping molue in the scorching heat? God forbid! Money talks in Nigeria and by the time these young traders finished their apprenticeships, they were swimming in the stuff, with a doctor or lawyer wife to boot. And they did not stop there. Mindful of the ridicule they had themselves faced, they invested heavily in their wives' and children's education: further degrees, private school and so on. They took chieftaincy titles and insisted on being introduced as 'Chief and doctor (Mrs)' or 'Chief and lawyer (Mrs)', the rules of the market playing out in real life: louder and bigger equals better. A typical introduction would go something like this: 'Chief and Architect (Mrs) Boniface Nwogwugwu, alias machine-printing-money. You're very welcome sir, please make your way to the high table'.

The rivalry between the educated and not, stems from the idea of women as a scarce commodity, which is really just a struggle for power and influence, which in turn is a fear of irrelevance and a desire for legacy projected outwards. It is a shame that this exists for both sides have a fair bit in common and a lot to learn, each from the other. Or rather because the so-called benefits of a formal educa- tion are immediately apparent, there is a lot to learn from markets and traders themselves. Markets in Igboland are not just places for buying and selling but are also hubs of industry and innovation. Ariaria Market in Aba is known for its leather goods industry, Nnewi for spare parts, including fabrication of new parts or alteration of pre-existing devices. Main Market in Onitsha is famous for having everything and most people when they talk about it will add the affirmation 'even a human skull'. Being in possession of one myself, I have not been curious enough to find out how legitimate this claim is. There is a deep, abiding appreciation in Igboland, and indeed the whole of Nigeria for artistry, workmanship and the sweet, sweet spot between flair and functionality of an item. I used to turn a blind eye to artisans at work: roadside furniture makers by the market in Onitsha, carving, staining and selling elaborate thrones and stools, or blacksmiths in Awka birthing guns, tools and expansive scrollwork for gates and banisters on forges that burned blistering hot before the sun had risen. I became inured to the rustic charms employed in basket-weaving, the magic that is to venture into the marketplace with a verdant bush on one's head and to emerge triumphant, hair spelled into an intricate coxcomb inlaid with beads. I miss the hope that I had (interwoven with the fear of being thought foolish) of explaining to traders what I wanted, of finding out if the things of which I dreamed had already been dreamt into existence by someone else. Often, I went straight to the artisans who were always up for a challenge. If it is not available for purchase, traders will point you to someone's cousin's uncles' aunt's brother who will listen patiently and make you what it is that you need. My parents own a Lister plant that is as old as I am and yet works perfectly, thanks to the resourcefulness of craftspeople in Awka and Onitsha.

Occasionally, there is a fight where a customer insists on a particular method for a desired outcome which is rejected outright by skilled workers in the market and replaced with a favourable alternative. Other times, the client receives a bespoke product which is entirely beyond the specification, outside the realms of possibility in fact. A table that transforms into a bed, for example, in place of dining chairs as were commissioned, but that is genius for you. There is always someone willing to part with their cash over whatever Agwu, the god of creativity, summons into existence.

Supermarkets in the UK filled me with joy. The pristine displays, even flooring, soothing muzak and uniformed staff, not to mention signposted aisles. My trips were in and out, wide trolleys preparing a way before me like John the Baptist so that I did not bump into fellow shoppers. Nigerian supermarkets have narrower aisles, but the spirit is the same – long, clean lines, baskets and inside voices. I would grit my teeth and traipse a farmers' market for fresh produce but crumple at the mere suggestion of visiting a Nigerian market. I am as yet not properly married, they tell me. There is one final ceremony outstanding, but the last time my in-laws mentioned it, the process involved shopping at Main Market for the required items. I turned into my mother, waved gaily, and told them that I was coming.

It has been twelve years.

Nowadays, I know myself better. The market might make me anxious, but it is residual stress, not hatred after all. Nobody touches me now. When I lived in Nigeria, I was a 'Sisi' or 'Miss' and I have since skipped steps 'Sister' and 'Aunty' and arrived firmly at 'Mummy' with a girth to match. I understand what the market – and my mother – was trying to teach me. The rules of the market are the rules of life: walk fast, own your space, be watchful and surround yourself with the right people, customers, whose interests align with yours. If you are jostled and fall, do not stay on the ground. The world is not yours alone, but to share with many others. However, the market has no owner. Regardless of how much or how little power you have, in the end, we are all just buying and selling, and once the market closes up, we each go home.

Rites of Passage

Anietie Isong

When I answered my mobile phone, the caller cried: 'Papa has gone to be with the Lord!' My immediate response to the news was numbness. I broke out in a cold sweat. I wanted to reject the message and return it to the sender. I was broken. My entire life was suddenly disarranged. How would I fill the void he left behind? How would I cope without him? Grief is a difficult thing to bear. I began to search for sources of consolation and found comfort in the Scriptures. The Bible does not prevent Christians from grieving when we are bereaved, but it does advise that we should not 'grieve like the rest, who have no hope'. I had hope.

Over the next couple of days, I made many calls – to relatives, friends, pastors and event planners – to discuss the burial rites, including the final resting place. Saying goodbye is a thoughtful and essential step in the grieving process and my family immediately agreed that the burial should be delayed to accommodate the needs and considerations of close relatives travelling in from afar. I was also informed that the funeral needed to be conducted in line with traditional and religious practices observed in my hometown. I was not familiar with these practices and didn't look forward to them. I loved my culture – the food, the clothes, the music, the dance, the people, but I was not a fan of customs. I never associated with village rules, considering them to be harmful rather than helpful. I avoided and denied anything to do with rites, including traditional marriages. I struggled to see the relevance of local institutions in a democratic country. We had councillors and legislators elected to represent people at the various levels of government. Why did we need village chiefs and the elders to make separate laws for the village? I was of the view that traditional modes of thought, behaviours and institutions impeded our development as a nation. In this regard, and given that I had never really lived in the village, I was rather apprehensive of the burial that needed to take place there.

*

The taxi driver at the international airport in Uyo was a thin, bald man. He was wearing a t-shirt with 'God is Good' inscribed in huge letters across the front. I was relieved that his car was fully air-conditioned. It was a long drive from the airport to my hometown – not a journey I intended to undertake in a scorching automobile.

'What brings you back home?' the driver asked in Ibibio, as he zoomed off.

How did he know I was from this state? How did he know I could speak the language? I wasn't wearing our traditional stylish wrapper specially designed to go around the waist. My neck was not adorned with a piece of knotted cloth and neither was I wearing a local belt loosely tied around my waist. When I informed the driver about the purpose of my visit, the man immediately offered his sympathy. Then he launched into a circuitous tale about burying his grandmother – a ceremony that had lasted for three days and three nights. I didn't doubt his story. Little expense was usually spared on our elaborate funeral celebrations. The driver wanted me to understand that these ceremonies, designed to pay respect to the dead, were also an act through which to honour one's roots.

My village, Ndiya, shares a boundary with Ikot Ekpene – a large town, located in Akwa Ibom, a state in the Niger Delta region of Nigeria. Inhabitants of my community subsisted mostly on trade and agriculture. A lot had changed over the last few decades. Power lines now criss-crossed the streets, providing the much-needed electricity to light up the neighbourhood. Back in the Eighties, many homes depended on kerosene lamps for energy. It wasn't a pretty picture. Tarred roads had replaced our once-dusty thoroughfares and elaborate duplexes with tiled roofs were springing up everywhere too. My village had morphed into a town. Gone were the many mud houses with thatched roofs. I often recollect how those palm-thatched roofs were usually light-weight but unusually waterproof. They were equally porous, permitting air circulation during the hot months. I was glad good fortune had visited my village and people could live decent lives.

As the taxi eased into my family compound, I was greeted by relatives, friends and neighbours. Condolences were expected and often encouraged in times like this. All of a sudden, I was surrounded by people who looked like me, spoke like me and acted like me.

I was home.

'I know you don't know much about our customs,' my aunty said to me. 'Don't worry, I will tell you what to do. Get a notebook.'

I was grateful for her support. First, she advised me how to receive the sympathisers who thronged our compound to pay their respects – and many of them came with gifts. My father's long-time friend presented us with a goat, tubers of yam and drinks. Another acquaintance came to return money he had borrowed from my father – a gesture that made me quite pensive. Had the person not mentioned the debt, I would never have known about it. In a country where honesty was in short supply, it was reassuring to see it displayed in surplus in the village. Although the well-wishers appeared at different times at our family compound, their speeches and actions were remarkably similar. I was moved by their deeds and marvelled at how our unwritten customs were commonly understood by the members of our society. I had thought that rapid urbanisation would cause oral traditions to disappear. Suddenly, I had an epiphany. What if, during the burial process, I kept an open mind regarding our customs?

'You are doing well,' my aunty told me after I had gone back to see her.

I was doing well? Something inside me shifted and I began to reflect on the set of values which my people considered worthwhile and necessary for the preservation of our culture. Like the procedure for breaking the news of death. There is much importance tied to relations involving the in-laws. It is strong family relationships that constitute a fulcrum upon which my community thrives. On an appointed day, elders from my village – bearing crates of drinks and food – drove to my mother's village to inform the elders there of my father's death. A phone call could have done the job but this face-to-face act was a sign of respect for my mother's family. Once informed, the in-laws were then called upon to play active roles during the burial, and I welcomed their involvement.

'Your mother's people were very happy,' my aunty said afterwards. 'That's how it should be.'

Was this the custom I had been avoiding? Perhaps my fears of primitive rites had been unfounded. No one in the village had asked my family to conduct a dusk-to-dawn wake. No one had asked us to wear 'mournful clothes' or to shave our heads. No one had asked us to sacrifice an animal to accompany the dead to the next world. No one wanted masquerade displays. Instead, everywhere I went in the village, people – including strangers – were eager to offer help, to show love, to share advice, to mourn with me, to share their own grief. I considered how, within the city, such devotedness was hard to find. The demands of urban life had siphoned many people away from charitable pursuits.

I took one step at a time, and with each passing day learnt something about my customs and myself. I am by nature a private person. I don't have many friends. I usually feel more comfortable behind the scenes, rather than in the limelight. I often avoid unfamiliar social gatherings. But in my hometown, I found myself at ease with large gatherings, interacted freely with the villagers, listened to their stories. I was made to understand that in my hometown, there is no particular day for burying the dead. But ensuring a burial does not take place on a market day is key. Furthermore, no two burials can take place on the same day – to ensure the presence of mourners and well-wishers. When my family received the all-clear from the village chief for the funeral to take place, there were no written documents or signed forms. Everything was done orally. Despite the advent of modernisation, the customs of my culture have remained largely oral. I wondered if beliefs, orally transmitted from one generation to the next, might one day be distorted. Why don't we write our laws down? I asked an uncle. I received a long lecture on orality that day.

'It is not everything we say or do that must be written down,' my uncle explained. 'Our forefathers passed these laws down from mouth to mouth, and that's how we want to keep it. Notwithstanding that these customs remain largely unwritten, they have been strictly observed over the years. In fact, writing could drain our customs of its colour. Since the elders in the village know our statutes by heart, it isn't necessary to convert them into written texts.'

I didn't share his views. I saw the importance of documenting our customs – for people like me who were not conversant with them. I was aware of the tradition of families burying a loved one in their ancestral home. What I wasn't aware of was that, as the only son, I had the task of choosing the grave site for my father. The final resting place of the departed is of such personal and communal importance and I didn't want to make a mistake. But there was no way I could talk myself out of this duty. Accompanied by some members of the family, I traversed my father's compound, inspecting and contemplating. Where would I choose? I prayed for guidance and felt at peace when the job was done. That solemn act taught me a lot about myself – that I could take major decisions on behalf of the family. I could step out of my comfort zone to do the needful. It didn't matter that I was younger than my uncles and aunties.

In the midst of the many stages of the funeral, I found it necessary to focus on the overarching goal of celebrating and honouring my father. Whenever my emotions overcame me, I took a deep breath and reminded myself that I was celebrating my father. I didn't want to be judged for being ignorant of our customs. I also sought comfort in my own private farewell rituals. Like choosing the casket. I had moments of tremendous self-doubt and second-guessing doing this. Was there a 'right' casket? Their quality often suggested the financial status of the deceased or that of his family. Could I get a design more aligned with my father's personality? I wanted to say goodbye – in a way that was respectful and not boastful.

My perception of traditions underwent further changes as the burial date approached. I slowly let go of my great preconceptions, judgements and concerns about villagers. So far, no one had asked me to do anything out of the ordinary. When it was suggested that we accommodate both the invited and uninvited guests during the ceremony, I didn't protest. Unlike in Lagos, or other bigger cities in Nigeria, burial services are usually conducted in open fields in my community. For my father's, we rented a nearby football field, which was a fairly large venue. My sisters and I, as well as the extended family members, wore white. This uniformity of dressing among key mourners symbolised our common grief.

It didn't take long before the seats in the field filled up. I had no doubt that the large number of guests at the ceremony was an indication of the character, status and position in the community my father held and how sociable he was. He was a philanthropist who never stopped helping others, even in sickness. I knew of several relatives and friends who ran to him in times of need, and he remained committed to community service, spending much of his life helping to improve the lives of others in our village. As the preacher spoke about my father's life, I felt incredibly proud of what he had achieved and the many people who had come to bid him farewell. I was grateful for the unity in my family that had enabled us to put together such an elaborate ceremony. Although more villagers turned up than we anticipated, there was order during the service. I had deep admiration for my parents' church who conducted the funeral service.

The burial formalities over, we celebrated the life of my father through merriment. There was heavy feasting accompanied by singing and dancing. Food is one of the most important parts of burial ceremonies as it is meant to unite all surviving members of the family and the community. Serving a variety of dishes to guests is also an important part of showing respect in the village. My family had carefully considered the food to be served, who would prepare it, who would be sitting at what table, and who would eat first – all cultural practices with deep meanings. We hired different caterers to ensure every guest was fed. A man I didn't recognize came to tell me I had made him proud by giving my father a worthy burial and that his soul will rest in eternal peace. The sincerity of his appreciation caught me off balance and I was lost for words. As the man walked away, I began to wonder if he would have said the same thing, had he not eaten to his satisfaction. My family considered returning a year later for 'death remembrance celebration', some sort of memorial in honour of my father to commemorate a year of his passing.

Later that night, my childhood friends and I traded our time watching sports for discussions on culture. We talked about the culture of respect for the dead and filial devotion in our village. What would have happened if I didn't follow traditions? Would it have been considered an insult and have forced my excommunication from the community? Given the oral nature of our laws, it was impossible to conclude what the outcome could ever have been. I couldn't refer to any printed statutes. Nevertheless, I was proud to have been able to abide by the burial rules that turned out not to be heinous as I had feared. As discussions with my childhood friends continued, larger issues of identity and belonging also surfaced. Due to inter-ethnic marriages, many families were not speaking Ibibio, Annang or any other language spoken in Akwa Ibom. Many parents in the city were increasingly refusing to teach their children our language, perceiving it as a potential waste of efforts – because we are a minority ethnic group. While speaking Ibibio with some elders in the village, I had found myself struggling to keep up with the conversation without using English. It wasn't something I was proud of. My language is my identity, and I needed to preserve it at all costs.

One of the final formalities involved paying homage to the village chief, who had been a friend of my father. I had met him years earlier during my sister's wedding. His palace was a bungalow that could have passed for any other house in the village. There were no guards stationed outside the gate and I was struck by the simplicity of the chief. I met the queen, sat in a raffia chair, watching a soap opera on her mobile phone. Nothing about the royal family appeared boastful. Their humility had earned them well-deserved respect in the community.

'You have made me very proud,' the chief told me. 'You and your siblings have not only given your father a befitting burial, but you have raised the bar.'

Then, he handed me an envelope filled with money. Apparently, it is customary for the village to make a monetary contribution to the deceased family – rules handed down from generation to generation. I didn't need their money, but refusing it would have been interpreted as an insult. My visit to the palace was also an opportunity to understand the role traditional leaders played in our society. I soon discovered my chief was adept at managing conflict and arranging peace-making meetings when tensions were high in the community. The work that he did every day contributed to holding the community together and keeping it safe and prosperous. People went to the chief when there were land disputes, and he ensured that all contributions in the village were debated and agreed upon by members of the community. The traditional leader was one of the main keepers of our customs. I realized the job that he had been entrusted to do was no small task. He held a great responsibility in providing services to our village and was by far more accessible than the elected councillor chosen to represent our people in the local government. As I left the palace, my perception of traditional leaders changed. I no longer saw chiefs as a great contradiction in the democratic system. I saw instead a gross underutilisation of their talents and felt incredibly hopeful about the future of our village. Faced with fast urbanisation, we were lucky to have a chief who continued to use his wisdom and skills to preserve our cultural heritage.

Saying goodbye to a loved one is difficult, but my father's funeral proved to be a fulfilling journey and an opportunity to memorialize the person who meant so much to me, my siblings and the community. Working with my sisters, other relatives and friends throughout the ceremony provided some comfort and the beginning of closure. Yet, regardless of the many ways I said goodbye, I knew my father would always be around. The funeral taught me so much about my culture. The ways in which burial rites were conducted gave me a powerful insight into the religious and social mindset of my village. When I came to the realization that these rites were put in place to discourage chaos and to promote community cohesion, I began to fully embrace my identity. The burial was a rite of passage for my father as well as for me.

Until We Meet Again

Hafsa Zayyan

Grief is a strange thing. A thing without words; a shared humanity which we will all experience, yet we struggle to find a way to express ourselves when it comes to pass. As Muslims, we borrow from the verses of the holy Quran in times of grief: *Inna lillahi wa inna ilayhi raji'un. Surely to God we belong and surely to Him we shall return.*

In the summer of 2020, we lost my father's younger sister, and with her, I lost my closest connection to Nigeria. Half a year has passed now but my throat tightens and my eyes still swell immediately when I think about her large, gap-toothed smile and the regal way in which she filled every wrapper she wore. It was through my Aunty, who regularly came from Nigeria to live with us for several months at a time in my pre-teen years, that I had my first taste of Nigeria – quite literally, burning pepper soup down my intestinal tract. She was a qualified obstetrician receiving her Membership of the Royal College of Obstetricians and Gynaecologists (MRCOG) in England and would go on to open her own clinic in Kaduna, named – at the suggestion of my younger sister who also wanted to be a doctor – the Diamond Hospital.

My formative experiences of Nigeria were thus made in England, where my Aunty swept like a whirlwind into our lives, bringing with her the cardboard starched stiffness of unmalleable batik wax, showing me how to tie the material around my soft hair, which didn't seem to have enough grip to make it stick, and always gave me a headache. But the way, once worn in, the wrapper complemented my figure, was new to me – this did not fall limply over the limbs like the Pakistani shalwars I was used to wearing from my mother's side; no, these were tight-fitting, hugging every curve of my body, giving Nigerian shape to my form. Not quite the demure image of a Muslim woman I had imagined. 'And that is why you wear this,' – and my Aunty would throw a huge shawl over my shoulders, so that only a peek of the colourful print remained visible at my toes – 'over it.'

And what other delights she brought with her! My mouth waters when I think about the bundles of kilishi she snuck across borders that I would raid any time my parents weren't looking – blasted in the microwave first, of course, for safety – but the chewy, spicy deliciousness of it. My Aunty would eventually get caught by Customs and was forced to stop bringing it back. But of all the edible Nigerian exports that came with her visits, gyada – salted groundnuts, roasted in their papery skin in sand – were the most superior. Nothing compares to Nigerian gyada, though I have seen, sampled and dismissed their competition from neighbouring countries.

'You know you are descended from royalty, my dear,' my Aunty told me as she packed the twenty perfume bottles she'd picked up from the local market for a tenner among the clothes in her suitcase. I stared, still baffled by the meaning of the custom of not returning empty-handed, and intrigued at the mention of royalty. 'You are a princess,' she declared, sticking her tongue briefly between the gap in her teeth, partly in an effort to close the suitcase, partly between a smile. I had never been to Nigeria before, and imagined a palace waiting for me upon my arrival.

And so, not long after my Aunty's departure, I was on my way to Nigeria for the first time. It was at the turn of the century, and the occasion felt suitably momentous – I was about to meet my wider Nigerian family for the first time. My grandparents had visited on occasion when I was a baby, but I couldn't remember them. One of my father's other sisters lived in Vienna, but other than her and my Aunty, I didn't know my Nigerian side of the family well at all.

Two things struck me at once when landing: the redness of the earth (my father informed me it was full of iron) and the dry heat – which has a particular smell. My father's family are Hausa and live in Katsina; the drive from Abuja was a long one, not, I understood, to be undertaken overnight. Potholes and checkpoints, mud-hut villages and goats passed by in a blur. I slept through most of it, shifting uncomfortably as I sweat through my wrapper. My grandfather, Alhaji, lived in a large compound in one building – his two wives, and the many children, lived in separate buildings. Everyone was so excited at our arrival – touching our skin, our hair; knowing our names – I didn't know anybody's names – and laughing hysterically at our attempts to speak a little Hausa (which, I am constantly reminded, is one of the easiest languages in the world to pick up).

Omelettes and homemade fries would be brought to our room by a nameless face with a flask of hot tea for breakfast, while we were introduced to yam, tuwon shinkafa (pounded rice) and miyan kubewa (okra soup) at dinner. Like all young children, I hesitated at first in the face of these strange, foreign smells and tastes – particularly the miyan kubewa, with its mucilaginous texture – but the taste on my tongue made it slide down my throat and into my belly with no persuasion at all. I was quickly made to understand that we were not expected, and in fact discouraged, from assisting: housework was not for guests and certainly not for the English children of Baba Kassim. My sister and I instead spent our days playing havoc with the chickens running around in the yard – one in particular had a little set of chicks following her – until we understood that the crispy fried chicken we'd so delightfully been devouring had come from none other than our feathered friends. I cried when I watched little Freddie's throat being slit – and ate no fried chicken for the rest of that trip. We would launch ourselves into the sprawling mango tree that asserted its dominance in the courtyard, its branches so low and wide as if they were built for the very purpose of climbing, and chase lizards into the leaves.

On occasion we would be called to my grandfather's building where – as I had rapidly learnt – the custom was to bow very low or kneel on the floor upon entry, and then sit on the floor while my grandfather assumed the higher seat and spoke. His English was impeccable and he would ask us questions or – worse – to recite the Quran, which made me sweat even more than I already was. Better, then, when he would lecture and we could just listen – stories about our Prophet (peace be upon him), or the rules and regulations of Islam. My sister and I would listen as his words gently lulled us, in the heat, to the Land of Nod. My grandfather was known simply as Alhaji – one who had completed the Hajj – and was a devout Muslim and Islamic scholar. My father followed his example and instilled a very strong sense of connection to God in both my sister and me. But it wasn't all religious lectures with Alhaji. Best of all would be when he would talk about my father. My sister and I would try to stifle our giggles as we heard stories of my father's escapades during a childhood we'd never been able to imagine.

And then there were Alhaji's other interests – the stack of yellowing Khalil Gibran novels he gifted to me on the last visit that I would see him before he peacefully passed away in his sleep at the age of 80. For a long time after I returned to England following that first trip, I would write him letters, which he would mark up for grammar and spelling and send back to me with his response. *You have a flair for English*, he wrote. *But I fear you're getting arrogant and allowing yourself to make mistakes.* He wasn't impressed with my choice to become a lawyer, but when he eventually accepted it, he gifted me a gold Waterman fountain pen. And when he came to England to visit us not long after our first trip, he gifted us copies of the Guinness Book of World Records 2003, inscribed with his careful, purposeful cursive – *From your loving Grandfather.* Inspiring us to break records. Those precious items – the books, the pen, the letters – each took on such significance after his death. They symbolised his encouragement to me to tell stories, to write, to exercise creativity.

On my second trip to Nigeria, I was treated to a further example of the Hausa capacity for storytelling when we stopped at Kusugu well – from which my father drank (but would not allow us to) – and the story of Sarki and Bayajidda was relayed to my eager ears. Legend has it that Sarki, a serpent, guarded the well and only allowed the villagers to collect water from it on Fridays, until a non-Hausa speaking visitor to Daura, Bayajidda, slayed the creature.

We spent some time in Daura district that trip and, having decided I wanted to pursue a career in law, I arranged work experience with an uncle, who was a magistrate there. 'You need to be very careful, Hafsa,' he explained to me as we sat in his office, a fan spreading hot dust around the room over our heads. I wiped perspiration from my upper lip. 'Let me tell you something about this country. We have a robbery, yes? A police checkpoint, a car, except they are not really police. They have weapons – AK-47s. They take everything. So the victim goes to police, he says: "Sir, they took my car, you can identify it?" The police ask whether these robbers were armed. "Well, in that case, there is nothing we can do," they shrug. "The robbers are better equipped than us."' My uncle drew a long, deep breath, as if dragging on a cigarette that didn't exist, and closed his eyes. 'It is like living in a Western, Hafsa. This country lawless.'

Even though I couldn't understand the Hausa, I began to recognize the sound of my father's voice darkening when he called back home; I began to listen for the snippets of what he would say to my mother. And in the end, my poor, righteous uncle gave a judgement someone powerful didn't like. He was shot in the head at a police checkpoint one evening after they had verified his name. This was one of many incidents I would come to learn of over the years that left dread hanging between my thoughts of Nigeria, like an unfriendly shadow. Scams by organised criminal networks, kidnappings, ransoms, being held hostage in the Bush. It was part of the reason our visits to Nigeria weren't so frequent; part of the reason my father shook his head when we begged to attend my cousin's wedding: 'People know you aren't from Nigeria straight away. It's too dangerous.'

Something had changed then, from when my parents had left. My maternal grandfather – my Nana – always spoke of Nigeria with such reverence, the memories of his twenty-five years there inflected with the rose-tinted glasses of nostalgia – he would speak often of his garden in Zaria, and even at the grand old age of 90, he remembered it all, right down to the last detail – guava, mango, pawpaw, fig, pineapple, oranges and lemons. My mother tells me that the Pakistanis left Nigeria when things started to worsen – access to running water, electricity, the security situation. The first few times we went back, I heard my parents lament how things had changed; my father's silence echoed around us as he stood looking out over his old university in Zaria. What did I know of that Nigeria, accessible only in my parents' heads?

Between the breaks of our brief visits, Nigeria stayed with me. After our second trip, I wanted to associate more with my Nigerian side – being black was suddenly in vogue, and I wanted to show up for it. My sister and I had collected a few pirated CDs on our trip and began to hold rap battles in the playground. We'd also returned with our hair braided tightly into beautiful little rows and we had learned how to do it – for a few quid, we would cornrow the hair of anyone who asked. For a brief period, almost every white girl in our year had a head full of braids, of which my sister and I were the proud, juvenile authors.

Later in life I came to understand what it meant, separate to being 'Black' or 'Black culture' (if there is such a homogenous thing), to be associated with Nigeria in particular. It was always a Nigerian con artist claiming to be royalty to get you to wire him funds. It was the awkward-ness of experiencing one of my bosses discussing Nigeria with an oil and gas client at work: 'Oh God, not Nigeria – avoid that shithole if you can.' Clearly not knowing I, sat there as a junior, taking a note of the meeting, was a Nigerian myself. I ground my teeth, gripped the pen tighter until its shape carved grooves into my palm, and said nothing. This person did not know me or my family. He did not know, and would never understand, the beauty of our cultural practices, the elegance of my grandfather's house. What he knew – the chaos of a part of Lagos to which I had never been, the dusty outskirts of an oil production facility – they did not encompass *my* Nigeria. But I did not have the courage to try to explain it to him.

If there was anything to be admired by my white peers about my Nigerian heritage, it was my association with the splattering of Nigerians dominating the arts – John Boyega, Tinie Tempah, Skepta, Shola Amoo, Yinka Shonibare. But among these, I could not identify any Hausa/Fulani Nigerian. Where were the creatives of the North? I myself came from a line of creatives – from my grandfather's interest in literature, to my father's passion for drawing and painting – a hobby he exercised regularly throughout my childhood. From an early age, he had taught me how to make watercolours diffuse into sunsets on paper, leaving me comfortable in the company of easels and crusted paints. If there was ever to be an opportunity to translate our creativity into the public arena, and I would do so proudly, hoping that it might inspire other Northerners sitting in the shadows to emerge and represent.

The last trip I took to Nigeria was after my grandmother's passing in 2014. This trip had a new meaning – with both my paternal grandparents now gone, I felt as though I was watching a favourite film, tracing the steps we had previously made, but the scenes were somehow different, something amiss. As we went from house to house to receive and pass on condolences, all the faces of the extended family began to blur in the absence of my paternal grandparents; like the roots of a tree, dug out, all the branches began to disintegrate as the structure collapsed. Thank God, then, for my Aunty, a lifebuoy of familiarity to whom I could cling and grieve.

In or out of Nigeria, I always felt uncertain of acceptance – in Nigeria, I did not look like them, and I could not speak their language; outside of Nigeria, I was not of the better half, and the Nigerians I met did not recognize me as one of them. Only with my Aunty did I find my Nigeria. She had a way of involving herself with the members of the family (sometimes to their annoyance), but she would not allow anyone – including my sister and me – to be left behind. She never let more than a few months pass without contacting us. She was my constant connection and reminder of home.

When she passed away, having not even reached 60, it was devastating on multiple levels. My dear, sweet Aunt was never coming back. She was never going to advise me or guide me again. There was so much we hadn't discussed, so much more that I wanted to talk to her about, but her time was up. *Inna lillahi wa inna ilayhi raji'un.* With her departure, I felt like my last remaining connection to Nigeria had snapped. I did not go back to Nigeria after she died – too late for the burial, which happens immediately after the death, and mid-lockdown anyway. My heart broke for her sons, three of whom were studying or working in England at the time she passed away.

But there was suddenly an outpouring from my Nigerian relatives over phone calls and messages, reminding me that they were there. These were people I hadn't spoken to in years, all of a sudden reaching out, like a web, catching me as I fell. Telling me they looked forward to seeing me and that now that Aunty was gone, I shouldn't forget them. These messages pulled me back from the edge of the chasm of grief, and turned my thoughts to the Nigeria from where I come. It has been nearly a decade since I have been back, but to Nigeria I belong, and surely – one day – I will return.

Nostalgia is an Extreme Sport

Lola Shoneyin

Being Nigerian means you are a work of art before you are out of your teens, shaped and moulded by accidental triumphs and traumas. When you are my age, recollection can be an extreme sport, where memories can either reinforce your faith in strangers or fill your heart with revulsion at their power to bend you out of shape. Nevertheless, in times of confusion or disillusionment or when I cannot recognize my own country, I find myself returning to the country of my youth.

I was born in Ibadan, a populous city that is famous for its kings, its markets and the spread of rusted corrugated iron roofing sheets across uneven hills; and although I was comfortable with the label – Ibadan Girl – I could sense that a time would come when it would no longer capture my life experience. At 16 years old, with O-levels and the Joint Admission Matriculation Board (JAMB) results in hand, I left for Ogun State University. I bucked the family tradition and picked an institution that was far enough from home that, unlike my older brothers, I could not commute. I was 16 years old and I yearned for freedom and independence. I'd grown impatient with the adults in my life telling me what was best for me when they knew so little about what kept me up at night, what inspired me or what made me unbearably restless. I'd learnt to keep my aspirations close to my chest and I swore my friends to secrecy. No one in my family knew that I had joined a band earlier that year.

The band was called Spectrum. We were gradually making a name for ourselves in the music circuit in Ibadan, albeit as an opening act – the seat-warmers, the band that played in the background while people ordered drinks and the house filled up. Femi, our bass guitarist, was by far the most streetwise. He was already smoking Rothmans cigarettes and playing bass guitar with more prominent acts. It was on one of his tours that he got us an invitation to perform at a jazz club in Lagos.

Of course, I'd travelled through Lagos before, but it was always to get somewhere else. For many of us who grew up in Ibadan, Lagos was a city of debauchees, home of the so-sweet-it's-rotten life, a land veined with never-ending traffic and Bar Beach. So the thought of walking through the wild Lagos streets made me shimmy with excitement. A couple of weeks after I resumed at university, I packed my toothbrush and travelled to Lagos to meet up with my bandmates at the Lagos motor park garage. Stoked for our performance, we agreed on our set and made our way to a spot in Lagos called Jazzville.

We shuffled through the metal side gate and navigated the poorly-lit stairs into a garden where a stage backed the far wall. Femi introduced us to Majek the owner, who seemed to genuinely delight in his role as host. To put us at ease, he donned a look of exaggerated concern. 'How do you people live in Ibadan?' he asked. He told us how he'd visited Ibadan once and had come away feeling that it was the perfect place for funerals. I was taken aback by this assault on our beloved Ibadan. I wasn't alone; my bandmates were unusually energised during our pre-performance pep talk. And when we were invited to perform, we were determined to restore Ibadan's honour.

Gaga, in his well-worn batik shirt and baggy jeans, sat behind the keyboards. Femi picked up the bass guitar, played a few chords and signalled to the sound engineer in a control box hidden behind the glare of coloured lights and billows from the smoke machine. Petite Dapo, who rarely spoke a word, settled onto the stool behind an intimidating drum set. Decked out in black jeans, black t-shirt and black beret – and hoping no one would recognize me – I opened our set with my Randy Crawford numbers: 'Time For Love' and 'You Bring The Sun Out'. We ended with 'Intoxicated', a song that I wrote:

> *I was intoxicated by the music I heard,*
> *It was enough to take you to another world,*
> *A world of your own, a world unknown . . . . . .*

I don't remember a thunderous applause. Like all the performers, we left the stage for the exit, straight-faced and in a hurry. We would make this trip at least six more times during my first year at university. I never discussed Jazzville with my family or the new friends I made at university; very few of them knew I could hold a tune. Jazzville was a secret getaway, the place we went to be passionate about our passions, without fear of being ridiculed or shut down. We were teenagers, all living on pocket money from our parents, but standing one metre away from other regulars like Femi Kuti, Maya, Tunde Obe Wunmi Aboderin, Daddy Showkey . . . In the cacophony of horns and the horny hecklers in office wear, a feeling of gratification would wash over me. In that moment, I was safe, certain that I was right where I ought to be.

Four years later, I had graduated. Sporadic rehearsals had dulled my confidence so I'd put my singing days behind me and turned to poetry, which didn't require musical accompaniment. I was on my way home with news that I'd been posted to a town in northern Nigeria for the three-week orientation period of my compulsory Youth

Service year. I wasn't sure how my parents would react. A couple of years earlier, when I was on the university 4 x 100 relay team, my father had turned down my request to attend the annual inter-university games. Although I often snuck off to places without his knowledge, I didn't dare disobey when I was expressly banned. I didn't know how to tell the coach or my teammates so I just stopped going to practice. I couldn't face them. In any case, if I'd told them, they wouldn't have believed me. Restraint and prudence were not qualities that people identified with me. Believing I had nothing to lose, I was carefree, fun-loving and I actively sought adventure.

When I opened the door of my dad's bedroom, Mum was seated on a stool, wading through a bowl of cold water and gari with a spoon. Daddy was at the desk, taking apart a wad of fifty-Naira-notes and rearranging them until all the pictures were face up and leftward. I broke the news and a discussion commenced. I resisted the suggestions of a chaperone. 'It's only for three weeks and I will be careful,' I reassured. 'You've been to northern Nigeria,' I told my dad, remembering the time when we'd drop him off at the railway station to catch a train to Kano for Lodge meetings.

*

I'd never heard of Wukari. Taraba State had only recently been sculpted from Gongola State and named, unimaginatively, after the Taraba River. The well-travelled people we asked for directions droned on about the Mambilla Plateau, where the hills were draped in leaves of rich, wet green. Everyone knew how to get to a place that was on the way to Wukari but never Wukari itself. I would come to understand why.

On the way to the airport, my father reminded me that he'd deposited enough money into my bank account to get me home, should the need arise. I was humbled by his faith in me. I grabbed my suitcase in one hand and slung my mattress, rolled up like a fresh newspaper, over my shoulder. At the airport information booth, neither of us thought twice about trusting the attendant who squinted at a map. 'You need to go to Jos,' he said, counting the money we'd given him for an airplane ticket. My father waved goodbye. I turned back to hug him. I knew he wouldn't leave the car park until my flight had taken off. The attendant suggested that I sit and wait for my flight. Every so often, he resurfaced to remind me that the journey from Jos to Wukari was one quick car-ride. 'From the airport, go straight to the motor park,' he said. What he didn't tell me beforehand was that my flight would touch down at 6 p.m.

We landed just as dusk was throwing indigo dust over Jos skies. I hailed a taxi. I prepared myself for the usual chaos of motor parks, bracing myself for sweaty men grabbing my bag and my arms, picking up the pong of privilege through my pores and punishing me for it. As I was closing the taxi door, the last station wagon belched past me, boot weighed down by yam. It was darker now.

I walked over to a food seller in front of her stall. She glanced up at me and returned to the dishes she was busy washing. Perhaps travelling in jeans and an old t-shirt from Notting Hill Carnival was a bad idea after all, I thought. I'd dressed this way to blend in, to smudge myself into the surroundings so no one would suspect I had ten-thousand Naira cash in my bum bag. Before I could repeat my question in Pidgin English, my ears had picked up a Yoruba dialect. The source was a woman wearing iro and buba in two starkly different prints. A stream of Yoruba erupted from my mouth as I marched towards her.

It turned out that I'd have to return the next day to make the trip. She could sense my reluctance to accept this alarming news. 'The only way you can start that journey tonight is by walking,' she said.

I was strangely comforted by her sassiness. It was so unmistakably Yoruba. When I asked about hotels nearby, she pointed me in the direction of the white Toyota, about twenty feet away.

The man leaned over to wind the lever and lower the passenger door window but looked straight ahead, tilting his head towards me very slightly, as if listening for a musical note. I fished out my crumpled call-up letter and pointed at the word 'Wukari'.

'But why did you come through Jos?' he mumbled and reached over to open the door for me. I was in a strange city where people spoke a strange language, in a strange man's car with no idea where he was taking me. He stopped abruptly by the roadside and ordered suya. The aroma of the groundnut coating on the strips of beef filled the car. He handed me a suya wrapped up in a newspaper. I was starving, but I put it in my handbag.

'You should have travelled via Yola,' he muttered.

This was the first time anyone seemed to have concrete insight into my destination and how to get there.

'You can have my bedroom and I'll drop you at the motor park in the morning.' He waved off my protestations and pleas and I felt brutally vulnerable and powerless. I thought ruefully about the karate lessons I'd neglected to take. He asked me questions and I answered openly, volunteering information about my life and my family, as if making myself memorable could save me. In my mind, I was listing everything I'd packed to see what could double as a weapon.

There was no electricity at his tiny bungalow – one of many on a dark, quiet street. He ushered me into the living room and dropped my suitcase and mattress at my feet. It was pitch-black and I could barely make out the walls. The glow from the kerosene lantern he brought into the room spread light on two sofas and a wooden dining table covered with files and piles of paper. It was while he was in his bedroom preparing for the next work day that I remembered how hungry and tired I was. I had a moment by myself, but I didn't want him to think I'd let my guard down; I let the steam from my suya warm the newspaper wrapping in my bag.

By the time my host returned, I was frantically knocking my knees together to keep myself awake. Alone, in his bedroom, I took one of the fresh sheets he had laid on the bed and wrapped it around my bum bag. I set my host a lame booby trap by propping my suitcase against the keyless door. I held my nail cutter firmly in my hand. If he was going to kill me, I would leave him with a scar to remember me by.

It was hunger that woke me just before 5 a.m. and I'd never been more grateful to welcome daylight. I reached into my bag and devoured every last slither of suya. Yakubu, the driver, knocked. I licked my fingers and rushed to the door to find him standing there, holding a bucket of hot bathing water and a tiny bar of Joy soap. Just as he'd promised, he drove me to the motor park. After several interactions with different drivers, he returned to the car. The only way for me to get to Wukari was through Ibi. At Ibi, I would have to cross the Benue River in a boat.

Nothing makes you contemplate mortality like sitting in a rickety motorboat that has never known a lick of paint, in the middle of a river of brown, murky water. We left the dock behind and all I could see was water, all I could hear was water, bubbling from the motor engine; he switched it off intermittently to save fuel. There were five of us aboard: me, the spindly, bald man who manned the motor and three women, whom I suspected were heading homewards from their farms. They'd loaded the boat with baskets filled with fruit and shaded with broad leaves.

At first, they rattled on in an unfamiliar tongue, then their voices quietened. I could tell they were talking about me. Their lips moved, but they couldn't tear their eyes from me. I was too emotionally worn to stare back. I could swim a good number of lengths in the pool at the Recreation Club, but I couldn't unsee the large branches being waltzed downriver by heavy currents. I gripped the side of the boat with one hand and the bench I was sitting on with the other. The two women sitting beside me chuckled, but the third woman found my eyes. She raised her palm to her chest and repeated a downward stroking motion, as if to say, 'Relax, you'll be fine.'

For the rest of the boat ride, I thought about the unexpected acts of kindness I'd encountered from complete strangers. At 21, I had already grown so wary and untrusting that I was suspicious of kindness. I wondered if my expression of gratitude to Yakubu had been marred by my obsession with the worst-case scenario. I wondered if the endless boat ride was my penance, and if this river would be that pool of a final cleansing. The ripples on the river surface took me back to a forest river in Ibadan, where I bathed as part of a religious ritual.

*

I was 10 when my mother started attending the Celestial Church. It was a clean departure from the divining bowl my father kept in his wardrobe, and from the Methodist Church that my brothers were baptized in. I was fascinated by the flowing white gowns and quickly adjusted to shoelessness. I didn't expect that we would be there for long; my mother's inability to accept life's ebbs and flows meant she was on a never-ending search for salvation or redemption. For her, everything bad was the handiwork of the Devil. Friends and family members were frequently banished because they fit the description a church prophet had seen in a vision.

We'd been going to the parish for two years and I was a useful servant in the house of the Lord. My father had got my piano teacher to score some of the hymns, so I sat in church at the beginning of every service and played the pump organ while the congregation filed in. It was at one of these services that a prophet convulsed her way towards me and pulled me aside by the arm. God had a message for me but it was not the good news I'd hoped for; I was an emere – one consumed by a spirit. My mother was visibly disconcerted by the prophecy and we both looked ahead to the day of isegun to gain victory over the enemy.

In the meantime, I wondered about the silent spirit that had slithered into my body, uninvited and unannounced. And if there was a spirit inside me, why didn't it save me from being whipped in school when I failed to hand in my homework on time? Why didn't it help turn my brothers to dust when they teased me to tears? I'd done all the river baths that were recommended to keep me safe, stripping down to my skin and scrubbing my body with seven sponges and seven bars of soap in the river nearby. I'd rubbed my body down with seven eggs in their shells and dashed them against a stone to ward off evil. I questioned the spirit out loud, asking why it had chosen me.

In the Celestial Church, the enemy is best confronted in sevens. The senior church members, who had been invited to help battle my emere spirit, were standing in the formation I'd seen many times before. The leader's garment was gathered at his waist by a blue garter. To his left side and to his right, he was flanked by three co-warriors, also in white, each grasping seven palm fronds. I knelt before the leader on the hot concrete of the church veranda, eager to endure the stinging that would ensue. This was necessary to agitate the emere spirit. After the prayer, and to the chanting of heavenly war songs, the seven elders whipped me all over, making sure every part of my body was swiped by the palm fronds. The ritual should have ended with one of the warriors receiving affirmation of our victory. In my case, a warrior woman said she had seen an angel placing a sign on my neck that said 'damaged'. This single experience would cast an imposing shadow on the way I lived. Since my fate had been sealed, what was the point of resistance? Instead, I learnt to accept whatever was to come. Back in the boat, I placed my hands on my lap and shook the tension from my shoulders. Resigned to whatever was to come, I surrendered myself to fate.

I worry that my memories are fading; it scares me that I have to think extra hard to conjure a memory, to catch a glimpse, a scent, or a sound carried on the wind from somewhere in my past. The Nigeria I knew is receding, but that Nigeria has also taught me to be unafraid of the Nigeria that is emerging.

Amaechina

Chika Unigwe

Enugu is a city on a hill. Enu ugwu. It is the house on Edinburgh Road, its greenness now fading and mottled with age. A balcony with metal railings and flowers in pots that became ashy with dust in the dry season. Afternoons that smelt of okra soup and goat meat. A plastic Christmas tree in the parlour my mother refused to dismantle for years after she set it up because *Do you kids know how hard it is to put this all together?*

We had Polo Park for picnics and Sports Club for the pool. Water as blue as the sky. I never learned to swim, though – I inherited my mother's fear of water. Osimili adighi eli onye ọ na-afurọ ụkwụ ya anya. *The ocean does not swallow those with whose feet it does not come in contact.*

But it's a pool, not an ocean, Mommy.

Same thing. Water is water, biko.

Thick chocolate milk in tins to swallow down Sunday-Sunday medicine, a futile fight against malaria. A dog called Spaniel because it was a cocker spaniel. And another called Pet because it was a pet. And finally, one without an obvious name because we hadn't named him: Justice. A lab mix bought from a man who swore to my father it would grow as huge as a house. The only dog we had that could

133

sit on command. It even came with a certificate from a school in Onitsha that'd trained it.

Enugu was a charmed childhood. Thursdays at the radio station co-hosting a request show with a woman who would later become big in Nollywood. I called her aunty and after the show, she'd take me to the station's canteen. *What'd you like to eat, Chika?* My answers were always the same: *Dodo and fried egg stew, please. Thank you.* Still the one dish I can never get enough of.

One day after the show, the taste of my favourite dinner still on my tongue, she returned me home but my parents were out. *Uncle Frank is dead,* a sibling said. Car accident. The first death in the family I was old enough to understand, it filled me with dread. Death was something that happened to old people before one was born, like the paternal grandparents I never met. Or to uncles and aunts your parents spoke of who died during the war or before the war or *when you were so little you wouldn't remember.* To strangers whose faces appeared in the obituary sections of newspapers, *With gratitude to God for a life well spent* . . . Death also happened in films, but actors died to reincarnate so it did not count. When my mother returned and hugged me, her perfume filled my nose. It was new and sickly sweet, the smell of death. It immobilised me. I still cannot stand Dior's *Poison.*

Weekends, my mother played ABBA and Dolly Parton. When we karaoke, my siblings and I mostly choose ABBA or Parton. We can sing along with our eyes closed. My eldest brother loved reggae. U-Roy and Marley and Dennis Brutus. Musical Youth and Yellowman, blasting from his room. When Lucky Dube was murdered, I played him on a loop all day. I might have called my brother to condole with him.

There was once a library and a zoo we went to sometimes. In the place where the zoo was, there now exists prime real estate. Sprawling houses and heavy gates. Rumour has it that the animals died of starvation. Or were eaten by hungry, underpaid zookeepers. Who knows what the truth is? Fact is that to live at the Zoo now is to announce stupendous wealth. On all my trips back, I haven't been able to find my way back to the building that housed the library. It might just shatter my heart. So my memory preserves my heart that way. There are other things it refuses to remember. Like the face of our family physician, a man we called uncle, who asked if he could be my special friend, who touched me in ways he should not have. I think my memory knows that it is better for my heart that way, this forgetfulness that stops me from ambling around the city stunned with grief. That way, I can love Enugu still. Home of my birth, but not Osumenyi.

Osumenyi was Christmas spent in the village where our figurative umbilical cords are buried. In the past, umbilical cords were buried at the foot of a young tree that became known as the baby's, the ballast rooting the child to the earth. Born long after the tradition had died, we have no trees planted for us, but we went back every year, where people who did not know us asked, 'Whose child are you?' rather than 'What's your name?' because one's lineage matters more than one's name, folding one into a history bigger than just the individual. *Chika the daughter of Fred the son of Jonah the son of Ezike Unigwe the son of Ezike Nwamearaku of Umuomam, whose mother was the daughter of . . . and so on and so on.*

The preparations for Osumenyi always began long before the trip was made. On the day, we scattered into cars packed full of *stuff*. In one of my memories we are in my mother's red Volvo and she's driving. My father and the driver have gone on ahead with some of my siblings. My mother's well-tied scarves are on the heads of my sister and I. We are the human mannequins she's rented to keep them in good shape during the ride. The scarf is stiff and heavy on my head. Our house-help is holding onto a cake my mother baked. The car smells of fuel and food and my mother's perfume. When we drive through the narrow, spiral Milliken Hill, allegedly named for the colonialist who blasted a road through the hills in 1909 so the British could cart off coal more easily, my mother instructs us to pray. Looking out the window at the valley underneath is like staring into the jaws of death. I cover my ears with both hands: everyone knows you don't have to listen hard enough to hear the cries of ghosts trapped underneath. I'd later learn of the 1949 Iva Valley Massacre when colonial police killed twenty-one miners for daring to ask for better conditions.

From the day we arrived to the day we left, our house was always overrun with people, some asking for help. With school fees. With feeding their families. With paying hospital bills. My parents helped however they could. No one left empty-handed. Someone left with live chickens. Others with plastic bags filled to the brim with rice. Once, a man who'd been given a bag of meat so fresh it still dripped blood, told me we were family because his grandfather and my great grandfather suckled on the same breast. But everyone was family anyway, we came from the same village. That was enough. It meant we had a common ancestor somewhere far down the line. It meant that my father and others whose heads were above water had an obligation to help those who were drowning come up for air too. The word for poor in Igbo is ogbenye, which literally means (one) who is helped by the community. Some visitors came with their own gifts of fruit and food and live animals. Akara fried incandescent gold for us. Ogbaroti, a snack made of egusi we could never get anywhere else. Tubers of yam with dirt still clinging to them. People did not want to come without anything, my mother told me once. It embarrassed them, even if they had little themselves, to 'gbalu aka bia'.

My sister and I sank our feet inside the sand outside our home and raised red dust playing oga. We pricked our fingers on the cacti that lined our gate like dwarf soldiers. I raced my cousin on our Raleigh Chopper bikes. With our mother, we visited my father's numerous relatives. They packaged fresh vegetables from their farms and pressed them into my mother's hands. *Take. Make soup for the children.* They plucked gigantic guavas off pygmy trees for us. 'Those guavas are gone,' my father said recently. *Everything is gone.* There was a berry that transformed sourness to sweetness on the tongue. *Gone.* Soursop? *Gone. Everything is gone.* Even the New Yam Festival, afia olu, has been modified. For a while, churches have been discouraging their members from taking part in the celebration because it is 'heathen'. Parents no longer let their children be initiated into the masquerade cult. My father's sad to witness so much loss. His parents were early converts to Christianity, converting when he was still a child. In 2015, he was celebrated as the oldest-living Catholic in Osumenyi in a lavish affair that included mass with Cardinal Arinze. But my father 'pours libation' for his ancestors at the beginning of afia olu, so that *when their mates are enjoying, they also enjoy. It's not their fault their descendants are Christian.*

In the past, before the village converted, the libations carried more weight. Now, it's what people like my father perform – just trickling liquor into the ground – to keep attached to their roots. My mother says it's theatre. My father says every generation has to find their own way to keep their roots alive. *There's a reason we name our children Amaechina.* May the compound never be desolate. May it never cease to exist. For my mother, this means us also knowing her village, Lokpanta, as well as we know our father's.

Growing up, every Sunday after mass, my mother would drive my younger sister and me to her village to visit my grandparents. We followed a ritual we allowed to surprise us week after week. My mother would pretend we were going home for lunch, and not until we found ourselves on the express road, speeding towards an explosion of farmlands, would she admit that we were going to see Mamannukwu na Papannukwu. We always made a stop at the Nkwo Market right at the junction before we turned a long, untarred road to her father's house. We would get out of the car to say hello to relatives she pointed out to us but who we promptly forgot. It seemed like everybody we met at the market was related to her, and they were often never the same people each week. By the time we got to my grandparents', my grandmother would be standing outside waiting for us because an enthusiastic bearer of good news would have run ahead to let her know that we were on our way. Every week, she spread out her arms like a bird to fold us in, pressing our noses into her wrapper, exclaimed we had grown taller, prettier than when she had last seen us the week before. She'd ask my mother, *What are you feeding them? Agriculture food?* And we would giggle in delight. My grandfather was the quieter of the two. His welcomes were less exuberant. For that reason, I don't remember him on those trips but he must have been there, in the background, waiting for my grandmother to finish the fussing, to release us so we could come and say hello to him.

My grandmother cooked over firewood. Every Sunday, she made us something different but my favourite was her jollof rice, which tasted like party rice. To drink water, we had to dip a metal cup into the clay pot in a corner of her room. The water, as cool as the refrigerated one we drank at home, tasted of the earth after a rain. There is a word for it which I cannot now recall but each time it rains, I remember my grandmother.

I get nostalgic sometimes and google Lokpanta. Often, I see reports of abductions and clashes with herdsmen. Recently, I saw something on the murder of a young woman. Like the women who spearheaded SARS*, Lokpanta women led a peaceful agitation to their traditional rulers to demand better security for themselves and their children.

When I want to see Lokpanta as I remember it, I watch a video recording my uncle made there during a New Yam Festival. There is footage of my grandparents, now long deceased, explaining the festival to a city journalist. There's footage of my mother's sister, also dead a few years now, driving into the compound in her white 504 Peugeot. There's footage of me dancing badly as I have always done, my younger sister and a cousin dancing better than I was. There's footage of my mother, my other siblings, various aunts and uncles walking towards the camera, dancing, smiling, living. Carefree. Everyone looked so young and shiny that each time I watch it, I want to crawl into the TV, back into that time when Nigeria was a little safer. When Lokpanta was a little unknown. When I could travel with my beloved from Nsukka to show him where some of my best memories were made without worrying about kidnappers.

*

My beloved – who was a stranger then – came into my dorm room on a Friday night. He was wearing baggy Adire shorts and toe-strap sandals. The tallest person I ever saw, he bent his head to come through the door. I could not stop staring at his strong calves covered in fine, dark hair. I wanted to reach out and caress those calves. He looked like an actor playing Jesus, who'd taken a break to roam the grounds. The spectacle of him dazed me. How had I never seen him before? He'd come with someone I knew to invite my best friend and me to a party at his house. *Not a party-party*,

* Special Anti-Robbery Squad

his friend said once he saw me already saying no. I was notorious for avoiding campus parties. Someone once spiked my drink at one of those in my first year and tried to get me to sit on his lap. Luckily, someone else was watching out for me and drove me back to the hostel, depositing me with a friend of his. *Don't let her out of your sight,* he told her. *Something literary,* my future beloved's friend said. *Bring your poems to recite. Someone will play the guitar, I'll play drums.* So, we went. By the end of that night, I knew I liked this Belgian stranger enough to want to see him every day of my natural life.

Nsukka was destined to give me my love. It was where, years before, I had had my first crush. My first kiss. A boy with olive skin and soft curls on his head, I had never seen anyone so beautiful. His eyes squinted when he smiled. His lips were so soft I wanted to sink into them. He brought me gifts: bottles of perfume that never came packaged. My first *Chanel,* an open bottle I knew later was pilfered from his mother. I did not know it then. Young and in love, we said when we were old enough we'd get married and have many children. We went to the Arts theatre to watch university students perform plays. At the end of the holidays, we wrote endless letters to each other. *How are you? I miss you. When will I see you again?* Coy love notes that never said *I love you* but dripped it all over. We taped envelopes shut Sealed With A Loving Kiss (S.W.A.L.K.) and dreamed.

In my old albums, I still have a photo of him as a kid in love, a satin cummerbund around his waist, his hands behind his back, his eyes squinting as if he had the sun in them. He's leaning against a car at his uncle's wedding. Later, when I lived in Nsukka as an undergraduate, I'd become good friends with his younger brother and his best friend. Three of us in a Volkswagen Beetle owned by one of them. I'd cut classes to go into town and discover new joints where we could eat bush meat and abacha, and drink palm wine so fresh its sweetness was like sugar. Once, we went to a joint where when we asked for toothpick, we were asked to break off straw from its thatched roof.

The best friend, who was also my friend, died in a plane crash years later on a flight from Abuja to Port Harcourt. The plane crash landed. Two of 106 passengers, most of whom were students, died. Parents at the airport to fetch their children returning from boarding school heard the bang. Smelt the smoke. Saw the plane split in two like the dry shell of a nut. *In a country that worked, Okla wouldn't have died*, my friend who gave me the news told me. *Can you imagine? The airport's fire service had no water to put out the fire. Nigeria knows how to break hearts sha.* Hearts are broken because we love, I might have said.

And we know that there's no reasoning with love. Lagos taught me that.

Lagos is chaos. Noise and legendary traffic jams. Ubiquitous generators snoring through the night, chasing sleep away. Itinerant preachers announcing salvation and doom waking me up before the day has cracked open. And a love for a city that was sown in childhood.

As a young child visiting my favourite uncle's family in Surulere during school breaks, I could have whatever I wanted for breakfast. Bournvita. Nido. Milo. Slices of bread slathered with butter and jelly, filling my belly with sweetness and love. All the options and the freedom to choose, that was heaven. My uncle Simon was my father's youngest brother. We called him Daddy too because in my culture, your father's brother is also your father. One day, he asked me to make eba for him. *You know how to do it, okwa ya?* I said yes. I was maybe 11 then, so not an unreasonable ask. I brought out the gari. I froze. I had no idea how to continue, I had never learned. I knew hot water was involved – but how hot? My uncle

141

shoved me aside gently. It was okay that I didn't know. Was I hungry? He'd make enough for the two of us while he taught me. *Watch me.* He boiled water, poured it over some gari, stirred it with a spoon to a consistency I recognized. Every time I make gari now, I think of Daddy Simon's hands gently mixing the eba, his face looking up to make sure I was watching, the smile never leaving his face.

Weekends, he took us – my aunty, his two sons and me – out to hotels for lunch and drinks. Fanta and Chapman for us. Jollof and fried meat. Meat pies with crust so tender it almost melted in your mouth. Scotch eggs and crunchy chin-chin in bowls. *Don't rush your drinks, kids. You take a sip, you pause. Count slowly to ten. Then you take another sip.* Years after Uncle Simon's death, I had my own children; I taught them to count to ten between sips.

Lagos was also a life I didn't imagine existed outside of Hollywood movies. Once, I visited a friend who lived on an estate with one house for his parents and another for the children. There was a pool, bigger than the Sports Club pool. That day, there were a bunch of us hanging out in the children's section of the estate. My friend asked if we wanted cake, I said yes. *What type? Chocolate.* He picked up the phone and called the kitchen. He had their private chef bake us a cake dripping with chocolatey goodness. I ate so much of it I had a stomach ache. Later, on the drive home, we were stuck in traffic and some beggars came to the window of the car we were in to ask for *money to chop, sista, broda.*

Lagos was my best friend's family house in Ajao, where I stayed sometimes when school was on strike and I was tired of waiting it out in Enugu. For her elder sister's twenty-first, we had an all-night party with a DJ and over a hundred guests. Once my best friend and I went with her sister to see *Death of a Salesman* at the MUSON Centre and I grew a crush on the actor who played Biff Loman.

Lagos was Ikeja, where my sister lived for a while. On trips back to Nigeria, I stayed with her. We would stay up all night talking like we had as kids, remembering when that happened. And that happened. And that happened. Working our way through our past. Nothing spoken about ever ceases to exist. Amaechina. It is both a prayer for continuance and a hope for better days. It is mine too for my beloved Nigeria.

One Season, Many Decades,

Abubakar Adam Ibrahim

1.

The Decade of Sprouting Memories

We were children playing in the sands, digging holes to plant seeds of memories and a love for a space we were yet to grasp the sheer enormity and complexities of. Seeds that would burrow deeper until their roots would curl around our hearts, squeezing them to give us the adrenalin rush, the pizzazz and passion it takes to live in this space. Yet, somehow, inexplicably, these roots smother us.

In those days, in Jos, that city nestled atop a plateau, feathered by knolls and boulders and often shrouded in the morning mist, we thought the world was still fresh, still grey from the unsettled dust of creation. On one or two occasions we bandied together, the other children and I, to walk to the world's end, that place just beyond the horizon where the fiery sun sets.

As children, there were very few things to look forward to or to worry about: playing in the plot down the street or the one in front of Ngo's house, where sometimes, her belligerent grandmother, wispy and bent over, would chase us with insults and her walking stick. The festivities – the Eid when there would be rice and robust chunks of meat in tomato stew, when Ngo and her siblings, the Ndubuisi children, Kayode and his brother Ben would treat us with veneration because they longed for the feast our mothers were preparing. Like little lords in our starched kaftans, we would delight in taking bowls of Sallah food to their houses. At Christmas, the roles were reversed.

When we played in the sands then, no one was Yoruba or Igbo or Berom, Hausa or Egbura, and we only became Christians or Muslims when it was time to pray, or when Ngo's crazy grandma chased us, screaming, 'Bastards! Forehead bangers!' our laughter riling her up further. Most times, we were just children with hearts open to loving, to living, to laughing, to moulding dreams from the dust. We were just children of a city nestled on the hills in a country whose name was immaterial, whose fault lines we were blissfully unaware of.

*

I became conscious of having been in love with stories and my country at the same time. It was an awareness because I didn't know when this falling in love happened, only that it had happened sometime earlier in my life.

I was about 6 or 7 then. In the evenings, we would gather in the courtyard, sometimes sitting on the dakali or at the foot of Binta, an older girl who seemed as wise as the griots of old. Under the starry night or the solemn gaze of the moon, she would tell us stories of the cunning spider and the wily tortoise, of gullible birds and proud lions. We didn't know this at the time, but we were to be one of the last generations of children to be handed down these stories. Television, a rarity in those days, happened to those who came after us.

While our evenings were expended in storytelling and the revelries of moonlight plays, our days in school were garnished with flag-waving fervour and our teachers' promises that we were going to be the future leaders of a great country.

In those days, residues of the post-independence glow from two decades before still lingered, a glow that even a civil war and several military coups had not been able to eviscerate entirely. There were moments of national pride surges, such as the time the football team won the first ever Under-17 World Cup in China, birthing a contagion of effusive nationalism.

'Nigeria! The best in the whole world!' my father said, cranking the knob of his National colour TV that went kat, kat, kat as he searched for a clearer image, a channel with better pictures. No one cared that most of the boys in the team were from Bendel in the far south, or what name they called God by or what language they spoke. They were just Nigerians.

It was the first time I recall thinking of myself as one. In the midst of those dancing adults and their excitement, I recall first catching the Nigerian bug.

*

It wasn't until much later that I would realize that even in those days in the mid-Eighties that despondency had already set in, and more people were investing their hopes, not in the promises of a 'Giant of Africa' but increasingly in the God bandied about by mercantile priests, clerics and new-age charlatans.

In the first Buhari years, this despondency had driven a good number of professionals to flee the country. The hit song in those years was Veno Marioghae's 'Nigeria go Survive,' whose standout line advising a certain Andrew against checking out and imploring him to stay and build the country became an instant pop culture reference.

Veno was a patriot who, like most others, believed whatever was

147

happening in the country then was only a glitch in the matrix, that things would reset themselves if all Nigerians 'do their work' and the journey to greatness would resume.

But deep down, our parents and teachers felt this despondency. In the dark, it gnawed at their souls, hearts and conscience. We were too young to understand it then or maybe they were just reluctant to admit it. Somehow, it felt wrong to acknowledge it. In a country of growing religiosity, it would feel like confessing to masturbating in an office. How could a dream of a country like this go so wrong?

2.

The Decade of Withering Stalks

By the time I was in my teens and had started writing love poems for a girl I fancied in secondary school, I knew what my country was, is. She is a dream. A mirage. An idea. Something that is both alluring, yet unattainable. When she is sober, she is celestial like a deity whose laughter and cadence enchants. A magical being (or realm) for whom adoration comes naturally. But for her, sobriety is rare. Something that comes flittingly, increasingly so as time progresses. God knows it is hard to love her. But it is harder even to unlove her, as I have discovered. As we all have.

One learns of such things, of the true nature of this place, as one would the infidelity of a lover: the silence of the neighbours as one walks by, the whispers that start off behind one, sometimes the secret histories of indiscretion scribbled on the walls, in the corners of the room, on the bed, tucked in secret private smiles. One learns of such things in the markets, from snippets of conversations gathered from others, from reading the newspapers and news magazines, from conversations with the other boys in school about how bad the military dictatorships were, how abusive they were and have been to Nigerians. Sometimes, one learns such things from experiencing these abuses and social injustices, and how they have violated the country, leaving her bedraggled and reeling from trauma; one collects this knowledge.

*

The birth of this contraption that is my country was a product of the business interest of the British. It was a colonial enterprise, one from which much was taken, repatriated to enrich a foreign country, one that was patched together and named Nigeria, one that was handed to 'our founding fathers' on 1 October 1960. It is telling that they failed to build a nation out of this enterprise and the men who murdered them in a failed 'revolution', and those who murdered those who murdered them in retaliation, decided that maintaining her as an enterprise, not a nation, served their venal interest the best. Hence began the perpetuation of the colonial industrial complex by those who inherited the scraps of a country that could have been great.

And so you imagine that this place, this country, is like a sozzled goddess in a convoluted process of birthing a nation, an interminable labour made longer by those intent on delaying this birth, even at the risk of smothering the children. Yet, in those sweet, naïve teenage years as we sat, our intentions clean like our white uniforms, legs swaddled in navy-blue nylon pants swinging off the classroom desk, debating what was wrong with our country, it was easy to imagine that my generation would be the one to salvage that illusion. I imagined, rather naïvely I admit now, that my peers across the country were having similar conversations like the one my friends and I were having then. That we had all, through some telepathy, come to the understanding that the task before my generation, I surmised, was not to lead a great country, but to create one for our children and the generations that would come after. I would realize not long after, that even that was yet another illusion.

3.

The Decade of Dragons

Illusions sometimes burn quickly, like tissue paper kissed by fire. And this decade, it seemed fire-breathing dragons, conjured by George R. R. Martin, had swept across the land, spewing fire, embers dripping off their wings, scorching cities, towns and villages. These dragons were not called Rhaegal, Viserion or Drogon. They were called Democracy, Politicians and Men of God.

As anxiety over the 'Millennium Bug' grew, the juntas, inspired by the sudden death of the last strong man, realized that they were going out of fashion across the world. General Abdulsalam Abubakar rushed the country through a transitions programme and handed it over to a former dictator who had swapped his smart khaki for flowing robes. New vistas opened, the democratisation of shares in the Nigerian enterprise meant intense power brawls among the ruling class and to secure or advance their places, the new overlords reached into the depths of darkness and unleashed the monsters.

The first time this behemoth breathed in Jos, I was standing with my old school friends, as we had formed the habit of gathering every Friday to nurture the bonds formed in our teens, when someone arrived, panting. 'They have started,' he announced.

'Started what?' I asked.

'Started fighting,' he said.

'Who and who?'

'Muslims and Christians.'

News of such occurrences had filtered from elsewhere, from places like Kaduna, Lagos and Sagamu. Not once did I, or my friends, imagine that something like that could happen in Jos, this place where people of different tribes and religions were just Nigerians.

That demon roared through the streets of Jos, raining fire and death as neighbours turned on neighbours, hacking at each other, torching each other's houses because they called God by different names. In the decade that this violence reoccurred with the frequency of seasonal rains, in this period when our politicians played the religious card and turned us against each other to advance their interests, the extent of our disillusion hit home. This truth, sad and bitter as it is, is that this country is the way it is, not only because of the failings of the people who should have made it a nation, but also because of the people who should have insisted it is made one. We are both her victims and her abusers.

*

In the black steel trunk I had inherited from my uncle, I would discover, years later, my very first notebook when I started school. I was looking for some document and my search led me to the trunk when I chanced upon this book.

I flipped through the pages and discovered my very first class work. The memories of that day pour in, slowly, heavily, like honey from a jar. Our teacher had been called off to some meeting and to keep us busy, he had asked us to draw anything we fancied in our drawing books. Instead of drawing a bird or a lion or some exotic animal as the other children did, I drew a montage. A convoy of cars, sirens blazing, driving down a street lined with flag-waving children.

All these years later, I could see the image coming alive in my mind. I could hear the children cheering these men who were speeding off to go whip our country into shape so that when we became old enough, we would become leaders of a great country – as had always been promised. That notebook, and all the content of that trunk, and all the possessions I had in my life would be lost years later in a fire some boys up the street, boys we had played Sunday morning football with, would light. By this time, the hate-spewing beasts of Politics and Men of God had embraced them. They had become Children of the Dragon. The friendship we had growing up had become secondary because politics married religion and reminded them that people of different faiths must be enemies.

That day, all of those memories, all that juvenilia and the dreams of a great country went up in furious curls of smoke, ignited by furious children of a country too furious for her own good.

*

The other day in the crowded Shasha flea market in Ibadan, a man was killed over a squashed tomato. Several people died because a man was killed over that squashed tomato.

A porter bearing a cargo of tomatoes had an accident and lost his load. The content spilt all over a woman's stall, making a proper mess of the space. He apologised and agreed to clean up, but without water, the task could not be completed satisfactorily. Sometimes such encounters end with a shrug. Other times with a conversation like this:

'Goat! You no dey see road?'

'Madam, sorry, nah. No vex.'

'Sorry for yourself?'

'Madam, e don do, please. See how you dey vex like my mama? And you come fine reach her sef.'

That may draw a smile, maybe even an exchange of jokes and both parties would go their way laughing, shaking their heads. At the very least, it would draw a long, dramatic hiss before the woman or the man pushes through the crowd and goes about his or her business. On some days, it could turn nasty, like that Thursday in Shasha.

Because the woman and the porter both spoke different languages and were from different regions of the country (the man was even said to be a foreigner), another man decided to intervene on the side of the woman. He slapped the porter. The porter slapped him back (some accounts said he stabbed him). The interloper fell and died. That sad incident agitated underlying ethnic and regional tensions and led to the death of dozens of people. All because an anonymous Hausa-speaking porter accidentally spilt his cargo in front of an anonymous Yoruba woman's stall in the middle of a crowded flea market.

This is the nature of this place now. This is how volatile this space can be. This place, beautiful and fatally fragile, but mostly unpre-dictable.

*

4.

The Decade of Endless Grieving

When Andrew, in Veno Marioghae's music video, was convinced to stay back to 'do his work' and help Nigeria survive, it was all a happy scene. Chubby Andrew shuffling at the end of the music video became an instant pop culture reference that has endured over several decades and even today, those who are unfamiliar with the song are familiar with the references.

I wish every Nigerian story ended with the protagonist shuffling happily, like Andrew. But the reality is that those who have stayed back are doing so either because they can afford a bubble – constructed from all the things that make their lives comfortable (a source of power, water, food, walls swaddled in the love of their families, some level of security and the other constituents of their happiness – into which they could retreat every evening. In there, they escape the constant dose of frustration and despondence that this country forces on its citizens daily. The other half stay because they can't afford to contemplate leaving, or they are not stupid enough to sit on a cargo ship's rudder – like those four stowaways pictured in Lagos – to risk the Atlantic crossing that their forefathers, in chains, were forced to make centuries before. For those who can afford neither, hope is incredibly fragile but not even the vagaries of this country have managed to perish it. And it comes at absolutely no cost. That is what sustains people here. That is what keeps people trapped in this reality.

*

My cousin's husband, Sa'ad, was driving into his house in Bauchi when some men jumped on him with the intent to abduct him for ransom, as has become the rage here. Through the window of her apartment, my cousin watched the shadowy figures, her husband and the assailants, tussling in the night, wrestling for the gun. There was a scream for help. There was a crack of a gunshot. There were men running in the dark and then there was her husband, slumped, drenched in his own blood, at first presumed dead.

He is only lucky to be alive. But as I write this, he is having a second surgery as doctors try to make sure he is not permanently damaged in some way from this incident.

Tales of encounters like these are a dime a dozen these days.

Thousands of Nigerians have been kidnapped in this fashion from the safety of their homes, others waylaid on the highways and herded en masse into the bush, where the kidnappers have their camps. Many never return from these forests.

In the last few months alone, nearly 1,000 schoolboys and girls have been abducted from their hostels, sometimes 300 at a time. From Chibok to Dapchi, from Kagara to Kankara and Jengebe. Each time these abductions happen, the country falls to its knees, grovels before these kidnappers and begs them to spare the children and save the government from the infamy. Not one person has been arrested or prosecuted for any of these kidnappings. Bizarrely, some of the bandits who claim to have repented are feted by the government. Their victims, some murdered, others forced to sell their valuables to regain their freedom, are abandoned to their financial ruination.

When Boko Haram raided a school in Buni Yadi in 2014, and slit the throats of 59 boys, there was no reaction from the government: no retaliatory strike, no arrest, no justice. Not even a monument to remind us that a terrible thing like that happened. Not one to remind us of all the massacres that have been inflicted on us, and the ones we have inflicted on ourselves through civil unrest, religious riots, farmers'/herders' violence, political riots, banditry and terrorism. Not even the civil war.

We are too inundated to even mourn the losses we suffer. We are afraid to learn the names of the children we lost. Nigeria doesn't really care and Nigerians don't have enough patience to learn all these names because new ones would be added to them before one would even have moved his or her tongue to form the syllables that make up their names.

*

The reality that has birthed all this creative verve to have come out of Nigeria is often stranger than the fiction we write and the overly dramatic movies we make and the laugh-out-loud comedy we create or the pop music videos we are famous for. It is darker, grimmer and far more bizarre.

So many things do not add up here, like how a country of such brilliant minds is always often led by middling men.

So when we retreat to the bubbles of comfort we create to escape this reality, we go all out. We party hard, the better to flee from our nightmares. It is no surprise that humour is one of the biggest industries in this country. We make fun of our misery and laugh at ourselves. Gently, with the greatest care in the world, we bury the bitter pills of our reality into the lush art we make so they are easier to swallow. With words, with art and music, we deconstruct our realities – the bizarre, the fantastical and magical, the tragic, the exhilarating and titillating – and cobble them back together in ways that would make it tolerable, beautiful even, sometimes even incandescent.

It takes courage to admit that loving this country is like being in love with an abusive partner, one who needs help but refuses to accept it, one who bites and punches, whom you wake up to find staring down at you with a look you can't comprehend but one that frightens you, one who, when he or she reaches for you, you are never sure if they wanted to hug you or hit you.

Nothing hurts like loving what frightens you the most.

War and Peace

Okey Ndibe

Late in 2020, I shocked some family and friends by announcing my desire to travel to Nigeria for a month. At the time, the Covid-19 pandemic seemed resurgent, mounting what looked like a vicious second wave. In that bleak context, few applauded my plan. It made little sense to them.

For me, however, an extended escape to Nigeria was both a risky idea – how could one deny it? – and a bravura move to save my sanity. I'm a creature of wanderlust, giddiest when on the move, hopping from one enchanted destination to another. I'm also notoriously gregarious, energised by the warmth and gaiety of others. After nearly a year of universal hibernation – a friend described it as the world going to jail – I was reeling. I was desperate to breathe again in an accustomed, freer manner. Nigeria was *the* place to do so. And the Christmas season was the particular time. So off I went, after assuring anxious family and friends that I would do whatever it took to stay safe.

Nigeria is quite simply the place where I feel happiest. It is also, in a strange twist, the place where my sorrows are at their most intense. The thirty-two days I spent in Nigeria reinforced my sense of the country as a space that springs countless surprises. Or – as I sometimes argue – Nigeria is a country of steady habits: my wry way of remarking that things hardly ever happen as planned. At any rate, my month-long trip yielded a rich harvest of the myriad ways in which Nigeria both buoys and disheartens me.

I had booked a Dana Air flight for 20 December to take me from Lagos to Enugu, a south-eastern city that's less than a two-hour car ride to my hometown, Amawbia. The morning of the trip, the airline called to announce the cancellation of my flight – no explanation given, much less the offer of an alternative itinerary.

Had this happened in the US, where I have lived for a little more than thirty years, the development would have left me deeply distressed. Not so much in Nigeria. Familiarity with the frequency of such happenstances has bred in me – as in many other Nigerians – an inventive spirit, an almost evolutionary genius for anticipating and planning for disappointment. The day before, I had called a childhood friend who was travelling by road from Lagos to my home state, to ask that he save me a seat in his car – just in case!

The road trip became sheer adventure, the kind an acquaintance of mine – a former Lagos-based correspondent for an international newspaper – once characterized as a source of exhilaration and exasperation. For most of the year, the 310-mile journey took between six and seven hours. For us, it was a thirteen-hour ordeal. Nigerian highways are infamous for stretches so rutted and gutted that vehicles must progress at a crawl. This was part of the story for us, but only a small part.

Far more taxing was the ubiquitous presence of security check-points. As we drove out of Lagos, I began to count these checkpoints – where a portion of the road is blocked with logs of wood, sand-filled drums or disused tyres from trucks. I abandoned the exercise after breaking twenty. Many of the checkpoints were within a mile of one another.

Every sentient Nigerian knows that these roadblocks were never designed to fight crime. They might as well be called by their proper name, extortion points. Beleaguered commuters know they must press cash into the hands of the unsmiling, sweat-slicked police officers, soldiers and customs agents who man the roadblocks – or risk being delayed for hours, or even brutalised. In October of 2020, Nigerians – most of them youngsters – had swarmed the country's cities demanding an end to police brutality. In a country where such protests quickly fizzle out, this one appeared set to go on for some time.

Rattled, President Muhammadu Buhari promised to institute reforms. Yet, in a sign that his rhetoric was hollow, he had hardly finished delivering his sweet pledge when soldiers blockaded protesters in Lagos and then unleashed deadly force, maiming many and killing a few.

That devastating denouement notwithstanding, I had arrived in the country expecting to see a measure of courteousness from police officers, not the old devil-may-care, swashbuckling deportment. My expectation proved immodest and naïve! The officers at the extortion points were just as brash, and as rough with hapless civilians, as I had ever seen them. In a season when most residents of sprawling cities travelled to the countryside to celebrate Christmas and usher in the New Year in their natal communities, the police presence exacerbated snarling traffic.

At the least sign of slowing traffic, too many drivers seemed to activate their selfishness quotient. They attempted to edge ahead of other vehicles, or created extra lanes of traffic. Often, these frenzied drivers' inconsiderate actions led to minor accidents, like fender thumps, but also to a few more serious ones. At any rate, their wretched choices always ramped up the gridlock.

Why, I wondered, did it not occur to these drivers that a little self-restraint, a smidgen of consideration for others, would serve them and their fellows? Why did they take the same ruinous steps time after time, but (perhaps) expect a different result?

It all enraged me.

Yet, once we arrived in my hometown, all that disenchantment took a backseat. After months of restrictions in the US, of masked faces, I shivered with shock and a little illicit delight to be among people who didn't wear masks, who teased me when I wore them, who didn't abide by the new regime of social distance but often exchanged hugs and handshakes, who staged revelries for traditional marriages, funerals, title taking, the outing of colourful masquerades. In the howl of their laughter, the sound of their instruments, the sway of their dance, in the ambrosial aroma of their cuisines, I glimpsed both a flirtation with danger and – more crucially – affirmation that we were still alive, the earth was still stirring.

Gosh, I basked in it all! I relished the foods of my childhood. I quaffed the sweetish, slightly fermented palm wine that my forebears put at the centre of their festivities and communions. I had a heady time reuniting with friends and relatives, especially those I hadn't seen in many, many years. I treasured the wit, wisdom and exquisite stories told by elders, the ones Chinua Achebe might have called 'owners of words'. I was having one big ecstatic time.

Yet, in the midst of all that joy, I suffered intrusions of that dimension of Nigeria that engenders shattering pain. Covid-19 felled two close friends of mine. Another friend and a cousin were hospitalised with the virus, but scraped through. Even so, I encountered many people, some of them educated, who insisted the virus did not exist, or that it was a Euro-Asian-American thing, or that its mission was to menace the affluent. I saw, close-up, the contrast between the obscene, wasteful lifestyle of Nigeria's privileged class and the grinding poverty of the vast populace. I took trips to other towns, even to another state, to visit friends. Again and again I witnessed monstrous traffic jams caused by unnecessary police checkpoints but aggravated by maddening drivers.

For years I had ranted about the disheartening conduct of Nigerian drivers. This time, I was finally summoned to a chastening epiphany. It dawned on me that Nigerians' driving habits represented a microcosm, metaphor and synecdoche of the country's broader malaise. That grating and selfish drive to get ahead – something too many drivers seek to do, at their and others' peril – struck me as mirroring the ethical bankruptcy of government officials who shamelessly corner public cash for their exclusive aggrandisement.

Nigeria has had a procession of Ministers of Works who amassed spectacular wealth, while leaving Nigerian roads in their perennially ghastly shape. Too many government officials talk a great game about fixing the country's schools and healthcare system. But far from delivering, they use their loot to send their wards to sound schools abroad and themselves – when they fall sick – to well-equipped hospitals in other countries. Instead of addressing their country's scandalous energy woes, some top bureaucrats and politicians are content to purchase generators for their personal use and comfort.

Why do I find these self-inflicted national wounds particularly hard to stomach? I'd specify four major reasons.

The first is that Nigeria and I are, in a manner of speaking, roughly age mates, so that I have come to feel a heightened emotional pang at the country's abysmal state.

I was born in 1960 in Yola, a dusty pastoral town in north-eastern Nigeria. I arrived exactly three and a half months before Nigeria achieved Independence on 1 October. My earliest childhood memories are linked to that quiescent town where my father was the postmaster, my mother an elementary school teacher.

Owing perhaps to the hardness that has marked the intervening years, the enchantment of my earliest childhood memories has acquired a tinge of eerie disquiet. But I fondly remember a tree that stood in front of our residence, one of a row of small flats called staff quarters. I remember Muslim men dressed in white, flowing jumpers. One of them, Musa, was close to my parents. I have vivid memories of sitting on his lap under the tree, absolutely absorbed in trying to grab at his white beard, while he, laughing, constantly moved his head from side to side, evading my little fingers. I remember when my father would leave our flat with a double-barrelled gun slung across his shoulder and return with his hunter's bag filled with game, often guinea fowl. I recall a day one of our neighbours took me to a brush clearing to watch stick fights. In the fights, young men took turns beating one another's bare backs with stalwart sticks, a test of endurance that heralded the youngsters' initiation into manhood. Any young man who survived the ordeal was counted a man – and became qualified to take a wife. I watched with horror as one of the men crumpled to the ground on being dealt a vicious stroke of the cane. Terrified spectators fled. I felt paralysed, my feet incapable of move-ment. Then somebody – the neighbour who had brought us – swept me up.

That idyllic life would soon expire. In mid-1966, our time in Yola came to an abrupt end. The Nigerian military had staged two bloody coups d'état. Ethnic and sectarian violence spilled out onto the streets in many cities and towns across the northern half of the country, most of it targeting south-easterners. My parents made a quick deci-sion. Our mother had to take us, their four children at the time, and escape to Amawbia. Father could not flee with us since he was a federal civil servant. The government had warned that its employees who abandoned their post would be sacked.

His decision to stay behind nearly cost him. One day, a mob showed up at the post office, armed with cudgels and machetes, chanting blood-curdling anthems. My father and his colleagues locked themselves inside. Their fiendish attackers were on the cusp of knocking down the barred door when the town's traditional ruler, the Lamido of Adamawa, happened to come around. He scolded the mob, dispersed them, and then took my father and his colleagues to his palace for safety. Two or three weeks later, he personally escorted them to the banks of the River Benue, where they boarded one of the last ships to sail to the south-east.

Soon after, Nigeria was at war. It was called a civil war, but fought on ruthless terms. The war was occasioned by the desire of the south-eastern zone to secede and create a new nation called Biafra. I was a child of that war, and lost my innocence to it. Hunger was pervasive and vicious. Despite relief agencies' best efforts to ferry in food, little of it came into Biafra, the Nigerian government having mounted a blockade of the secessionist territory. What miserly supplies made it in were quickly mopped up and hoarded by corrupt Biafran officials. Death became a staple reality, for children and adults alike. In the final reckoning, most of those who perished were felled not by bullets but extreme starvation. Children – who were much like me, except less lucky – and women, were overrepresented in the war's two million casualties. I barely held on to life. I had the fortune of having a cousin who was adept at setting traps for game as well as using a catapult to hunt lizards and birds. We were sustained on such unaccustomed diets as roasted lizards and fried locusts.

Ultimately, Nigeria's superior firepower triumphed; Biafra, and the dreams that animated its proponents, went prostrate. For me, however, the war rendered urgent my ongoing dialogue with Nigeria. It utterly dispirits me that a country whose corporate existence was underwritten by the shedding of so much shed blood could afford to wobble and stumble. Two of Nigeria's greatest writers, Wole Soyinka and Chinua Achebe, have often painted unsparing portraits of their country. In sum, their contention is that a nation does not yet exist in the space called Nigeria. Their critique deeply resonates with me. The two writers' critiques speak deeply to my own concerns about Nigeria.

My vocation as a writer is inextricably linked to a perceived obligation to be attentive to Nigeria's odysseys. Did I choose to be a writer because – as I often tell it – I couldn't think of a better thing to do with myself? Or was I chosen for the vocation, commissioned by forces whose nature and authority I know only in the dimmest of ways? Depending on my mood, I sometimes incline towards the former theory, sometimes towards the latter. But about my subject, I have no doubt. It may be fortuitous that I became a writer, but I believe I have been handed the confounding subject called Nigeria. Achebe has spoken of it as a country versed in the art of snatching defeat from the jaws of victory. I have often described Nigeria as conceived in hope but tragically nurtured – mostly by its leaders – into hopelessness.

Here's a final reason I can't help bothering about Nigeria: I am haunted by my grandfather's pain. Let me explain with a story.

I once had a memorable conversation with an elderly man from my hometown. A retired teacher, he had just read and admired my debut novel, *Arrows of Rain*.

'How did you get this gift for writing?' he asked. He held me in a gaze, expectant.

There was, I felt, no mystery to it. I told him that my mother, a schoolteacher, had made me into an absorbent reader. Quite early in childhood, I had developed a sizable appetite for getting into trouble. My mother, a stern disciplinarian, felt that occupying me with books would keep me on a tight rein. Often, to earn permission to join my friends at play, I had first to satisfy her that I had spent significant time reading. Out of that compulsion grew an enduring passion for reading. That interest bloomed – years later, once the opportunity presented itself – into a desire to write.

An odd expression wreathed the man's face as he listened to my account. It seemed a cross between fascination and incredulity. 'I'll tell you how you became a writer,' he said finally, his air confident and knowing. 'You became a writer because your grandfather was the first person to bring English to Amawbia. Did you know that?'

I didn't.

'I was a child, but I remember it clearly. People gathered each evening to listen to your grandfather speak English. You, his grandson, have inherited that gift. That's why you became a writer. If you doubt me, go and ask.'

My father had died, so I went to his immediate younger brother, Uncle Ochendo. I had double fortune: he happened to be with Aunty Mgbogo, his and my father's only sister. I told them what I had heard about my grandfather and the English language.

'It's true,' my aunt stated immediately, with glee. 'Our father was the first speaker of English in Amawbia.'

My uncle flashed a wry smile. 'Forget my sister's word. Our father did not speak real English.'

I watched as both siblings squabbled playfully. At last, my uncle said he would tell me a story to clear up the puzzle.

One day, sometime early in the twentieth century, a party of British merchants appeared in Amawbia with their retinue of factotums. They were seeking to hire strong young men for timber-sawing jobs in Nigeria's thickly forested deltaic zone – notorious today as the country's trouble-prone oil-producing hub.

My grandfather and a handful of other adventurers elected to take a chance with the British entrepreneurs. At the time, Britain – for good or ill – had welded more than 300 disparate ethnic groups into a fledging collective it named Nigeria. Indeed, imperial Britain had profoundly reshaped the lives of all inhabitants of this new space. The creation of a variety of new wage-earning jobs was one of the salient by-products of this transformation. A cash nexus undergirded the novel economy and its multiple forms of transactions.

My grandfather seemed quite suited for the arduous demands of hewing wood. He was youthful in age and quite famed for his strength. An agile wrestler, he was fondly called Kaodiechi. The nickname, literally 'let it be tomorrow', arose from his verbal exchange with a would-be opponent during a wrestling festival. My grandfather, who was near-invincible as a wrestler, had challenged another well-known virtuoso to a duel. Dreading the prospect of defeat, the other man pleaded that the match be postponed until the next day. But my grandfather retorted, 'Why not today?'

On their arrival in the delta, my grandfather and his fellows realized that they were in for unrelenting agony. The British were cruel taskmasters, quick with their whips. Day-long, as they strained at the saw, the workers' backs were steeled for scourging by sadistic white men. And a torrent of curses accompanied the incessant flogging.

Within a few days, my grandfather and his fellow recruits had had enough of British brutishness. They set a date to return to their hometown – and to the familiar rhythms of their lives as farmers, hunters and traders. But when the departure date arrived, my grandfather had taken ill. There was no way he could make the trip, a trek of close to 150 miles. He asked his townsfolk to assure his parents that he would travel home, alone, once he fully recovered.

Several weeks passed before he returned to Amawbia. As he had spent a little more time with the abusive merchants, my grandfather had picked up some of their pejoratives. He became a small sensation, offering delectable entertainment to small crowds of people who wished to hear him 'speak' English. He obliged his audience with mangled pronunciation of choice insults. Scallywag became *sukali-wagi*, nincompoop turned into *ninicompoopoo*, bloody fool incarnated as *buladi foolu* and idiot was reborn as *idiotu*. In his heavy, inflected accent, he would render fiery phrases like 'I'll deal with you!' and 'Get to it!'

My uncle's account buttressed what my elderly fan had told me. I embraced the idea of my grandfather as a linguistic pioneer. I also began to imagine his broad wrestler's back rife with a latticework of welts, scars etched by the whips of white men.

That image, hideous and persistent, has layered my conversation with Nigeria. My grandfather's scars, even if they existed only in my imagination, became one way I could enter the subject of Nigeria. The cascade of whips on Grandfather's back informed me – and us – that pain was from the very beginning part of the equation of Nigeria. Those who flogged him were, with each stroke, engaged in the high-minded 'mission of spreading civilisation'. They were founding and naming this space called Nigeria. When I remember my pangs of hunger during the Biafran War, and my grandfather's shuddering back as the whips landed, I can't help thinking of all the stories one must tell about Nigeria if time permits.

There's this mystery I hope to resolve some day – hopefully with help from my grandfather's ghost: how is my pain connected to his, or my joy to his joy? If he had handed me the heirloom of a new tongue, have I used it well enough to chronicle the annals of a country he saw from afar as the whip flashed in the air?

A Banner Without Stain

Ike Anya

. . . Our flag shall be a symbol
That truth and justice reign
In peace and battle honour'd
And this we count as gain
To hand on to our children
A banner without stain . . .

    Nigerian national anthem,

           1960–78

It is July or August. The rainy season. I can smell the loam-rich scent of freshly rained-on earth wafting through the lacy brickwork of the airy main corridor of our bungalow: 614 Odim Street, University of Nigeria, Nsukka. Through the mosquito netting covering the bricks, I can see the frangipani tree with its gnarled grey branches on the lawn my mother has carefully planted and nurtured. A sea of pink flowers laps at the foot of the tree.

I am lying on the carpet of the room I share with my brothers, Chidi, who at 8 is three years older than me, and Nazo, who is only 2. I frown, concentrating, trying to make out the unfamiliar words on the page. I should be waiting for my mother in the parlour. Usually, she sits in the armchair that faces the door to the kitchen and I squeeze in by her side. Thus, comfortably ensconced, her familiar warmth cocooning me, she opens the latest in the Ladybird reading series. They are all about an English boy called Peter and his sister Jane and their various activities. I have scythed through level after level of the numbered books, faster than expected for my age. And the hunger for the written word, a constant companion through the next five decades, is already establishing itself, as I try to read everything that has writing that I see. Even when the words are unfamiliar and difficult to pronounce. 'By a . . . ppo..int-ment to Her (those two bare easy) Majest . . . tie, (rhyming it with sky),' I read aloud the writing on the Robertson's Marmalade jar, the one with a picture of a golliwog, which is on our breakfast table each morning, together with the Anchor butter (Made in New Zealand) and the packet of Kellogg's Corn Flakes with the drawing of a crowing cock in yellow, red and green.

This rainy morning, restless for my reading lesson, I wander into my parents' room where there is always plenty to read. Foraging in their wardrobe, in an old handbag of my mother's I find a small, plastic-covered diary for 1974, the previous year. The diary gives off the characteristic smell of the interior of my mother's handbags: echoes of hand lotion, Horlicks' sweets, glycerine, Vicks and other familiar smells that I cannot identify.

Opening the diary, I see the Nigerian coat of arms – two horses supporting a black shield emblazoned with a white *Y* – the Rivers Niger and Benue. A red eagle perches on the shield, which itself sits on a bed of scattered flowers, not unlike the one beneath our frangipani. I recognize the coat of arms from Colouring, a favourite activity at Floyd Nursery, on the street next to ours. It is in a corrugated zinc shed built at the bottom of our teacher Auntie Floy's garden. Her husband Chris works in the university personnel department and has been firm friends with my father since their undergraduate days at the University College in Ibadan.

I turn the page of the diary, immediately spotting something familiar – the national anthem – which we shout-sing at assembly each morning. I begin singing softly, the familiar 'Nigeria we hail thee', but by the time I end where we usually do, with the words, 'Nigerians all, and proud to serve . . .', I notice that there are still two clusters of words below, all unfamiliar. I apply the same tune to the next line, which begins: 'Our flag shall be a symbol that truth and justice reigns . . .' As I progress through the second and third scarcely used verses of our national anthem, a sudden flash of new knowledge dawns. For the first time I realize, in a way that I have not before, that I am Nigerian. That is the day I learn our national anthem has three verses. It is also the first time that I appreciate that I am Nigerian. I cannot say why. What does not occur to me is this: Had I been born just eleven months before my actual birthday, I would have been born Biafran. Perhaps I would even have been one piece in the haunting mosaic of round-bellied, stick-thin infants whose images, travelled around the world at a time when 'viral' was still only a biomedical word.

Years later, I would meet people – English, American, Australian – who on being introduced to me, would exclaim: 'Ah, you are from Nigeria, which part?' If I judged them to be the right age, I would sometimes venture: 'The part that was Biafra.' Almost invariably, I would be rewarded with variations on the theme: 'As children, we were told to clear our plates because we were lucky to have food, not like the poor children starving in Biafra.'

Decades on, I reflect on my idyllic childhood, middle child of educated, middle-class parents in Nigeria's oil boom years – the 1970s. Reflecting, I muse on what unseen pain and trauma from the war hovered behind those sunlit days spent playing in the garden of the bungalow at Odim. How did my parents, their colleagues and friends create this haven, this close-knit university community out of nothing?

How, having returned, ragged and penniless just three years before, on the losing side in a harrowing, brutal, thirty-month war, had they created this idyll? How were they able to put aside the bitterness and hurt from three years of fratricide to live so seemingly untouched by those events? And how were they able to do it so well that a mere four years after the war ended, on a campus whose lecture halls' walls were still riddled with bullet holes, their precocious 4-year-old had no hesitation in declaring himself Nigerian?

The war was often mentioned in passing, but matter-of-factly, devoid of context. So, asking why the ivory-handled cutlery set (a wedding present to my parents) lacked two knives, I would be told, 'They were lost in the war.' Similarly, when my brother, peering at an album photo of our youthful father standing next to an unfamiliar relative, asked, 'Who is this uncle? Where is he now?' The same answer would come: 'Lost in the war.'

Little else pointed to any sign of the war as tragedy, to any lingering trauma. I had no idea, for instance, what my father's younger brother, Uncle Boko, and his fellow undergraduate friends who flocked to our house at weekends had been through in the war. Watching them dance raucously to The Wings' 'Catch That Love', Afros bobbing, wide-bottomed trousers falling over caterpillar shoes that sweep the floor, no one would have believed that just three years before, they were fighting in trenches, slipping behind enemy lines as almost-child soldiers, part of the Biafran Organization of Freedom Fighters.

Nothing about what they or my parents said or did indicated that we were anything other than Nigerian.

When they sang 'Nigeria, we hail thee, our own dear native land', it was not tinged with regret, at least as far as we children could tell.

There has always been an inexplicable symmetry in my mind, between the events leading up to that most uncivil of civil wars and that old national anthem, with its snippets that seemed to presage

the carnage to come: 'Though tribe and tongue may differ, in brother-
hood we stand, Nigerians all, and proud to serve . . .

'. . . help us to build a nation where no man is oppressed.'

And then of course there was that other phrase, attractive to me
perhaps by its mention of children: 'To hand on to our children, a
banner without stain . . .'

A banner without stain?

*

Perhaps Nigeria's military leaders shared my perceptions of this strange
symmetry. Perhaps they felt uncomfortable with the words of the old
anthem, dreamed up by a British housewife to win a pre-independence
competition run to select an anthem for the new nation. Perhaps
they sensed that the words held within them, an indictment, a
reminder of how far we had fallen from the ideals of those early days.
And so perhaps that is why, in the year that I turn 8, reading fluently
and in my third year at primary school, I join my classmates in
learning a new national anthem. The old verses with their uncomfortable reminders of our diversity, dated in language and guilt-inducing
in their talk of a country 'where no man is oppressed' are discarded.
In their place, a shiny new anthem, written by a committee of Nigerian
academics. It has only two verses. And there are no mentions of
difference, of oppression or of banners, stained or clean.

The old anthem does not die, however. During the many student
demonstrations I witness, growing up and as an undergraduate, it
often reappears.

As successive generations of Nigerian students rise in protest against
successive military governments, at each demonstration, a lone voice at
some point rises above the hubbub, intoning: 'Nigeria we hail thee . . .'
and always, always, always, a ripple of recognition runs through the

crowd, who launch into the anthem, singing with a passion invoking a repudiation of the military, their new national anthem, and their authority, all rooted in illegitimacy.

*

On the night that Auntie Nkadi tells the story of how her father died, I am the person who opens our front door to her. The doorbell rings and I sweep aside the thick brown, cream and orange curtains to her gap-toothed smile, her jerry-curled hair teased out in a soft, frizzy cloud.

'Ike, doctor! Are you home for the weekend?'

I nod, bashfully ushering her to an armchair covered in the golden-brown velveteen fabric my mother picked out on a special visit to the vast Onitsha Market. I am only a second-year medical student, but older friends and relatives have taken to calling me 'doctor'. I go upstairs to tell my mother of her visitor, to her palpable pleasure. Auntie Nkadi has been a firm favourite in the couple of years since, newly returned from the US with her scientist husband, she started teaching biology at the boys' school where my mother is vice-principal.

I serve Auntie Nkadi a Fanta and retreat to the adjacent dining room, a favourite vantage point for eavesdropping on my parents, to continue reading a novel.

'And then they asked the men and the boys to move to one side. My mother and the other women started crying and begging them not to separate us, but the soldiers ignored us. That was the last time I saw my father and brothers . . . so many were killed in Asaba that day.'

Auntie Nkadi's voice is calm, steady, as if simply describing an incident observed that morning at Ahia Ogige, the Nsukka main market.

I abandon all pretence of reading and put my head round the partition separating me from the living room. Auntie Nkadi sits bolt upright, my mother clasps both her hands in hers. Auntie Nkadi sees me. She smiles wanly as if to make light of her story, to lighten the horror she sees inscribed on my face.

That is how I first learn of the Asaba Massacre, the despicable episode in the early months of war, when the Nigerian Army overran the town of Asaba on the western banks of the River Niger. Rounding up the town's inhabitants, then separating the men and boys from the women, they killed hundreds of unarmed civilian men and boys in cold blood. The Asaba people, straddling the border between Nigeria and Biafra, had been caught in the diabolical position of being considered saboteurs by both sides.

Long after Auntie Nkadi has gone, I lie flat on the carpet, looking up at the white ceiling and wonder how it is that I have only just learned of this tragic incident even though I have devoured book after book on the war. How is it that the commander of the troops who committed this atrocity rose to become Military Head of State, and is still revered like a martyr, having been assassinated in an abortive coup attempt when I was 6?

In the years that follow, more massacres, more unlawful killings, more miscarriages of justice come. Odi, Zaki Biam, the Apo Six become familiar names, often cited examples of instances when the Nigerian state turned on its citizens.

*

August 2001. I stand at the gates of my soon-to-be sister-in-law's family compound in Victoria Island. Loud juju music blares. A throng of gorgeously, flamboyantly dressed men and women in blue and gold and lilac, the wedding colours, bustle in and out of the spacious compound. The traditional engagement ceremonies done, there is a lull before the all-night engagement party starts. I am seeing off Dupe, fiancée of Endee, my closest friend and colleague at the National Hospital in Abuja, where I have worked for just over a year. Dupe has flown alone from Abuja to attend the ceremony. Just a week before, Endee left to begin postgraduate studies in Illinois. I too will be leaving in a fortnight, to London to begin my Master's degree.

'Wait, let me give you my number,' Dupe pulls a mobile phone from her handbag as her driver manoeuvres the car towards us.

'Ah, you have got a GSM? Let me see . . .'

GSMs are still a new luxury for young professionals like us, it is mere months since the new civilian government awarded licences to a few mobile phone companies. As they roll out their services, for the first time, middle-class professionals can at a stretch acquire mobile phones, with prices just within reach.

The mobile phones and student visas that Endee and I leave on are direct and indirect results of Nigeria's re-engagement with the world. We have staggered into the murky sunlight of a third attempt at civilian government, emerging from the dark military dictatorship of Sani Abacha, when it seemed our only remaining friend was North Korea.

I leave for the UK in September and do not return for another eighteen months. In those months, I go through the new immigrant rituals of juggling cleaning and security jobs with study, while marking the longest time I have been away from Nigeria as an adult.

A couple of months after graduation, now a senior house officer in the NHS, I can afford a ticket home, returning to act as best man at my friend Chinedu's wedding.

As our plane begins its descent, preparing to land, I sight the familiar palm trees and lush greenery, the patchwork of rusty roofs, and my heart is full. Through the open aircraft door, I step from the refrigerated cool into the welcoming warm wet embrace of Lagos.

Pushing my luggage, having run the gauntlet of hawk-eyed customs officials, I make my way to the agreed place where my parents' driver Moses will pick me up. As I manoeuvre the trolley, piled high with luggage, I am assailed by calls of 'Change money', 'Oga, you need taxi?', 'Taxi', 'Change money', 'Taxi' . . . the alternating chants become irritating, and I am tempted to shout at the harassing men and women, 'Don't you think if I wanted to change money or get a taxi, I would have done so by now?' Yet there is a tug of admiration for their persistence, that distinctively Nigerian spirit of hustle that refuses to give up.

That resourcefulness is even more evident on the streets, as I hungrily take in the familiar, long-missed scenes on the drive from the airport in Ikeja to my parents in Victoria Island. On virtually every street corner, men and women sit at small tables, often protected from the relentless sun by small canopies in the bright yellow or bright red colours of the two leading mobile phone companies.

Hunched over the tables, these people, who eighteen months before had never seen a mobile phone, let alone touched one, are now offering handset repair services. Without formal training, without any preparation, mostly without any basic knowledge of mathematics and physics, let alone technology or engineering.

Perhaps these are the children who were handed the banner without stain.

*

Nigerian noise, Naija flamboyance – these are traits I cringe at, still in many ways the bookish little boy, in the corner, reading quietly. I am often the one who, when we go out as a pack of Nigerians in London, keeps hushing the others, pleading on behalf of the other guests that my people tone it down.

This attitude persists until 2007 when, invited to the TED Global Conference in Arusha as part of the first set of one hundred Fellows, I first visit another sub-Saharan African country. I am struck by how docile and pliant the Tanzanian air staff are on the connecting flight from Dar es Salaam. And in the safari lodge where we stay, I find myself wishing that the waiters would occasionally be rude, rebellious or slapdash instead of the almost constant servile bows accompanying the tea, meals or whatever they are serving. For the first time, I yearn for Nigerian sass, Nigerian noise.

I am not alone in noticing this. On the last day of the conference, Dr Ngozi Okonjo-Iweala, newly returned from the World Bank to be Nigeria's minister of finance, and Pulitzer Prize-winning journalist Dele Olojede are just two of the Nigerians who deliver thoughtful, inspirational talks. Afterwards, we pour from the hall, an exuberant effervescence of Nigerians, into the flower-filled outdoor space, where white-linened tables stand, set up in rows for lunch. We all, speakers included, coalesce around one long table, loud and raucous.

We occupy all the set places, then take it in turns to visit the buffet. At one point, two fresh-faced young white American men approach, gesturing to two empty spaces, asking if they can sit. We explain that the seats are occupied, the owners gone to fill their plates, but half-jokingly, one accuses us of being racist, of not wanting them to sit because they are white. We smile awkwardly but one Nigerian – it may even have been me – quips, 'Well, you know on that front, we have a lot of catching up with you guys to do.' The men blush, scurrying away as the table erupts in laughter.

Going to fill my plate, I almost bump into June, the young Kenyan activist introduced to me by Binj, our mutual friend, also a Fellow at the conference. She stands by a hedge, her gaze trained, as one hypnotised, on the spectacle of a group of celebratory Nigerians loudly colonising a shared public space, characteristically oblivious to recriminatory stares or disapproving tuts, completely at home.

'Come and join us, you can take my chair,' I invite. She looks at me, then again, wistfully at the table and says in a soft voice, 'I wish I was Nigerian.'

More used to hearing the opposite, I ask her why.

'Just look at the way you guys are carrying on, not even noticing if there is anyone else here . . .'

When I return to London, my frenzied hushing of my friends, my embarrassment at their spectacle is gone.

Part of my ambivalence with Nigerian pride and swagger stems from a knowledge of how poorly, how woefully we have deployed our extraordinary resources, how badly we have failed our weakest. Through my life, lurching from military government to military government, with brief interludes of civilian government, a phrase recurs. Through the demonstrations and protests, as each flickering of hope fizzles into nothingness, constantly repeated in roadside bars and bukas by the roadside philosophers ubiquitous across our nation: 'Until people are ready to die, to lay down their lives for Nigeria, this country will not change.'

Last November, five decades from the end of the Biafran War and from my birth, the bitter reality begins to seep in: the knowledge, that like my parents, I may never witness that Nigeria that I have often dreamed and worked for.

And then the EndSARS movement happened, bursting into my melancholia. Young Nigerians, techs, creatives – two areas providing the sustenance the country had denied them – rose against the tyranny of the police Special Anti-Robbery Squad and the nation erupted.

Watching in awe as they deftly deployed technology to crowdfund, to organise litter picking at the demonstration sites, to despatch

179

funding for legal fees for arrested comrades. And getting ambulances to the points where they were needed within half an hour. This last something the Nigerian state in sixty years could not ever achieve.

Energised, I poured all I could into the bank accounts advertised – buoyed by the transparency in the way accounts were published daily; and by how, as the government clamped down on each bank account, the young people would move to another and from cash to cryptocurrency, outwitting their pursuers. One of the key moving spirits was the Nigerian Feminist Coalition, and seeing Nigerians rally willingly behind an organisation with the F-word in its name seemed too momentous to take in.

One Sunday, a lockdown-enforced long walk to Trafalgar Square saw me join other Nigerians demonstrating in support of those back home. Well-organised and energised by a sense of possibility, we sang the national anthem, the 'new' one, its words echoing in the vast space of locked-down Central London. For the first time, I felt moved by the words, 'The labours of our heroes past shall never be in vain' in a way that I had never before been.

*

It was almost inevitable that it would end in sorrow, tears and blood as our national musician-philosopher-prophet Fela would have put it, and yet when it came, it was still a shock.

The footage of uniformed men opening fire on a crowd of young people singing the national anthem draped in the green-white-green of the national flag.

This – young people taking refuge behind the national symbols, the flag and the anthem – was something that happened in the West and in communist countries when I was growing up, not in Nigeria. And that unfazed by this, the uniformed men still opened fire, wounding and killing some, the number destined to remain disputed forever. Yet, in many profile photos on social media and elsewhere, an image endures: the Nigerian flag captured by a camera at the site of the Lekki Massacre. Its usual vertical bands of green and white are there, but where usually the white is spotless, blank, unstained, today, a map of red spreads, seeping across the flag. Infused with the blood of Nigeria's children, who, holding it up as a talisman, still fell at the hands of their own country, victims of those who were sworn to protect them, it takes on a new power, new meaning . . . Harking back to that old anthem's words . . .

To hand on to our children, a banner without stain.

Pride and Punishment

Chigozie Obioma

When I was a child, developing a voracious reading habit, I happened
upon a newspaper story that remained, even now, indelible in my
mind. I had retrieved the piece from between piles of old papers which
my father, a relentless reader himself and hoarder of newsprints, had
kept. What had struck me the most about the story had been the
surreal brutality of the event it described and the fact that it was not
fiction but recorded history. At exactly midnight on 16 January 1966,
soldiers stormed the houses of several top officials of the Nigerian
government, including the Prime Minister. One of them, Festus
Okotic-Eboh, then the Finance Minister, was taken out of his bed,
blindfolded, beaten and driven to the edge of the city. From
here, the account would become even more grisly – the minister,
seeing the imminence of his death, had babbled, sobbed, sweated,
vomited. On an empty road outside Lagos and with the country
peacefully asleep, the soldiers drew their guns and shot him dead.
Later, at a conference after the successful overthrow of the government, the slightly agitated leader of the coup, Major Kaduna
Nzeogwu, would speak at length about the motivations behind the
coup and the murders. Of that speech, all of which was transcribed
in the newspaper, I still remember this line: 'We promise that you

[the citizens] will no more be ashamed to say that you are a Nigerian.'*

The fate of the coup plotters and the explosive, unintended consequences of the coup are now well-known history. But reading that story as a child, I had found myself admiring Major Nzeogwu's courage and vision. What he wanted, I thought, was what most reasonable people should want: to take pride in their country. For a long time, despite the political and social climate of 1990s Nigeria, I pursued this goal. Family archives are filled with photos of my patriotic engagements. In 1993, only then 7 years old, I was enthralled by the presidential election campaign of M. K. O. Abiola as most people in Akure were. I had seen the fear in the eyes of my parents and most adults throughout the General Ibrahim Babangida years. The dictator had assumed power in '85, a year before I was born, and had been leader all my life. It had become drilled into me that whatever hardship we felt at home was a result of the dictator's whim. When therefore the chance at salvation came, myself and everyone joined in. I marched with a group of children to welcome Abiola to Akure on his campaign stop – an event I fictionalised in my first novel, *The Fishermen*.

When General Babangida annulled the election that same year, throwing the nation into chaos, I was shattered. The dark days and months following were etched in my memory as transitional both in my civic consciousness but also in the development of my aesthetics. I began reading more and writing more about the aspirations of

---

* Note that there are variations of this speech now available. The one from Stephen Ellis's indispensable book, *This Present Darkness: A History of Nigerian Organized Crime*, for instance, puts it as 'You will no longer be ashamed to be Nigerians.' https://www.vanguardngr.com/2010/09/radio-broadcast-by-major-chukwuma-kaduna-nzeogwu—announcing-nigeria's-first-military-coup-on-radio-nigeria-kaduna-on-january-15-1966/

people whose 'HOPE' – the rallying cry of Abiola's '93 campaign – had been quashed by the military leader. One of such writings was a play, *Vegetable Kingdom*, which sought to eulogise the country and its citizenry in the face of persistent hardship. This play was acted at my school and church at the time and gave me my first shot at fame in Akure. It bred in me a consciousness whose convex attributes was one of patriotism but whose interior was filled worms of disillusionment. It did not occur to me at the time that I was idolising the country – that in idolising, we defend, in defending we turn on blinders, in blindness we believe in lies, and in believing in lies, we settle into stagnant conditions.

My pride in Nigeria was not much shaken even in the withering years of the Nineties when Babangida was replaced by Sani Abacha, a more brutal dictator than his predecessor. He declared Abiola enemy of State, assassinated one of his wives and imprisoned him. Swiftly, Abacha pounded his heavy fist on the desk of the nation so loudly that everyone began living in acute fear of him. Having established the repressive climate of fear, Abacha ruled the country according to his whims. One event captures this whim succinctly: wanting to lead the African union, he declared in December 1996 that French would become the second national language of Nigeria and began forcing all the schools to teach it. But when in 1998, a severe harmattan was blamed on France's 1960 testing of nuclear weapons in the Saharan desert, he threatened sanctions against them.

In those years, I struggled to hold on to my pride, wanting mostly to see these setbacks as mere blemishes, like the perpetually forgivable errors committed by one's beloved. I loved the earthiness of our cultures and histories so much I was able to look beyond the lack of development to appreciate being Nigerian – being Igbo and Yoruba. I believed in a golden future, that someday, Nigeria would emerge from its troubles and redeem itself. This was a common belief – one not based in reason, but rather imbibed as an act of faith. It is an eccentric kind of hope whose provenance is located in the people's acute religiosity, and which fosters a resilience that has become wholly characteristically Nigerian. Its axiomatic premise holds that every individual is a unique product of God and holds an auspicious future. Therefore, unfavourable outcomes must often be treated as temporary setbacks, with that auspicious future pre-ordained.

In 2005, I found myself at Caritas University, a new private university in Nigeria. It had been advertised as a Catholic school, administered by nuns for a priest, Father E. M. P. Edeh. But it was in fact a repressive encampment, where students were put under the strictest rules, spied on by student spies and where the smallest missteps could trigger an expulsion. Twice, I was punished, detained and after two painful years holed up in this establishment, under the threat of unjust expulsion, I fled the school.

My experience at Caritas University was the first time I allowed myself to be truly angry at Nigeria. I had left there unable to get legal redress. No lawyer would accept to take up a case against the university for fear of the priest's influence and power. I entered a place of psychological stasis in which I felt abandoned, alone and broken. I felt strongly that there was a systemic failure in Nigeria which had allowed such an establishment to exist. My pride in Nigeria had endured for years despite assaults on it – finally, a crack had appeared on the wall of its fort.

For months after my escape from Caritas was followed by an unjust expulsion letter, I had wandered about unsure of what to do. My parents, anxious and afraid, tried to get me into a school in Britain. The visa, which was a difficult thing to get for a middle-class Nigerian student at the time, was granted to me at first, then withdrawn at the last minute. Crushed by this blow and starting to see my chances at higher education dying out, I seized on a chance encounter with a neighbour who mentioned that he knew someone who had gone to school in a remote country near Europe named 'TRNC' (Turkish Republic of Northern Cyprus). Months later, I had secured the visa. This was a country so foreign I did not know of its existence two months before. But now, it was to be where I would get another chance at an education.

At the airport in Lagos, I felt my pride crescendo, feeling impressed by the edifice my beleaguered country had, despite its youth (it only got its independence in 1960 while the US had been independent since 1776), its recent internecine civil war (which only ended at the beginning of 1970) and its infant democracy (it only became a fully 'democratic' state in 1999). The light shone in my face and cheerfully, I gave the airport workers money, waved at my dad and siblings. When the plane ascended, I fixed my eyes on the window, wiping it and reframing my gaze at the disappearing land, swaying out into the amorphous hole of the distance. Then, as the plane entered the planetary darkness of clouds, I started to weep.

It took two days of opening my eyes into the daylight reality of the new country for the first internal shift about Nigeria to occur. It had been minuscule, as if the change had happened behind some subconscious curtain and its appearance now, at the shop window of my mind, had surprised me. That day, I noticed that most of my speech had started to end with the phrase, 'I am disappointed.' I had just uttered this word in reaction to the fact of the electricity being constant since we arrived in Lefkoşa, the capital of the TRNC. It had surprised me to find that a country so small, with landscape so dry and under international embargo, could have such reliable infrastructure where Nigeria did not. Then I went into the city and, confronted with the cleanness of the streets, again, I uttered those words. Soon, I had become disenchanted, bothered so much I was struggling to sleep. My settling into the country was going well, I had brought much of the resources I needed for my first year of study. But I found that, increasingly, as I discovered more of Northern Cyprus, I came to see in it everything my own country lacked. And the accretion of these deficiencies, in time, came to compose in me a tower of afflictive rage.

My rage, at first, baffled me. In its essence, it was a reductive force, which soon enough had poked a wound at my vision of Nigeria. It occurred to me that in a warm entanglement with a country, one spends many years trying to sew the country's badge to one's coat with fingers continuously injured by the fabric of the coat itself. My rage gave birth to ardent curiosity: why was it in truth that Nigeria had been so inadequate? What happened to us, to our brilliant, smart, leaders who assiduously and heroically fought for independence? At what point was the march into the future with the flaming torch – an Olympian metaphor so often used in poems and rhymes to refer to Nigeria's future – fully halted, and by what? Was it the civil war? Was it the many decades of military rule? Was it the ascendance of a shaky, graft-ridden and acutely corrupt democracy, which began in 1999, at the threshold of the new millennium?

My curiosity, at first, sustained me. There was certainly something I did not understand, a nuance hidden beneath the surface of things. I had seen videos of times past, of good office buildings, strong, European-standard development in the Fifties and Sixties. And surely, something had happened along the line. I began to read in my spare time, paying little attention now to the goings-on in the new city and the exotic foreign university life. I read about Nigeria and Africa, from the Sixties to now, I searched the library at the universities in North Cyprus and the internet. I read and read, trying to understand the source of the lack of development, of the stark poverty, of moral decadence, of blatant insecurity, until I could no longer find an oath through the worn path through the post-independence years and now. During this period, I learned much from reading the works of the older generation of Nigerian writers – mostly Wole Soyinka, Chinua Achebe, Akachi Ezeigbo, Elechi Amadi, Flora Nwapa, Sola Osofisan, among others. There were writers who were writing about the history of the country, but also about its misalignment. Of this lot, Soyinka's plays about the ravaging of the 'nation's soul' by the military in *Kongi's Harvest* held a fascination for me. I saw that what I could do as a writer was to reveal to my readers not my opinion about society but my observations of it. In observing, I would get closer to the truth about society, about its true shape and the true content of its character, and that the end result of that observation would be a revelation of things concealed, things not clearly seen by others. But by the end of my first year, I had only found fragments of what I was looking for, and had to keep looking.

My panic, at first, spurred me on, if I were to have looked in these fields this long, combed this strenuously, to find no answer would have disheartened me. So, I decided to look at where I had not wanted to look – the distant past. The precolonial, African, traditional society. This was 2008, the world in its turn of the new century had started to become 'progressive'. Only a gaze forward was encouraged; in the past lay nothing but an ocean of senseless darkness. And nowhere in Africa was this sentiment – in its basic form at the time – more persistent. Before the 'enlightenment' brought by the Europeans, what we had were superstitions, deities, bad customs and shameful patriarchies. So, I deterred. I read up the scant materials I could find, feeling much like the anxious man in a well-known Igbo proverb who, for fear of sunlight, walks during the day with his eyes closed, bumping into objects and risking injury. But soon, I found myself pulled into the history of those years. And here, I found some of the answers I had been looking for. In the past Nigeria had not existed, and now it had been artificially created. The result of its creation was that the former nations and their civilisations had been upended, reducing them to a contraption in search of a cohesive national identity. Thus, it became clear to me that the answers to my quest lay in the circumstances behind its creation.

This answer, at first, satisfied me. My people, after all, were not to be blamed for the contraption in which they now lived, given that it was imposed on them. The vision of the foreign entity coming into this place where it was not wanted and proclaiming how their lives must be, almost in a form of prophesy, constituted the narrative core of *The Fishermen*. In the months following, satisfied with my answer, I poured my energy into this work, which encapsulated the condition of my country and sustained my pride in it.

But soon, as the number of Nigerians on this tiny island nation, unrecognized by the United Nations, swelled and their living conditions worsened, I began again to feel disappointment. Then, early in 2009, a man I have come to know simply as Jay arrived. He arrived already broken, having been duped into selling all he had by grifters posing as Study Abroad agents. They'd conned gullible students into thinking the place was a wealthy Western country, where their dreams of the successful émigré would be met. Most of them had lost something to these agents, but none had lost everything. This was what had happened to Jay. He stayed with me and my roommates for days until another new student asked to take him in. Days later, he was dead – he'd jumped from the attic of a tall building to his tragic death.

Jay's death shook me like nothing ever had. I saw in the senseless wasting of his youth, a cosmic wrong inflicted not just upon his family but upon all of the Nigerians in Northern Cyprus, upon me. Nigeria had failed him twice: once when it forced him to escape to Germany, only to be deported. But he'd survived that first blow with that resilient spirit characteristic of Nigerians, believing that if he tried again, he would succeed. Much of the time, this resolve can propel one through adversities with uncommon drive, and this is one of the reasons for the success of most Nigerians who have risen to the top, wading through huddles which would have crippled others. But it is often also responsible for irrational courage writ large – for instance, in the numerous deadly journeys through the Sahara Desert or the Atlantic Ocean in search for greener pastures. If Jay's faith at first had helped him find his footing, this second time, it failed him. Having been psychologically damaged by compatriots, he came to North Cyprus, a desert in a foreign land, to die.

I saw in his death, a fatal consequence of Nigeria's failure. This was a grievous wrong, one for which, for days, weeks, months and now years, has battered my pride in Nigeria. I came to see that the country has never once rewarded my pride in it, but has often punished me for it. For my trust in its systems, it has disappointed me. For my investment in its culture – in telling stories, in seeking to preserve its history and in seeking to celebrate its culture – it has returned to me ingratitude. And now, as I grow older in a country not my own, pining daily for Nigeria, I realize that I am spending my life trying to bridge the distance between my love for the country and a hatred for it, between hope and despair, and between pride and punishment.

In the years that have now passed during which I have mostly lived away from it, Nigeria has become for me a forced companion – a thing to which I'm inextricably bound by virtue of birth and ancestry, and from which I also do not desire to remove myself. What I have resolved to do is live with it as one would a completely incapacitated parent. I stayed away from it and sought refuge in the comfort of other places. But for at least two months of every year, I live there. And even while away, I find that I am incapable of writing about anywhere else because, as Aleksandr Solzhenitsyn once said, 'I only hear the pain of my homeland, therefore I only write about my homeland.' What sustains me now is a sense of brutal peace cleaved from my experience in Northern Cyprus. For that experience had yielded in me an understanding. I had for a long time realized that the ethical exigency of patriotism did not render it an ontological necessity. Therefore, while it was right and certainly beneficial for me to love Nigeria, it was not necessary for me to do so. Patriotism is a choice I could choose to make or not make. This, I know now, is the teleology of positive patriotism.

Contradictions

Bolu Babalola

The first time a boy called me beautiful was in Nigeria. When I say 'boy', I mean a male person my own age in a context of consent and comfort; not a catcall, not a grown man leering out of a slid-down window, not 'hot' or its rather nauseating variant '*hawt*' – which I have had the grave misfortune of experiencing – but 'beautiful'. That elegant, unequivocal word – solid and unmalleable. Timeless.

Make no mistake, I have experienced lascivious and lecherous approaches in Nigeria – intensely – but I am pointing out a fact that perhaps doesn't fit neatly into those other facts. The first time a romantic interest called me beautiful, was in Nigeria. If Lagos is the Regency ton, then I would have said that this experience occurred during my coming out, my entrance into season. It was during the Christmas holidays, the period of time within which the diaspora converges into overstuffed clubs and pours into raucous parties that beget other parties that have you coming home when others are beginning their commute. I was a 22-year-old debutante, experiencing Lagos in my first real blush of womanhood (or so I imagined). I'd been coming to Nigeria for about fourteen years already, and at this point it was as familiar to me as my nook of the East London/Essex border. However, the Nigeria I had known previously had been limited to visits to my grandparents' compound in Abeokuta, the church my dad had gone to as a boy and our compound in Lagos – where my cousins would pile in and essentially form our own version of summer camp, in which having the same ancestral lineage was a requirement.

While all these things had their own glory – particularly the Saturday Baptism classes in which we were fed dry biscuits and over-sweet cordial – this time was different. I was wearing strapless bras, my parents let me stay out after midnight, I had friends with cars and I switched between two tubes of lipstick. This was a new, refined me. My spindle-thin eyebrows proved it. Lagos: meet Bolu, new and improved, *grown*. I now had my *own* group of friends. It was an aggregation of my parents' friends' kids, *their* friends, my Nigerian friends from university and *their* friends. It was a whole new world, bright and sultry, Henny fumes, celebrity perfume and the crisp-toasted scent of straightened weave. Friendship groups layered up in a diasporic smorgasbord; American Nigerians, Canadian Nigerians, Brit Nigerians, Nigerian Nigerians, Nigerians who tried to sound like American Nigerians, connected and separated and then connecting again, a reunion ritual, a homecoming. Even if some of us didn't feel it was home, it was understood that it should be recognized as home, a formulaic acknowledgement that 'This was where my ancestors were from, where people see my surname and know what town my people are from, what village, and so forth.' Therefore, it was home.

Though British-born, I had been coming to Lagos at least once a year since I was 7 years old, even before my father moved there for work, even before our house was built. It was a conscious decision from my parents, a proud pair who once asked a young me, 'My dear daughter, how many English people do you know with Yoruba names?' when I asked why they hadn't given me a Sarah or a Louise as a first name, names light enough for English tongues not to get tangled up in, names that I wouldn't have to immediately repeat when uttered. 'But you can call me my Yoruba name at home!' I countered, recalling my many Nigerian friends that only went by their English names at school. 'Oh,' my father's tone would be coloured with a blithe, easy smile, 'because your Yoruba name isn't good enough for them? Should your Yoruba name be a secret? My dear, they will learn.'

And they did. I learned to say my name louder with each repetition. The tongue is a muscle, and as I used it to assert my culture, it got stronger, surer, more comfortable in correcting in a world that saw me as someone that needed correcting. They forced us to speak English, my father said, why should your name be too much trouble? There was no back-up, no nickname, no 'You can call me, This Slackened Version Of My Name if it's easier'. This was me: you could take it or you could take it. This, alongside their commitment to bring my sisters and I to Nigeria, was part of a concerted effort for us to *know* ourselves. Sacrifices were made to create that privilege, and it wasn't always easy – it rarely was. However, they felt that some knowledge of Nigeria was necessary to complicate the notion of 'home' for me; yes, home was the UK, or rather, London, a world within a world – but home was also within the stucco walls of the Yaba apartment we crammed into in December 1998, my first time in Nigeria, where I met my grandparents, my cousins, where I had my first sweet, fluorescent, effervescent dose of heaven from a glass Fanta bottle, where I felt that new sense of peace and knowledge and grounding. A place where my name was familiar. They knew that in my life there would be a complication of identities, but they didn't want there to be a *conflict* of identities. They wanted me to know that there were no disparate, warring parts, but one of me, built of tessellations of cultures and sub-cultures. I am British, yes, but really, Black British, and within that a Black British Londoner, but also British Nigerian, and within that, ancestrally Nigerian, and enclosed in that, Yoruba. In retrospect it was my first introduction to the notion that complication does not necessarily mean conflict, but rather allows space for an ease and grace in understanding ourselves and life. The notion that I need to make space for contradictions. Truths can be found within them.

The result of all this was a base note of confidence that was part indigenously Nigerian – an innate Yoruba swagger and sauce, one part instilled by the efforts of my parents, and the rest I managed to cultivate myself, bolstered by the aforementioned. The indigenous vitality is sourced from a mystical, primordial source, it is beyond words, beyond dogmatic cultural paradigms, it is just something I feel at an owambe when the deep reverb of a gangan being hit jolts both bone and blood and holds conversation with my heartbeat. It is something I feel when we are together and we are laughing, there is a transcendence in the movements and in our sounds of joy and communication. The lip purses, in the tonality of the words more than the words themselves, but sometimes it is the words themselves, the alchemy we make with English and the tone of our indigenous languages. It's why, 'Suit yourself' can sound like a slap, why, 'My friend' can be more of a warning than an endearment, why 'Ah, sorry o' can be a sting. It's in our praise poetry when we meet, 'My sis, my oga on top, ah, so is it that you want to hurt me?', like someone can look so good it can cause actual, physical harm. It's in our drama. Of course, this can be said of so many Black and African cultures, but perhaps it is in the specificity that makes it more potent to me. I still contend, from a position that is undeniably underpinned by bias, that Nigerian swagger has a specific note that is immediately, universally recognized *as* Nigerian. It's an energy that is bolstered by osmotic understanding of culture and sweetened by community. I had always felt it with family, but when I entered university I felt that within an African-Caribbean society comprised of both British-born Nigerians and Nigerian-born Nigerians, it was my *own* iteration of it, a generational legacy of communion, someone cooking jollof rice for the squad in their flat, Afrobeats parties in tiny student houses. It was joyful for me to hear a sharp quip from a friend uttered in Yoruba. Somehow we found ourselves within ourselves.

Despite the regular insecurity that one might have had being a young person feeling their way out into the world – or a young woman feeling her way out into the world; or a young Black woman feeling her way out into the world; or a young, dark-skinned Black woman feeling her way out into the world – I had an immutable surety that I could grab onto in the darkness, and though I might not have known exactly what it was, I knew that it was solid, I knew what I was, even if I was still trying to figure out the shape of who I was. Knowing I was both British and Nigerian helped with that. I understood the rudimentary components of the raw mass.

This is all to say that this obscenely handsome boy calling me beautiful was not crucial for a sense of validation. It was the way he said it that was, perhaps, noteworthy. It was on the balcony of an apartment that had been fumigated – cleared of any parental presence – and during a house party. I discovered he was sweet when we escaped to the balcony to talk without the intrusion of Wizkid. He maintained eye contact and asked me what I was into, what I had studied, and seemed delighted by my blog, charmed that I wanted to be a writer, said something like 'Wow, man, that's so dope. I can tell you're a smarty pants,' and I smiled at his astute observation. He was a model: he showed me his Instagram, the handle of which was a portmanteau of the first three letters of his name and a popular brand of cognac. 'Cool! Witty,' I said. There were a lot of shirtless pictures. Throughout, a conversation that was delightfully light and clearly a respectable conduit for us to make-out on the balcony, we started to inch closer to each other. Cars honked below in anticipation, the stars winked at us with glee, and so, given this encouragement and support, the model looked at me through heavy eyes that ran an electric jolt through me, tilted my chin up while I was mid-sentence, stroked a thumb across my skin, and murmured something.

He followed up quickly with, 'Do you know what I just said?'

I did not. He squinted his eyes in a way I now know was configured to look seductive (and I now would find slightly nauseating), but at the time found deeply erotic and said, his mouth now inches from mine, 'I just said you're beautiful in Igbo. Because you are, you are beautiful.'

He was, of course, an expert. He had learned I was Yoruba from my name and our conversation, so knew I could not check the veracity of this claim, and as a good-looking straight man attuned to the base politics of heterosexual desire, he correctly guessed that in a low-stakes context (the stakes being we make-out or we don't) a woman who is already attracted to you would find being called beautiful in a language she did not know – with immediate translation – incredibly hot. Then, of course, we kissed. It was okay. My admittedly limited experience hinted at the fact that he might not have been technically great at it, but most of the thrill came from the fact that he had called me beautiful in Igbo.

This is what intrigued me; not the compliment itself, but its *essence*. It seemed to me to be something that could only occur in Nigeria. It was only when he called me beautiful that I realized that I hadn't ever been called beautiful by a man in the UK. To be clear, I knew I was generally attractive due to the aforementioned confidence, but I came to the knowledge that in Nigeria, I felt my appeal more acutely. Perhaps, I thought, because there was less for that knowledge to go through. Though colourism is present as a colonial vestige (in 2011, the World Health Organization recorded that Nigeria has the highest amount of bleaching in the continent), we are still, largely, a hegemonically Black country. Blackness is still the default – this, arguably, disallows for the clear de facto hierarchy of beauty that is present in the UK. In the UK, you have, of course, white women, and then lighter-skinned Black women, and then dark-skinned Black women, and though it might not have been said explicitly, it was clear in the way people you might have been attracted to interacted with you. In university, I once got into a debate with a Black friend who insisted that I wasn't 'that dark'. I believe the discussion came about because I casually mentioned how little attention I got from the boys in university and wondered about the reason out loud. During my summers and Christmases in Lagos, I was approached. I was sought after. I was flirted with. I was wooed.

'But I *am* dark-skinned,' I countered, confused that she was insisting that I was not, and as to what the definition of '*that* dark' was, and why it even mattered. My parents had told me to take pride in my deep skin that had the sun baked into it, and though bouts of self-hatred tried their luck, they slipped and slid on my latent self-assurance. Our equanimous dispute over my skin tone went on for a few bizarre seconds until she conceded: 'Fine, you are, but you're still beautiful.'

'Still' as in 'despite'. I noted it and rejected it.

The second thing to note about my model's comment is that he said it in Igbo. Though Yoruba myself, there was something at once grounding and sublime in being flirted with in one of Nigeria's numerous indigenous languages. I was home, *Home*, and I was Yoruba and this boy was Igbo and Nigeria was a world of worlds enough for this to be both foreign and familiar. I think most of all, however, it affirmed how I *felt* in Nigeria. When I hear Afrobeats – wherever I am in the world – my hip and my waist are cajoled and called, the beat speaks to my soul. When I hear Yoruba spoken (loudly, always loudly) on public transport, there is an immediate somatic smile; a warmth floods through me and fills me up.

At 11 years old, when I felt plump rainy season droplets rapidly punching kisses into my skin as I rode my bicycle around the compound in humid air, I felt like a superhero, invincible. When I sit on the beach with my friends and drink hastily mixed drinks with fast-melting ice, laughing and joking and dancing, I feel like a deity charged with merry-making. When I went to Abeokuta to visit my grandparents in their compound and sank my knees into their peeling lino in greeting, and watched the smooth folds of their faces crease further in delight, as they prayed for me and squeezed my hands in theirs, I felt *bonded*, protected, held snug by lineage and love. That boy was vocalising something I'd always felt in Nigeria: beautiful. It was beyond my physical appearance, rather it was something visceral. And yet, his utterance of it landed slightly askew just as my previous description of Nigeria sits slightly askew. For the truth, as long as it is from humans, is always askew, never pure.

I get to enjoy Nigeria in a very particular way when I am in my vacuum, and though it is a reality, it is not its totality. Without looking at Nigeria in its totality, it might as well be a mirage.

You can go to a street in Victoria Island and find it lined with G-Wagons that are haunted by the dusty handprints of those who beg to be able to eat. The first time I came to Nigeria, my comfort was confused by the fact that children my age were selling wares in the hot sun, in traffic, while I sat in it. Privilege and poverty sit clunkily, uglily next to each other, and though the latter is the default, those within the former may sometimes slip into the fallacy that their gold is enough to make up for the dust that coats the country. On the way back from a party in Lagos once, my Uber got stopped by the police. They banged my door with assault rifles, threatened to strip me naked and beat me, and tried to force the door open. I'd just had one of those, 'I am my most beautiful in Nigeria' nights. Almost laughable. I was close to my house and managed to call someone. I was able to leave by giving them money. I was still shaking three hours afterwards. I could not sleep. I was lucky, and I am privileged.

There is something we can learn from ourselves within the friction of two conflicting truths: the war and the peace and everything in between when one opposing fact converges with another. How a boy can call you beautiful and not text you back? How you can find a boy beautiful and not want him to text you back? How you can enjoy the components that comprise a moment but find issue with its discrete parts? Nigeria is nothing if not conflicting truths. Wherever we are globally, one will notice. We are loud and proud: literature, medicine, finance, politics. However, as of 2018, Nigeria had the largest number of out-of-school children in the world. Those are truths: uncomfortable and painful, glory that should be mired in a shame that galvanises us, but does it? Nigeria boasts Afrobeats, musical pioneers with an unmistakable élan, but do we seek to capture and cultivate and cherish those talents within our children? Nigeria itself is a question mark unanswered; it is baffling, potential posed, energy coiled. Range Rovers rove on unpaved roads in a city, chickens cluck outside of elegant restaurants, at night, a woman sits with a small boy, on the concrete, with a face that could be 30 or 40 – abject despair eludes time – a meter away from a five-star hotel that Nigerian businessmen will use to woo their European suitors.

Nigerian women are some of the most powerful, intelligent, formidable people I know, and still, patriarchy lines the interior of Nigeria, with feminism still considered edgy, unentertained as something that should be default. The organisation Feminist Coalition raised funds for legal aid and medical care during the 2020 EndSARS protests with the funds allocated in full transparency, and yet they are penalised by those they attempt to assist, with feminism being called an 'agenda', as if seeking equality is a nefarious masterplan. The only

201

people who fear equality will render them impotent are those who consider themselves on the right side of an imbalance.

We glow strong, our verve is known. However, we can also be loud and wrong, and often we allow the glow of a few to blind us from the suffering of the many. Wherever triumph is, you will find us. However Nigeria has not triumphed over itself. Yes, we were joined by arrogant white men with guns and greed, and we are also plagued by arrogant black men with guns and greed, attacking what is good and necessary for growth. Societal dysfunction twines with communion; there is a togetherness bound by innate brilliance that arches over ruptures from wounds not yet healed. Can we move towards peace if the brokenness of past wars has not been examined? And this communion we have, it is fragile, for can it truly be sealed if we do not take the time to accept that we are a culture of cultures and truly hold space for the fact? To take joy in it rather than ignore it, or grudgingly accept it, or violently reject it? We need to face our contradictions.

When Nigerians progress individually, their Nigerianness assists yes, but it is often in spite of what Nigeria *is*. Nigerianness and Nigeria are not always synonymous. Nigerianness often operates best outside of Nigeria; that surplus energy and power needed for survival allowing us to thrive in conditions that allow for it. Nigeria is my home in the rooted sense, the ancestral sense, the intangible spiritual sense, but Nigeria is also nonsense. We are renowned for being welcoming, joyful, entrepreneurial, ambitious, but all of these traits are an antithesis to our state, a patriarchal megalomaniac that eats his own, fearful of being usurped. Murder instead of nurture; a young person stopped on the road because they have a computer, arrested because they have a computer, vanished because they have a computer, by law enforcers who have permission to bend laws till they are a mockery, who have not been paid a salary for months, who are hungry and are given a gun. Often those who witness the unnatural crime of parent consuming child suffer a spiritual damage, a corruption of the soul. We were assembled into a mass by colonialists, who had to destroy souls to be successful, interlopers who had to tempt corporation with greed and skewed power from the indigenous, and that psyche has seeped into the soil of our land. We are a nation with a strong identity, but our swagger does not know which direction to saunter in. All that is good is constantly in a state of battle and insecurity.

*

People are often surprised by my affinity to Nigeria, expecting me to feel disconnected, and I find myself surprised by their surprise. They feel the fact that I was born in Britain would mitigate my concern with the land of my blood. They do not understand that it is in me, that is part of me, that my concern should not be a novelty, that I am not an outsider, that I could never be an outsider. Nobody can make me an outsider. I know myself. Nigeria calls to the beauty in me and the beauty in my people because our energy is something that is impervious to corruption. It is as if, despite its brokenness, despite the ugliness of the state itself, that call of beauty is an energy within our core that is crucial for our survival, for our reconfiguration, for our healing. It is a cry from within the rot. Within our raw matter, those diamond flashes of light – our loudness, our boldness, our strength, our talent, our intelligence, our charisma – can be gathered in the right direction to form hope, and that hope can be collected to move us forward. In the contradictions, in the friction, let there be a spark to light our way. I want Nigeria to be as beautiful as its potential.

Nulli Secundus

Nels Abbey

Whenever I start a new job or venture the first thing I do is look around for who the super-Nigerian in the room, industry or business is. Once identified, I immediately go and make friends with them. Not because I want to, but because I have to. I know the risk associated with competing with Nigerians, and I'd rather we pre-emptively get the truce out of the way and cooperate.

There is no corridor you walk into in the West (and around the world) where a Nigerian has not decided they are going to dominate. From sports to academics to medicine to banking to . . . well, let's just say the more informal areas of financial opportunity: dominate we do.

Remember the doctor who removed an unborn baby from a woman's womb, treated the baby for cancer and then placed it back to enable a natural birth? That doctor was Nigerian.

How about the superdiverse school in working-class East London that consistently produces nation-beating A-level results and gets their students into the best universities (in the world)? The principal is a Nigerian.

The 26-year-old appointed as Covid adviser to President Joe Biden? She's a Nigerian.

The first woman to head the World Trade Organization? Nigerian.

The founder and owner of the Shade Room? Yep, Nigerian.

The world's best (or most promising) boxer, basketball player, UFC fighter and rugby player? All Nigerian.

The first Black man and the first Black woman to win the Booker Prize? They're Nigerian.

The two brothers who confessed to helping the actor Jussie Smollett stage a white supremacist attack? Okay, yes, they too were . . .

Jest aside, Nigerians achieve amazing, globe-beating feats. But there is one issue that I've long been bothered by, especially in modern times: why are Nigerians able to walk on water abroad but often struggle to crawl on concrete at home? Why does it seem that these days, most Nigerians have to leave Nigeria to be great?

*

My childhood was a compendium of Nigerian parental experiments and trends. I was born in Britain to Nigerian parents in the early Eighties. Humble brag: I was actually born in the same hospital as generations of members of the royal family, St Mary's Hospital in Paddington (humble technicality, my siblings were, I happened to be born on a hood off-site of St Mary's, a couple of miles away).

In Britain in the Sixties, Seventies and Eighties there was a strange and widespread phenomenon in which Nigerian parents handed their children over to white foster parents to raise them, often in strange and racist-as-Mississippi corners of Britain. Why? Classic Nigerian ambition. As new immigrants to Britain these parents believed that white foster parents would better help their children integrate into society. Additionally, fostering out their children would grant the parents the time and space to study, work and pursue business interests in Britain and Nigeria. As a result, countless British-Nigerian children were fostered. I was one of those children.

I was handed over to loving white working-class foster parents (a German-Jewish mother and a Scottish father) as a baby. I was raised in a little-known, all-white village called Benson.

For much of my childhood I didn't know what a Black person was, let alone a Nigerian. I don't think I even considered myself British, I was an English boy, nothing else. I didn't know I was different to the other children until I was approached by some teenagers offering me ten pence to see if my hair would attach to Velcro. Dripping with sincerity, they informed me that they had heard that 'the soft part of Velcro is made of Black people's hair' (this was the mid-Eighties, pre-Google). Moments later, for the grand price of ten pennies, the first money I ever earned in my life (and enough to buy me my favourite thing: a Belgian bun), 5- or 6-year-old me unwittingly agreed to enter the centuries-long tradition of Africans used as experiments by racially curious and confused Europeans.

Outcome: negative. Of course, it didn't stick. They left the encounter ten pence poorer and I left ten pence richer, but they also embedded a million-pound question into my head: what the hell is a Black person?

Prior to that moment, I didn't know what Velcro was and I didn't know what Black people were. After that exchange I didn't care for Velcro but I quickly figured out what a Black person was. And I then knew the exact number of Black people who lived in Benson: two. My elder sister and I.

There were significantly more bulls in Benson than there were Black people.

When I was 9, my biological mother picked us up for our regular summer holidays in big bad London, but this time she unilaterally decided we were never returning to our foster parents. This was an extremely traumatic moment for my foster mother and I . . .

Aaaand: CUT!

For the average Black British writer (Nigerian or otherwise) – that would be the story, the TED Talk, the book deal, the film, the white liberal tears and potentially even the Oscar. Not me, I was destined for much crazier stuff.

By the early Nineties, foster care was falling out of fashion and Nigerian parents came up with their next bright idea. Part punishment, part *'you have to know your culture'*: sending their children 'back home' to the old country.

Naija was the new Black. Or was it?

In the early Nineties being Nigerian in London was far from cool. This was the age of Shabba Ranks, Maxi Priest and the remains of Bob Marley. Lord knows Sir Shina Peters tried his very best, but *Shinamania* was no competition for *Mr Loverman* and *Housecall*. Culturally, this was the age of Jamaican supremacy: they were absolutely *killing* us. So, I did what all cold cowards do: I waved the white flag and picked up the Jamaican one. Yep, I *became* a Jamaican. My name made it so easy. In our ridiculous attempts to live up to the most vicious of Jamaican stereotypes, my fellow 'Jamaican' friends (years later I would learn that many of them too were West Africans pretending to be Jamaican) and I got into a little trouble in school. In order to scare me straight, my mother threatened to send me to Nigeria. My eldest sister, who is thirteen years older than me, upped the 'scare-him-straight' ante by informing me that 'Nigeria is too good for you, you need Kenya!'

What clinched the deal was my teacher, a white English man who happened to be a swirler* dating a Nigerian. To my horror, during a parents' evening he revealed that he saw right through my Jamaican act. This swirler could smell a Nigerian.

'Nels is Nigerian isn't he Mrs Abbey?' he asked.

'Ah-ah, of course he is, sir,' responded my mother, demonstrating her colonial deference to white authority figures.

'Erm . . . no I am not,' I chipped in, attempting to defend my Yardie credentials.

They both looked at me in bemusement. The rest followed the usual script: 'Nels is extremely bright, but he will waste his potential if he stays here. I spent the summer in Nigeria and saw the amazing structure and discipline in boarding schools over there . . .'

The colonial whispers of a swirler worked their magic again on my mother's African ears: a few weeks later, I was in a three-piece suit on a plane to Lagos, crying my eyes out. Six to seven hours later, we landed in Ibrahim Badamasi Babangida's Nigeria.

*

My first thought of Lagos: white people had lied to me about Africa all of my life.

It was far from the 'mud-huts, flies and absolute darkness' Africa that British television had led me to believe. What I saw was an exciting, dynamic, super-busy urban sprawl, with all the trappings of success. Of course, there was poverty but, selfishly speaking, my own standard of living improved fantastically compared to life in the UK.

---

* *Swirler*, noun, (derogatory or complimentary depending on application): person with a sweet tooth for people from other races – especially relevant to people racialised as 'black' and 'white'.

I met my father for the first time in my life at the airport. Meeting, hugging and holding your father's hand for the first time is a critical part of the life of any boy who grew up as I did. My father was funny, successful, popular with his peers, masculine and fatherly. He was a big man in all senses of the word. I quickly learned to love him.

Our home was in an amazing middle-class area called Bode Thomas in Surulere. We'd shop in a rather posh Westernised local supermarket called UTC. I had an abundance of successful role models – brilliant, strategic and ambitious people. Pillars of community, dignity, integrity and professionalism. Yes, the society was unorthodox in parts but it was, in retrospect, well-functioning and prosperous in many parts. In London, we were very working-class, but in Nigeria, we were part of a buoyant middle class.

The £10 note I took to Nigeria had me feeling like a millionaire when I found out it was worth 330 Naira. I felt so happy about the 33 Naira to £1 exchange rate, yet my father saw it as a sign of serious economic deterioration. Though I didn't say it, I considered him a little bit of a hater when I thought he was scoffing at the 'upgraded' status of my £10 note.

The joys of youthful economic illiteracy.

Although I thought things were amazing, my father and his friends would often speak of the nation crumbling. 'These guys don't know how good they have it,' I would think to myself as I sipped Fanta out of a champagne glass and watched *Voltron*. My new life in Nigeria was amazing and I loved it . . . until it became time to enrol in school. I quickly learned about life on the other side of Nigeria.

All of my proudly-held Great British certificates were placed neatly in a folder so we could show the school administrators proof of my academic and extracurricular achievements. I can still remember the wry smile curl on to the face of the official who was lucky enough to be presented with them, as he pushed the folder carelessly back across the table.

'This is just paper, we've seen this before. Oyinbo give their children certificate for anything. Wash their yansh properly? Oyinbo will give them certificate. I beg show me proper paper please sir.'

'He wants me to bribe him,' said my dad as we got up and left.

'I DID NOT ASK FOR BRIBE, *OOO*! PLEASE DO NOT ACCUSE ME OF SUCH NONSENSE!' shouted the official as we left his office.

At that point, in Nigeria bribery wasn't as usual as it would go on to become. Like most Nigerian businessmen, my father too was a sinner but he was strictly against bribing people for academic access or in pursuance of success for his children.

'Whatever you achieve, you must achieve it honourably. Your academics must be a true mirror of your ability. If the school system is corrupted or goes bad, everything this nation tries to do will fail. Everything will be rubbish.'

That experience of corruption in the education system in Lagos prompted the decision to send me to a boarding school in the place where my dad had gone to school: 'the city of Abeokuta'. Lagos was always just 'Lagos'. And Lagos was fairly amazing to me so I thought 'the city of Abeokuta' must be pretty magnificent. It was labelled a 'city' after all.

I learnt I had been enrolled at the Baptist Boys' High School (BBHS), but for some reason my father didn't take me along for a school viewing. Weeks later, we pulled into the 'city of Abeokuta' in my father's car.

My first impression of this 'city': white people were telling the stone-cold truth. This *was* the Africa they had shown me my entire life. This was do-they-know-it's-Christmas Africa.

When I heard the word 'city', imagery of New York, Los Angeles and Miami sprang to mind. Skyscrapers, underground train stations, McDonald's, all the comforting detritus of the urban high life. Abeokuta was and had none of the above. Labelling Abeokuta a 'city' was perhaps the single biggest advertising fraud I have ever been subjected to. Converting my little £10 into Naira, finding the Lagos school official and bribing him myself actually crossed my mind.

Anything to escape.

The three things Abeokuta did have going for it were: education, education and . . . education. It was a 'city' of education. And in this regard, it was a magical 'city', for Abeokuta – literally meaning 'under a rock' – was a global fountain of black excellence.

Fair enough it didn't have a KFC or, for the most part, widely available running water, which meant settling for Iya Kabiru and a well, but when it came to academics, Abeokuta was world-beating. This excellence was principally due to two schools: Abeokuta Grammar School and my alma mater. A who's who of south-western Nigerian life were educated in Abeokuta: Funmilayo Ransome-Kuti, Fela Kuti, Wole Soyinka and many others all went to Abeokuta Grammar School. Obafemi Awolowo, President Olusegun Obasanjo and would-be President M. K. O. Abiola all went to my school. In fact, that was the entire marketing brochure for my school: Abiola and Obasanjo went here. 'Say no more,' said many a Nigerian parent.

BBHS, which was (predictably) founded by British missionaries, did not subscribe to the Nigerian adage, 'Naija no dey carry last.' We were forced to aim a little higher. Our slogan was the simple Latin phrase: *Nulli Secundus*. We were to be 'second to none'.

I will not offer the truly gory details of discipline here, but the drive for academic excellence was unlike anything I had ever experienced. The average child in my school was not bright, they were truly brilliant. And if you weren't, you were weeded out and thrown away. Gifted was normalised, genius was over-represented.

Unlike in the British education system where you moved on to the next class no matter what, in Nigeria, moving to the next year necessitated meeting an academic achievement threshold. If you didn't meet that threshold, you were either forced to repeat the entire year or 'advised' to withdraw from the school. The use of the term 'advised' here was Nigeria at its most British in terms of polite subtlety. It wasn't advice, it was an iron-clad compulsory instruction.

Another area that was completely different from my experience at school in the UK was that students were in direct and open competition with one another. In my year there were nearly 200 children. At the end of each term we were all ranked against each other based on our grades. Everyone was informed of their position from first to last. Coming first was the epitome of cool, coming last was . . . like being a Nigerian in London in the early Nineties. I had never in my life struggled academically. But until that point I had never been in explicit head-to-head combat with over 200 brilliant students. I'd also never lived in Nigeria or in a boarding school. In my first term I came 194th out of 200. Even in these liberal times that is hardly trophy worthy, but I was so proud that I hadn't come last . . . until I was informed that I had technically come last as there were several tied places and each tied place meant a number was eradicated off the end. And there I was: meritocratically designated the 'dullest' child in my year. I never wanted to feel that sense of shame again so the following term, I threw everything into my studies. Out of fear of being asked to repeat the year and wanting to be taken seriously by my peers, I worked and worked and worked. And prayed and prayed and prayed.

I came 42nd.

Still far from trophy-worthy, but it was the biggest esteem-boosting achievement of my life. I scored the highest mark in English literature – hence I am here today! After a quick celebration treat of kuli-kuli and gari, the cycle of competition, commendation and potential shame started again, so I was back to the grindstone. And I have remained at that grindstone till this very day.

This triple force of competition, commendation and the threat of immense shame baked into the Nigerian education system is the secret sauce of Nigerian excellence. My school didn't care in the slightest about how good we felt, their concern was how well we did academically. Often to the disadvantage of my own mental wellbeing, this ethos remains my source of drive and determination today.

In the midst of the harshest austerity known to man (the infamous Structured Adjustment Programmes imposed by the IMF and World Bank), extreme political instability, economic collapse, gruelling living conditions, extreme punishments often spilling into abuse, malnutrition, no electricity, often unbearable heat, extensive teaching strikes and everything else Abeokuta did not have to offer, these children excelled. Imagine what they could achieve if they didn't have to contend with these problems.

Well, you don't have to imagine, you just need to look at what so many Nigerians achieve outside of Nigeria. We achieve what we achieve not despite being Nigerians, but because of it. Because excellence is often the bare minimum accepted from us. The root of this, I believe, is (or was) in the pressure of the Nigerian education system. We take this pressure wherever we go. And we instil it in our children too.

But the question remains: why are so many Nigerians able to perform miracles abroad but not at home?

Sadly, things fall apart. Or maybe they're blown apart? Whatever you may label it: I saw it happen in real time.

In retrospect, when I arrived in Nigeria in 1992, things were already on shaky ground. But following the inexplicably annulled

12 June 1993 elections, the Nigeria I came to love – especially Lagos – crumbled. And it was a devastating sight.

Nigeria was hit with 'Three Ss of Hell':

- Structural adjustment programmes (SAP);
- Sani Abacha, and,
- Sanctions.

From there, everything collapsed and crumbled.

Corruption, even in the precious education sector (as my father had warned about), became normal. Like the police, soldiers and other unpaid-in-months key workers – some teachers resorted to extorting bribes from students. Roads started to deteriorate. Electricity was always unstable but it got much worse. Armed robberies became normal. Political assassinations (including in the form of gangbanger-style, drive-by shootings) became a serious issue (my own father nearly lost his life in this manner). The health sector crumbled and life expectancy dropped. People began to die a lot younger and for a lot less serious of reasons.

My little £10 that was worth 330 Naira when I arrived had more than trebled in 'value' (you could now get nearly 6,000 Naira for that same £10). Practically all infrastructure was either poorly maintained or not maintained at all. Meritocracy was thrown out of the window. Many smart, accomplished, successful and creative Nigerians (of integrity) were finally muscled out of national leadership by incompetent corrupt clowns, principle among them: Sani Abacha. Bootleg American-style, prosperity-linked Christianity exploded (as did Islamic extremism). The UTC supermarket I once loved was abandoned by its owners and the beautiful vast complex it was situated in was to become an open market for sex workers . . . and extortionists in police uniforms trying to exploit them.

So many successful middle-class Nigerians – the professional class that underpins the progress of any nation – started to leave the nation in their droves. Business people and professionals who I would once see congregating in my father's living room to discuss and successfully implement mind-blowing business ideas, were now reduced to congregating to exchange tips on succeeding in the American visa lottery.

This wave of Nigerians leaving en masse resulted in several things: a Nigeria of economic extremes, the decimation of the Nigerian middle class and a class of great-Nigerians abroad. All of these super-high potential people should be in Nigeria helping to make it a great and cutting-edge First World nation but they were left with little option but to leave. They went abroad, often lost all of their status, and started again. Sadly, this exodus, this brain drain, continues till this day.

During my last visit to Nigeria, I asked a brilliant teenager I'd known since birth what he wanted to be when he grows up. He responded, 'American . . . or at least British.' There is not a single person I met in Nigeria who came to the West who is not doing exceptionally well for themselves. At the same time, many of the brilliant people – no matter where they stood on the academic ranking – that stayed in Nigeria are struggling. An email or message seeking financial assistance is a fairly regular occurrence. Deep down, I know that if I was not born with the (white) privileges associated with Western citizenship, there's a good chance I'd be the one sending those desperate messages (or I would be a super-successful Nigerian living the high life).

When I competed with these very people, they mopped the floor with me. These people who send those messages are not lesser people to me, they're are much brighter, better and more capable than me. They just didn't have the opportunities I do.

The sad reality is that for too many Nigerians proximity to the exit as opposed to brilliance, determination and drive is now a key determining factor in how well they might do in life. Many Nigerians are left with the fully justified belief that their dreams start to come true at Murtala Muhammed International Airport's departure gate. Nigerians are more likely to prosper in other people's lands than in their own. I cannot think of a greater definition of national tragedy that.

It wasn't always like this. And thankfully, it doesn't have to be like this forever. All we need to do is unleash the Nigerian brilliance we see abroad . . . on Nigeria.

With my secondary education drawing to a close, I too left. I returned to Britain with enough crazy stories, experiences and post-traumatic stress disorder to fill a dozen lifetimes. Nevertheless, every time I have visited Nigeria since, I have made my way to Abeokuta – just to see if they are still 'preserving' its 'natural charm and elegance'. Alas, they are.

Today, you could not pay me to sleep in my old hostel. If it was a prison in the West, it would be shut down and the people responsible for it would be arrested. Abeokuta lacked everything, it had little to offer in the way of First World trimmings – but somehow, someway in the middle of a seriously Third World 'city', I attained a first-rate education, supreme belief in myself and full knowledge that it is better to cooperate than compete with Nigerians. Abeokuta drilled performance, confidence and excellence into me. And for that, I'll be forever grateful.

#RepresentationMatters:
The Oppressor in the Mirror

Yomi Adegoke

Being British Nigerian means constant talk of straddling two cultures, at times questioning whether you feel true ownership of either, and on other days, feeling that you are doubly proud to be who you are. Grappling with two identities borne not from an uneasy marriage, but something more akin to rape. Possessing a bilingualism of sorts, even if you don't speak your native tongue of Yoruba, or Hausa, or Igbo, or any other of the over 500 languages spoken there. Two nations, so different but inextricably linked by colonialism and another 'ism': classism. While class distinctions exist in every single country and are often no more fluid than they are in Britain, in the UK class is something that is as central to our collective identity as tea or politeness. In turn, it is widely understood as something as integral to Nigerian identity as jollof rice or loudness.

I've been thinking more about my own class identity recently, which I first truly became conscious of at university. The day I received my admission letter from Warwick to study law, I distinctly remember full-on ugly crying. They were not gurning, gurgling tears of joy, I was beside myself at the prospect of attending a university where I'd be 'the only black person'. I never had been before. I was born in

Newham Hospital in Canning Town, a stone's throw away from Grime's birthplace in Bow, a place which by the 1930s was home to London's largest Black population – Crown Street became known locally as 'Draughtboard Alley' because of its Black and white population.* It only got more diverse as time went on and when we eventually moved, it was to Croydon, the home of Dubstep† and an area that is currently 50 per cent BAME (Black, Asian and Minority Ethnic) – on course for 55.6 per cent in four years' time.‡ Perhaps it was this backdrop that made me want to attend the notoriously diverse SOAS University of London, to study Yoruba no less. But despite my dad's lifelong hopes I'd learn to speak the language, he wanted me to attend Warwick even more.

Of course, when I got there, wiped my eyes and took a long look at the student body, it was clear that I wasn't the only Black person there at all. There weren't swathes of us – I pretty much knew at least the name of any Black student that attended between 2010 and 2014, because you could easily cram us into the space of a lecture theatre and we often did, during Afro Caribbean Society (ACS) events. But we were there. I had spent so much time fretting about being the only Black in the village, it hadn't even occurred to me to worry about being the only one without money. I didn't suspect that when I arrived, the vast majority of black people I did meet, who were also from Nigeria, would have more in common with the white, wealthy, Lacrosse players who they went to private school with than me. That they would speak the same language; not Yoruba or English, but

* https://www.researchgate.net/figure/Crown-Street-Children-circa-1930-C-Mary-Evans-Picture-Library_fig1_332483961

† https://www.independent.co.uk/arts-entertainment/music/features/dubstep-straight-outta-croydon-409487.html

‡ https://www.croydon.gov.uk/sites/default/files/articles/downloads/Annual_Public_Health_Report_2017.pdf

something only the monied can understand. That my first real experiences of classism would be from fellow Black people, and Nigerians nonetheless.

My secondary school in Purley had a large catchment area, and therefore kids in attendance who had grown up on Millionaire's Row and those who had come from New Addington council estates. There were many I deemed 'posh' – they had double glazing. They had the Disney Channel and PlayStation 2s. They brought Jane Norman bags to school, which meant they could afford to shop at Jane Norman. Those were signifiers of wealth to me – people who could get trainers or games consoles when they first came out, as opposed to waiting for them to be knocked down in price by the next release. People who had their own bedrooms. No doubt, there were people who would have considered my life comparatively privileged. I wasn't the first person to go to university in my family. We had a garden and went on holidays – I'd come back to school with tales of my adventures in Nigeria and my friends would listen in awe as I described plots of land and houses with swimming pools. But when I arrived at university, the blurred distinctions between the lower-middle class and skilled working class became entirely obsolete. When I talk about the culture shock I experienced at Warwick, the assumption is that it was down to coming from a predominantly Black area to an almost entirely white institution and it was in part. But it was also coming from a predominantly poorer area to somewhere where almost everyone, including those who had names like me and looked like me, was super rich. People whose parents bought them accommodation in Coventry, Leamington Spa and on campus 'for ease'. People who would casually spend a maintenance grant's worth on clothes in a day. While white British students were primarily posh at Warwick, there were still a handful of white state kids in attendance. The same with the Black British students. The African international students however, who were mainly Nigerian, were *all* within the 1 per cent – it's why they were there.

As freshers, the Black, state-school-educated students hailing mainly from South London had a few nicknames at university. Each was steeped in differing kinds of snobbery and all were given by fellow Black students: the 'too loud, too Black Freshers', as we were dubbed by the boujie second years. The referring to Black working-class students as the 'Brap braps' – an exclamation used to imitate the sound of a gun, once upon a time made by inner-city youths as part of slang – grated most, something that would have made me flinch or fight had it been from a white person of the same social standing. The 'fake Nigerians' was another, based on the fact that we hadn't, like they had, been raised in the country we were 'from from'. Two times in my life I recall my Nigerian identity being called into question; once in secondary school, when a white boy I sat next to in Year 9 German, perhaps surprisingly became frustrated when I said I didn't consider myself to be 'really British' and was Nigerian instead. 'That's where your parents are from,' he'd retorted, agitated, a stark difference to the 'No, where are you *from* from?' questions I'd already become accustomed to batting away. The second time was not a particular instance, but a general, ongoing feeling at uni, where your claim to 'Nigerianness' correlated with how many times you had been there and for how long on each stint. On whether your grasp of one of the many languages was limited to speaking or 'understanding but not speaking'. This was perplexing to me, when all my childhood had been spent defending my culture, refusing to fake Caribbean heritage as so many of my peers did at school to avoid the teasing that came with an African background. Even when I visited on holidays, and was ribbed by cousins and aunties about my 'Oyinbo' accent, I was still regularly reminded that this was where I was 'really from'. At uni, this was challenged, but if anything, was a more tolerable form of pomposity. These students not only sneered because of our comparative lack of 'Nigerianness' but also, covertly, because they were well off.

The similarities and differences between how class manifested among rich British students and rich Nigerian ones became apparent immediately, especially to a British Nigerian. The same affinity UK employers have for plummy accents and degrees from certain establishments in Britain is the same adoration Nigerian institutions have for affected American accents and overseas schooling. In both countries, there is a fixation with the impenetrable upper classes; the only place that loves classism as much as the UK, is Nigeria. In the UK however, where there is also a level of derision and at times even shame, Nigeria's rich are celebrated for being Nigeria's rich. British culture creates a quiet embarrassment around wealth, which Nigerians celebrate with wild abandon. Nepotism in the UK is rife, but doesn't tend to be shouted from the rooftops. If it is, it is swiftly pilloried. In Nigeria, it is part of the flex; it is hard to imagine a British artist crooning 'I am the son of a rich man' – as musician Davido, son of Nigerian billionaire Adedeji Adeleke, did in his hit song 'Dami Duro'. The presence of Femi Otedola, one of the richest men in Nigeria, cannot be extricated from his daughter DJ Cuppy's success.

When I was starting out in journalism, I would be constantly shocked to realize that a white peer had parents well established in the industry – it was often concealed by the use of a mother's maiden name or a refusal to raise their parents in conversation altogether. While rich kids in any context will attempt to divorce their parentage from their subsequent wins, in Nigeria, extreme wealth, even by ill-gotten means, seems to be treated with the same deference as the divine rule of the British monarchy. Even Prince Charles' kids go to greater lengths to feign that they're 'just like us' than Nigeria's elite do. It is not that Nigerians are not critical of corruption and the wealth gap that it has caused. It is simply that culturally, even affluence attained through corruption is not only aspired to but venerated.

The chasm between the rich and the poor in Nigeria is so large that for many, they may as well be living in two different countries. In 2018, when Davido joined Nigeria's National Youth Service (NYSC), a mandatory three-week work programme for Nigerian college graduates under the age of 30 who want to become part of the country's workforce, he arrived at the camp premises in a chauffeur-driven car. Before long, he flew to Boston ahead of his sold-out concert.* Such an obvious display of double standards in the UK could not take place without permanently sullying someone's reputation. Just look at how the reaction to Rita Ora's flouting of lockdown rules to host her 30th birthday party – the only way it could have only been worse is if she was also the daughter of a Tory MP, as well as a popstar. In the same year, after the media urged more young people in Nigeria to get their Permanent Voters Card (PVC), DJ Cuppy was reportedly able to walk past people in their droves who had been queuing for hours in order to get registered†. Even if this type of unfair treatment were taking place in the UK, people would be far more coy about it. Notoriously bad Nigerian roads do not affect those in government or their children, who simply use the money that should be spent on fixing them to pay for Range Rovers or to book flights. Children of the elite don't even attend the schools in their own country; any failings of Nigerian schools that the government are responsible for are mitigated for their own children by flying them out to boarding schools internationally. They avoid the unprecedented levels of crime they contribute to due to the poverty their

---

* https://punchng.com/nysc-sanctions-davido-for-violating-service-rules/
† https://guardian.ng/life/nigerian-lady-narrates-how-dj-cuppy-jumped-the-queue-to-collect-her-pvc/

policies cause by use of their own personal security. The inequality is perhaps best illustrated by SARS (the Special Anti-Robbery Squad), a police unit that was conceived to combat armed robberies and kidnappings, which were endemic at the time of its conception in 1992. For years, the force has abused its powers by profiling and targeting young people, carrying out unlawful detentions, arrests and unwarranted searches, driving unmarked cars, not wearing uniforms, as well as violently attacking, raping, abducting and murdering civilians. SARS isn't an issue for Nigeria's elite to circumvent however, it's something that operates specifically to serve them. It was created to work exactly as it does now.

To properly understand this, you must look at the context of the Nigeria Police Force. It was created in 1861 by British colonists and established with the sole purpose of quelling any potential resistance from Nigerians to colonial administrators and to protect the interests of the British. The suppression of Nigerian citizens was and remains integral to it: even sixty years after independence, the same elitist class system the British imposed on the Nigerian people through the police remains. As the previously white occupied positions of power emptied, a new class of ruling elite were moved in, emulating the same oppressive structures as their former colonial overlords. It is unbelievable how little has changed over the years.

When Afrobeat legend and activist Fela Kuti released 'Beasts Of No Nation' in 1989, he mocked the then General Muhammadu Buhari as an 'animal in a madman's body'. He wrote the song after a twenty-month stint in prison for currency smuggling – he'd been jailed in 1984 by Buhari's government, which Kuti was vocally critical of. With Buhari as head of state once again, it is eerie how so much of what Kuti outlines nearly forty years ago stands today.

Police officers in Nigeria exist to serve and protect Nigerian elite, as opposed to performing normal police duties that safeguard your average citizen. As they brutalise and terrorize the average civilian, they are deployed as the personal guards of politicians at public events, in their homes and on the streets. They are insulated from the discord and destitution they have created through their own governance by the police. According to Oxfam, the five wealthiest Nigerians have a combined net worth of $29.9 billion and could end the poverty affecting 40 per cent of the country.* In the same way the corruption and abuses at the hands of the police are not investigated meaning-fully by the government, the many corruptions and abuses by government officials rarely lead to criminal prosecution. Instead, normal Nigerians are harassed and detained on the basis of their age, hairstyles such as dreadlocks and clothes choices such as ripped jeans that their wealthy, Westernised Nigerian peers enjoy with impunity.

Nigeria's political elite are constantly looking over their shoulder, ever fearful that the nation is on the precipice of an overdue revolu-tion, and for years have hoped cracking down on even the smallest signs of perceived rebellion against the status quo would stop any potential uprising. These fears were partly realized during the #EndSARS protests of 2020, the second wave of a movement against Nigeria's police brutality that began in 2017. As the hashtag continued to spread, so did further scrutiny of those in the upper echelons of Nigerian society; it was the first time in years I myself had thought about a dynamic that had bothered me so much when I'd seen just snippets of it at university. It became a wider resistance against those who have ruled Nigeria for decades. Deference was replaced with defiance; the palace of an oba in Lagos saw protestors dragging around his throne, swimming in his pool and looting his home.† And while

---

* https://www.oxfam.org/en/press-releases/wealth-five-richest-men-nigeria-could-end-extreme-poverty-country-yet-5-million-face

† https://www.bbc.co.uk/news/world-africa-54662986

the momentum for #EndSARS was undoubtedly felt in the UK diaspora as the movement travelled globally, one particular tweet from the onslaught sent during that October caught my attention. 'It's very awkward, because when we are talking about the corruption and nepotism of Nigeria, it implicates a lot of the kids people went to uni with and formed friendships with,'* wrote Keziah Doudy-Yepmo, the Congolese, Cameroonian and British founder of the Black Narrative platform. 'Are people ready for the reality of a non-corrupt Nigeria . . . I don't know.'

The 'people' in question undoubtedly references many of us; the British Nigerians and Black Brits who are vocal about a want for revolution in Nigeria but cautious about what it would mean in practice, refusing to engage with the fact that the buck doesn't stop on Nigerian soil alone. We are almost more complicit by only being critical of Nigerian elitism in lofty, indeterminate terms and a vague referencing of structures in order to create a level of distance. When I was at university, what also amazed me was just how many people would decry the staggering privilege of white, middle-class students and with the same mouth ingratiate themselves with those whose status could be traced back to the oppression of Nigerians even more directly. People would fawn and court invites for summer stays in sprawling mansions, joke that they bet they lived like Prince Akeem in *Coming to America*. That same reverence and deference that we begrudge in Nigeria is present, but on British soil.

In 2018, when attending the Aké Arts Festival, I visited a secondary school in Surulere to talk about my co-written book, *Slay In Your Lane*. I was trying to explain to the children, most of whom were under 12, that it focused on racism, but they told me they didn't know what racism was. And why would they? Almost everyone is

---

* https://twitter.com/nd0uri/status/1318670784760524801

Black in Nigeria – and that includes those doing the oppressing. And while that's patently obvious to Nigerians in Nigeria, it's a conversation that is lacking among the diaspora. We are so fixated on #BlackExcellence and images of the affluent 'Africa they don't show you' that increasingly, the class conversation falls behind. This is an ongoing issue in the UK. We see the lived experience of the daughter of a Nigerian senator flattened into the same bracket as a state-educated student who was on free school meals. But in a country where racism is not the main axis of oppression, Nigerian men within Nigerian context are the white men of their nation. In *Americanah*, Chimamanda Ngozi Adichie speaks eloquently of this default that we only usually hear described by white people: 'I did not think of myself as Black and I only became Black when I came to America.' This was the same for many of the Nigerian people I met at Warwick who came to England for boarding school and university and were for the first time, minoritised; it is not an experience inherent to blackness. For well-off Nigerian men, it usually was where they had their first experiences of any form of discrimination. And it goes without saying that they will face racism in the same way as any black working-class person does in Britain. But the jaw-dropping privileges go unnoticed. There is no such thing as Black privilege, granted – but how much does that matter in a nation where there isn't racism?

What is most telling is that the Nigerian elite in the UK are also straddling two worlds too, both obsessed with class but with different approaches to it. You see it in the children of the rich obscuring their fathers' professions in UK publications, and leading with it in the headlines of Nigerian ones. As commentary on various other 'isms' in the UK is finally being addressed, the complex class differences within the Black population go overlooked, presenting us as a homogenous set of individuals with the same set of circumstances, even when referring to some of those within the upper echelons of society globally. It is worth noting that the class conversation is not a cut and dried one; a working-class Black Brit is instantly of a higher class than the majority of Nigerian citizens. When I hop on a plane to Lagos, I'm transported to the 'Nigeria they don't show you', which most Nigerians don't even see themselves. But 'Britishness' has been internalised as a shorthand for privilege, meaning that while the undeniable privilege of 'returnees' and 'repats' – the children of Nigerian migrants who come 'home' in search of opportunities that may have eluded them in their place of birth – is discussed, we rarely examine the relative privileges of rich Nigerians rebranding or outright cosplaying as working-class Black Brits.

It's why Kemi Badenoch, daughter of a GP and professor of physiology, can reframe herself as a living example of the 'British Dream' merely by being 'African'. She wrote about this in a *Spectator* piece titled 'From African immigrant to Essex MP'* as if her being an African immigrant inherently means she was impoverished and qualified her as having 'started from the bottom'. She speaks of 'going without electricity' in Nigeria, which pretty much any person does when the National Environment Policy Act (NEPA) takes light.

'There are few countries in the world where you can go, in one generation, from immigrant to parliamentarian,' she writes. But does that not depend on the type of immigrant you are? Many first-generation immigrants experience a shift in their societal position due to the move; many security guards and cleaners are degree holders in their home countries. But many don't. The students I graduated with, often privately educated at Britain's best schools, had no issue getting highly paid post-uni jobs.

---

* https://www.spectator.co.uk/article/kemi-badenoch-from-african-immigrant-to-essex-mp-i-ve-lived-the-british-dream-

Discussions in Britain around whether you can be 'middle class and Black' (spoiler alert: you can) usually revolve around the ways in which it is alienating; a lack of ownership of narratives, not relating to depictions of poverty and gang life on television. Valid gripes but comparatively First World problems, even if your family has hailed from the so-called 'Third World'. What we rarely look at are the privileges and freedoms that also make up that experience. It is a conversation that is lacking, but crucial. I say this as someone who grew up in an area considered 'rough', the home of the 'chav' and the 'Croydon facelift', and am now processing becoming part of the wave of its slow, steady gentrification, having purchased my first property there. While I was raised in the area, in a similar socioeconomic situation as the majority of its residents, pretending my experiences directly mirror theirs today, simply because I'm Black, is intellectually dishonest. It should really go without saying; this is by no means an indictment on *all* upper middle-class Nigerians, but the fact it's a conversation I feel the need to caveat – when the idea of saying 'not all men' or 'not all white people' is scoffed at as superfluous and pandering – shows how difficult we find it to grapple with it. Intracommunal classism is usually only discussed in terms of white people using it to oppress other white people or minorities. In the context of the Black community, it's largely seen as an 'over there' issue, as though it's only Nigerians on the Continent that have a blind, mindless idolisation of wealth regardless of its source. But as conversations surrounding inequality continue to take precedence, we must be willing to call out the types that take place and hit closer to home, however difficult it may be.

Education as Saviour

Cheluchi Onyemelukwe

'It is a truth universally acknowledged that all men in possession of a great fortune must be in want of a wife,' my father would intone, a grin lighting up his lightly browned face, his eyes sparkling with memory. 'I remember Mr Ealing reading that out loud every class.' On another occasion, my father looking through my books, and seeing the remarks of my teacher, said to me, 'Education is what saved me.' Or more literally, 'I went to school and that was what saved me.'

My father, Obidinma Isaiah Okoli Onyemelukwe, born around the mid-Thirties, was orphaned at a young age. His uncle, Samuel Onyemelukwe, made sure he went to school, following a promise to Eze Nwaka, my grandfather, his brother, as he lay dying. He promised that he would send Okoli to school so he could read letters like the letter readers of that time. At the school in Nanka, in the present south-east of Nigeria, my father was taught to read and write. Eventually, like his cousins before him (Clement, who became the first Nigerian electrical engineer at the Electrical Corporation of Nigeria, and Jonathan, who became the Anglican Archbishop on the Niger), he passed the Common Entrance into the prestigious missionary school, Dennis Memorial Grammar School (DMGS). He was one of only a handful of boys around the area to go to school. I can imagine his mother hoping for a future as bright as the sun after a shower of rain. I can imagine her joy, her hope and longing, as she saw her son off to Onitsha for what turned out to be the last time.

For that generation, and those before him, education was the key. Education, as obtained in school and rounded off by experience, was revered. It was the game changer, a saviour. Education was the avenue to success, to working with the Civil Service, the University, the Church. Education was the avenue to visiting the countries one read about, and to respect at home and abroad. Not everyone was fortunate to get it, but especially in the south much effort was made by governments, with Awolowo proposing free education for all in the south-west.

Education was therefore not a choice in my home. As my father would say to any of us when we were not doing so well in school: 'I have very little money to give you or to leave you when I die. All I have to give you is education. That was what saved me.'

And my father tried to give us the best education he could. Starting in about 1981, I went to school roughly until the early 2000s, acquiring an education to get me through the doors of workplaces. Today, I am a lawyer with multiple degrees, an academic teaching others, and a writer. One could argue that I have been saved by education: from penury and neglect by society. Although I have my doubts, I am now doing the same with my children.

*

At my first school, Air Force Primary, a school for children of the staff of the Nigerian Air Force, but which also admitted non-staff children, we were paid slightly higher than the regular public school. We had teachers for different subjects: a music teacher in the Music

232

Room who taught us the treble clef, the Yoruba teacher who taught us to sing 'Iwe kiko, Lai si oko', which I can still sing to this day, and a smattering of Yoruba numbers and greetings that I still remember too. An Igbo teacher taught us abichidii, the alphabets in Igbo. I remember it as a wholesome, fun environment to learn.

Later, when they increased our fees from 50 to 75 Naira, my father said any regular public school would still provide good education. Then we went to Ekulu Primary School. It was eye-opening in many ways. In Ekulu, we had a more diverse demographic, children from all classes of society. I met a child in a wheelchair. I became close friends with a child who happened to be albino and whose near-sightedness, worse than mine, required her to have a special chair made for her, in which she sat in front of the class. Sometimes, I squeezed in with her. When I think of public school now, I think of Ekulu. It was considered an outstanding school and yet many – though not all – families could afford to send their children.

It is hard now to think that public schools were the best schools in the not-so-distant past. Not only was quality high, it was the leveller – what brought the rich and the poor closer together, to the middle. As the government took over schools in the Seventies, many villages and towns fought to have government schools. I recall my father and others advocating for a secondary school in Nanka, my hometown, and the leaders of the day making every effort to support the school. Essentially, education was still a purveyor of opportunities. Although it cost money, it was subsidised significantly by government, and good public schools were the hope of many communities, of the rich and the poor.

This is no longer the case. Today, there are many schools run by faith-based organisations – from nursery to university. The federal schools are still considered relatively good, but private education is now the main source of education. This follows the significant reduction of government investment in education at all levels and the decay that has seeped into the very foundations of public education. There are private schools everywhere – in villages, in cities, on every street corner, it seems. Small houses, large compounds, there appears no limit to what can be employed as a school. The quality of the education, like the buildings, is often variable, depending on location, amount of fees paid, the motivation of the founders. Founders range from faith-based organisations, private organisations to individuals. Many agree that, in general, we do not appear to have better-quality education, despite the number of schools dotting the landscape. While it may be argued that this can be attributed to the usual syndrome of 'our generation did it better', there are many pointers to truth in the assertion, including the high failure rates at national examinations and the complaints of unemployability of graduates even amidst high unemployment rates.

The fees for good private education are, as I often say, an effective contraceptive, but also a divider of rich and poor, of upper class and the rest. In the high-end schools, the fees for each child are sufficient to pay the wages of a middle-class couple in some parts of Nigeria. In the poor income neighbourhoods, they are significantly less, but still difficult for persons living in those neighbourhoods to pay. Yet the importance of funding cannot be discounted. While Ekulu was a fantastic school, the infrastructure was not as good as Air Force Primary School. There was pee on the floors and maggots in the toilets. I tried not to use them all day. There was a grand piano in a large building in the middle of the school, but it was beginning to fall apart and several of the notes did not play. We had a school library but I do not recall being encouraged to borrow books. In retrospect, our generation saw the beginning of the end of public schools. Later on, I would study how the Structural Adjustment Programme (SAP), which was championed by international develop-ment organisations like the International Monetary Fund and the

World Bank, and which forced indebted countries like Nigeria to devalue currencies and downplay healthcare and education, which were, at least part of, the reason for the degradation of public education in Nigeria.

Many children and their families worked hard to go from those government primary schools to 'federal'. Federal schools (now unity schools) were considered the ultimate in education. Established in the 1970s by the Federal Government in order to foster unity after the Biafran Civil War, there is at least one in each state. It is still a terrific idea: bringing people together in an ethnically diverse countries, from different cities and villages across Nigeria, and placing them together to learn about each other and, hopefully, see the humanity in one another, while giving them a high-quality education.

In my time, every parent wanted their child to attend federal, as we called them. Making the cut-off for federal was the goal of most students in Year 6 and some in Year 5. As far as I know, children got in on merit. I took the examination in Primary 5 and my score did not hit the cut-off mark, I was a few marks off. I ended up going to secondary school at an Anglican school, much like my father. My secondary school, the Anglican convent, was an outlier, missionary schools having been taken over by the government in the Seventies.

Several of my friends got in, however. In the years that followed, I admired the fact that they had been able to meet and make friends with people from all over the country, from other ethnic groups: Yoruba, Ijaw, Efik, Hausa and other backgrounds. A few of my friends went to secondary schools established by universities. Others went to state secondary schools. Regardless of where they went, many of them did well at the Senior Secondary School Examinations (SSCE) and got into federal universities, which were also more competitive when we went to school. Products of public education, they are paying bills and, occasionally, even changing the world. Many of them – from the Seventies, Eighties and Nineties – are around the world doing great things, making the best of life and of opportunities.

Today though, I wonder if public education benefited the poor. How many people, whose parents were not in the middle or upper classes went to federal? How many children from villages, how many of those who went to work as help in homes got the opportunities to get extra classes and private tutoring that seemed a 'must' in those days for entering into federal? Even with public education, the class divides have remained apparent. At any rate, by the time my friends and I got into the university in the Nineties, great public education was already passing into folklore. First, we had to spend over a year after leaving secondary school and taking the university entrance exams, 'JAMB' (so-called after the Joint Admissions and Matriculation Board, the administering body) because university lecturers were on strike. Academic Staff Union of Universities (ASUU), the union of university lecturers, wanted better salaries, more resources to improve on the dilapidating structures, etc. Still, it was a big deal when I passed and entered the University of Nigeria to read Law.

Although I grew up in Enugu, I had hardly been to the University of Nigeria, Enugu Campus, except once in the Eighties when I went with my mother to visit my uncle, who was a student there. I am not sure now what I expected, but it was not the untarred roads that marked the areas between the hostels, not the dusty cream walls of the buildings that had been built in the Sixties. Still, there was a faded beauty about it, and you could see, if you looked hard, what Zik* and others around him had imagined when they thought to set up this campus for Law, Medicine, Architecture and others in Enugu, with that motto now embossed on the gates into the school: 'To

---

* Dr Nnamdi Azikiwe, Nigeria's First President.

Restore the Dignity of Man'. The staff quarters lined with flowers and no fences were serene and welcoming.

I remember us sitting in the main hall, after shouts of 'Lions and Lionesses', waiting to pick a ballot to determine whether or not I would get a bed in a hostel. I remember thinking that I must be really unlucky when my best friend got a 'yes' and I picked a 'no'. Many things were scarce: seats in some classrooms, water in the taps, enough toilets and bathrooms. All of which made for room for creativity, survival skills and resilience. Gone were the days of chicken and all you could eat in the cafeteria, but the generator still came on when the power went off at night. In the Faculty of Law, we still had world-renowned law professors, and while perhaps one could quibble over the improvements that could be made in pedagogy, I and many who went to school in my day felt able to hold our own anywhere in the world. We had such confidence and our lecturers imbued in us the thought that, even in the Abacha era, we could take on the world and win.

I spent five years there and left as the 2000s came in, amidst the Y2K furore, having never used a computer, but with a law degree. My degree has been the avenue to other things: scholarships, graduate degrees in Canada and several employment opportunities. Although I have had to learn many more things through the years, I have often felt that I had a solid foundation to explore the world. As my father told me on the day he took me to UNEC, as we walked on the red earth of Enugu and between buildings, where the dignity of men was to be restored, 'Now that you are here, as people used to say in the past, "You have increased your asking price."'

Out of these universities, there are now young people doing great things in the world, developing apps, still winning scholarships into the best universities in the world, and bringing their energies and passions to different endeavours. But it is not in doubt that the infrastructure is just as bad as it was in my day, and that the overall quality, particularly in the public schools, could stand significant improvement. Today, many suggest increasing the fees at public universities to fund them properly, with governments stepping away from the business of funding education and maintaining only regulatory oversight. These are interesting propositions, but I can't help wondering where that would leave people at the lower end of the income scale.

*

Some of the foundational schools – nursery, primary and secondary – choose their curriculums based on what will attract subscribers. So, in Lagos, particularly in the middle- to upper-class areas, but increasingly in other locations, many schools claim to provide only British curriculum education. These come with the testing requirements of the national curriculum of England, a celebration of the Queen's birthday and visits from English dignitaries. Others provide Canadian, others Dutch curriculums. Increasingly, many state that they provide an 'integrated curriculum', including both British and Nigerian curriculums, perhaps not to lose out. Many teach English history, Spanish, French, German. Only few teach Yoruba or Igbo.

It is eerily reminiscent of my father's days at school, back in the Fifties. My father, like others before him, and others after, was taught extensively in the English language, and his learning was steeped in English literature and British history. However, certainly more than today, he still had access to knowledge of the native customs, still spoke his language outside school, even if 'vernacular' was banned in school. (This is not to suggest that the traditional cultures were necessarily pristine and free from challenge. Many females, even in my father's time, did not attend school and many of those who did, were married early. The girl who beat my brilliant father in primary school, was married off early and never got a university education.) Education, as obtained through schooling as brought by the British, was also the means for entrenching colonialism. So some of that education needed much supplementation. The political part of education, was therefore not derived in school, but was rounded off by the activism of Zik and Awolowo, the fight for independence, the rebellion of Patrice Lumumba. Like Chinua Achebe and Chukwuemeka Ike, my father would go on to change names from his baptismal name of Isaiah to Obidinma, partly in solidarity with his Igbo roots. F. C. Ogbalu and others started to insist on the teaching of Igbo language in schools and wrote books to make this possible. These all became part of a much more rounded education. But, formal education was still a must, a saviour.

In the Eighties and Nineties, we struggled with these issues too. School turned us into a blend of Engli-Igbo children, learning English at school, singing English nursery rhymes – baa, baa, black sheep, have you any wool? But we also sang our Igbo nursery rhymes – nwa nnunnu nwa nnunnu nta, turu za nza turu nza. We were still steeped somewhat in Igbo culture at home. We learnt basic English grammar, wrote composition and learnt some Nigerian history. We were taught that Mungo Park discovered the River Niger. But we also learnt a song at my after-school lessons, where we sang about the lone, forlorn, white man who had lost his father and his mother, and who had nothing to eat and could not find his way home. Could this not be Mungo Park, somewhere near the River Niger, being pitied by the Onitsha people? How could he discover the River Niger when people already lived there, my 8-year-old self queried. I was too shy to ask my teachers and only discovered that I was right much later in life.

But we have gone back, it appears, to my father's time. Except, of course, that we have much less access to our cultures, and even our languages are fading away. Oh, and they play Davido and Burna Boy on Fun Days now. I often wonder what our founding fathers and mothers would make of this self-imposed re-colonisation, feeding off the ever-growing gap between the rich and the poor, the vanishing of a national identity and the neglect of the State.

The blame is, to be fair, a collective one.

Despite my own background and strong belief in public education, I teach law at a faith-based university, in part because on my return after graduate studies in Canada, it was almost impossible to get a position in a public university in my city. But even now, with the instability in the public system, I cannot fathom teaching there. My children all go to private schools in large part because there is no public school where I live in Lagos, but also because on my return from Canada, I needed a school that resembled, somewhat at least, the schools they went to there, especially in terms of infrastructure. Like many parents, I am looking for the best for my children, not often wholly certain what 'best' is, but sure of what it is not. Their schools are all right, with the basic infrastructure and learning. Inclusion is better perhaps than in my day, with my children learning side by side with their friends who live with disabilities. But I realize that so much of what I took for granted in the schools of my child-hood, in my public education – my Yoruba teacher, my Igbo classes, my History classes, my oga playing at break time, the vernacular that we all spoke in hiding, the friendships across all demographics – is lacking now. Many of us are making individual choices, easier choices, not based on principle, but based on survival and getting ahead.

Our governments carry on without much thought to us or to our children. For a time, Nigerian history was taken off the curriculum. There is little evidence that education is a priority. During the Covid-19 pandemic, as the government shut down all schools, the higher-end private schools set up schooling online and carried on. The public universities were on strike. I taught my private university students online while I read the frustrations of young friends on social media, venting at being unable to go to school, much like I did 25 years ago while I waited for the resolution of the never-abating issues between government and the university lecturers' union.

*

Today, I look around my sitting room, which to my dear husband's dismay, has been turned into an office and a classroom and a TV room and a reading room all at once. My children are in their classes, one in a secondary school which was physically not even one kilometre away, but which he hasn't been in for almost a year. The other is also online at his primary school, and the other is attending an American middle school online. All being saved. As I had been. As my father had been – by education.

I read to them from *Things Fall Apart*, 'That boy calls you father. Do not bear a hand in his death.' Perhaps they will remember this as I remember my father reciting those first lines of *Pride and Prejudice*, learning a love for literature that is, in itself, an education.

Recent news around the world about education in Nigeria, however, is about kidnapping. 'Twenty-seven boys have been kidnapped from a school in Niger State, Nigeria,' a broadcaster stated not long ago. He mentioned that this incident followed another only a few weeks before, when more than 100 children were kidnapped. He also mentioned that Nigeria has the highest number of out-of-school children in the world. Images of the school – a public school – appeared on social media. Later that evening, my friend, based in the US, wrote that no one would keep a dog in the rundown buildings which housed the children. I could sense the heartbreak in those words because I felt it too, that we, our governments, did not care enough to repair schools, to make them accessible to everyone. And, even as criminal as that was, despite all that had happened in the past, including the kidnapping of boys in December 2020 from their hostels, there were no efforts to protect children in other schools in the North.

There is more recent news about girls who have been kidnapped in Katsina, a state in the north of Nigeria. It comes after only a few weeks of the kidnapping of the boys. Another has occurred in Kaduna, where the governor insists that he will not negotiate with kidnappers, even if that means that the kidnapped young persons are lost to their parents forever. I watch as the BBC, CNN and Al Jazeera news present this news, as they describe the frequent recurrence of these events, and give those figures of out-of-school children.

I listen as a mother says that she is pulling her children out from other schools to stay home with her. I reflect now on what parents did without thinking, back in the Eighties: sending children across Nigeria to a boarding school, many kilometres away from home. Education is no longer a saviour for many in Nigeria, it seems.

Renewal

Sefi Atta

We arrive at the Consulate General of Nigeria in Atlanta, my husband Gboyega, my daughter Temi and I. It is 9.30 a.m. on Tuesday, 13 October 2020, and we have a morning appointment for our passport renewals without a specified time. I am thankful the weather is warm – enough for me to wear a linen dress and denim jacket. A crowd is already gathered outside the black wrought-iron gates, and we may have to wait a while before they are opened. Notices inform us that the gates are automated and the premises are protected by 24-hour video surveillance; others warn that photography and firearms are prohibited.

The Consulate is a red-brick, one-storey building, with what appear to be fixed windows. On our side of the gates is a similar, but taller building, which has a sign in its front yard, indicating that it has been sold to new owners and is ready for lease. A group of gardeners remove shrubbery behind this building as Gboyega parks our Toyota Highlander nearby. Ours is among several other vehicles with out-of-state number plates, some from places as far away as Texas.

Yesterday evening, Gboyega and I drove in from Meridian and Temi flew in from Chicago. We met her at Hartsfield-Jackson Atlanta International Airport and went to a hotel in Dunwoody. Temi, a management consultant, has been working online because of the

Covid-19 pandemic. She will come back to Mississippi with us and stay until the holidays are over – or until we begin to annoy her.

Earlier this morning, we found out, via an online Nigerian newspaper, that J. P. Clark had died. 'Uncle J. P.', as I called him, was a friend of my late father's and I came to know him after I introduced myself to him at the 2009 Garden City Literary Festival in Port Harcourt.

I have taken to introspection, as I do when Nigeria loses a great writer of that generation. I remember laughing and crying during a conversation we had about my father at the Lagos Motor Boat Club, and visiting him at his Lekki flat overlooking Five Cowries Creek. Gboyega was with us on the latter occasion and we drank wine, listened to opera and took turns to read out loud a poem Uncle J. P. had written. It was a change from the get-togethers my husband and I usually had, with his medical colleagues and their wives.

J. P. Clark was a poet, playwright and professor emeritus of literature. His intellect was intimidating and his memory extraordinary. In his mid-eighties, he could easily recall dates and times of events that I, in my late fifties, would have trouble stating accurately. He once told me about how he accompanied my father to a traditional poetry festival in my father's hometown of Okene, even though he couldn't understand the language, Igbirra. With similar precision, he shared a personal account of the military coups of January and July 1966, which preceded the Nigerian Civil War, adding that he was part of a delegation that met with the President of Ghana to discuss the growing unrest in Nigeria. Before he could clarify which coup he was referring to, and which president he had met with – Nkrumah or Ankrah – he got sidetracked when I asked why Nigerian writers of his era were constantly engaged in political activity. 'Because,' he replied, 'we cared about our country.'

The SARS protests in Nigeria have also been on my mind. Yesterday, on Columbus Day, we learned that they have spread further still. In

Lagos, scores of people gathered around the tollgate between Victoria Island and Lekki, chanting and raising placards and flags. As a Lekki resident, I have passed through this tollgate numerous times on my way home, and between the possibility of government reprisals and Covid-19 infections, I worry about the demonstrators, most of whom are millennials.

Last night, after we checked into adjoining hotel rooms, I went about disinfecting handles, switches and table surfaces with Wet Ones wipes. Later, as we ate Jamaican takeout, I asked Temi if she would take part in the protests if we were in Lagos and she said, 'Yes,' without hesitation. I said, 'You know I would be pissed off with you,' and she said, 'I know.'

In her senior year at college, she was chair of an organisation for minority students that facilitated interculturalism and promoted social justice. When she got the job in management consulting, I told her she could no longer change the system because she was now part of it.

We disagree on what constitutes activism. She is not idealistic about social and political movements, and recognizes when activism is self-serving or performative, but she thinks I ought to relax my definition of it. However, she did grow up in the United States and is accustomed to seeing activists on public-speaking tours and on the covers of glamour magazines. I was raised in Nigeria, at a time when African activists were more likely to be featured in underground newspapers. They didn't enjoy fame or fortune; they suffered infamy and financial hardship. Back then, protests were called riots, even when they were peaceful, and parents warned their college kids not to get involved in them because of the risk of being gunned down by the police. The story of a student who got killed by a stray bullet after stepping out of her hall of residence during a campus protest to see what the commotion was about was an urban legend. 'Stay in your dormitory,' parents would plead.

When I was 12 years old, Teboho 'Tsietsi' Mashinini, the South African student revolutionary, visited my secondary school, Queen's College, Lagos, to talk to us about the Soweto Uprising of 1976. He was 19 and living in exile. Twelve years later, I was at the 1988 anti-apartheid rally in Hyde Park, London, singing, 'Free Nelson Mandela,' and in 1990, while I was working as a trainee accountant in England, Mandela was released from prison. It took almost half a century to end apartheid.

This year, as some of my fellow African writers follow the internet blueprint towards branding themselves as global social justice warriors, others on our continent still face consequences for their grassroots advocacy. On 31 July 2020, my colleague Tsitsi Dangarembga, recently shortlisted for the Booker Prize, was detained in Harare, Zimbabwe, after participating in a protest against the government. We stay in touch by email. She is out on bail, but is charged with attending a meeting with intent to incite public violence, breach of the peace and acts of bigotry, as well as contravening Covid-19 regulations.

Temi is a Ransome-Kuti, and some of her blood relations played key roles in Nigeria's struggle for democracy – her great-grandmother, Funmilayo, and her great-uncles, Fela and Beko. These days they are celebrated, but when they stood up to Nigeria's military rulers, they were arrested and imprisoned by the government, and endured beatings and other assaults by the army and police. I believe that if change is truly transformative, it is bound to impact those who champion it as if they have charged into brick walls, especially in a country like Nigeria, where a powerful minority have a vested interest in ensuring that change doesn't occur. This is why I'm worried about the SARS protesters and why I would – well, *have* – strong reservations about Temi joining them.

I have never attended an organised rally in Nigeria. I once tried to organise a public speak-out in Lagos. It was supposed to take place during the Christmas holidays of 2019, but I ended up being blocked by the management of the venue, which was funded by the state government. One of them joked that I was an agent provocateur. I finally gave up on the idea and instead wrote an open letter criticising the federal government for suppressing free speech, failing to improve the economy and other issues I felt compelled to address. The letter, 'From All Sides', was published in January 2020 and the only backlash I received was from an old friend who called to berate me for putting myself and my family in harm's way.

I must admit that I'm not given to expressing my opinions in this manner. I would much rather, for instance, examine Nigeria's wealth gap, power imbalances and other national character flaws in fiction and plays. I have done so from the beginning of my writing life, and have sometimes questioned whether it is worth making an effort to research and chronicle periods in Nigeria's history that bring such issues to light. The SARS protests assure me that my works are in keeping with the concerns of Nigerians, and make me more committed to documenting incidents in which I'm confronted with the condition of being Nigerian. I have described this elsewhere as necessary optimism, but it is a constant search for agency, seldom collective, and primarily by individuals acting on behalf of themselves and their families, against the odds.

*

Temi decides to wait in the car as Gboyega and I join a haphazard line outside the gates of the Consulate. We both wear KN95 masks. Gboyega, an internist, has been tending to Covid-19 patients at the main and satellite community clinics he manages, and the nursing homes he covers, so we have to be careful. A couple of FedEx vans come and go. The gardeners are now attempting to uproot a plant using rope tied to their truck and they seem to be succeeding.

A masked man walks out of the Consulate gates and asks those of us who are standing in line to observe social distancing rules; otherwise, the police are liable to show up and shut the place down. I don't believe him and I'm further annoyed by a maskless man behind me who is on his cellphone and shouting in Yoruba. Two women, who were seated in a Jeep, alight with masks on and join their daughters, who are in the line and also wearing masks. The women carry on a conversation in Igbo. With or without masks, we all form a gapped queue, which is so long it stretches from the Consulate gates to a back fence that delineates the plot we're on from the one behind.

I befriend a couple of people ahead of me – a man with a white polyester mask who drove in from Texas, and a woman with a patterned mask who lives locally. The man tells Gboyega and me that he has three appointment forms for his passport renewal and Gboyega tells him we have two. The woman, like us, had an appointment on Columbus Day until someone in the Nigerian Consulate realized it was an American public holiday and called her to say her appointment had been moved to the next day. She is applying for an emergency travel certificate so she can attend her father-in-law's funeral in Nigeria. She complains about his church asking her husband to make a contribution towards the purchase of an electricity generator.

'I hate that country,' she concludes, and we all laugh.

A young guy with a mask and blue baseball cap emerges from the Consulate gates. He starts calling out names of applicants in a dodgy American accent. He's definitely not Nigerian, and I guess from the way he pronounces his Rs that he is from a francophone African country. His tone is arrogant – scornful, almost.

'Someone thinks he's important,' I mutter.

The Texas man shrugs. 'Let him.' He says he has a double dose of patience and will prostrate himself before Baseball Guy, if he has to.

The local woman begins to sing Wole Soyinka's 'I Love My Country'. Surprised, I join in and so does Texas Man as Gboyega falls silent.

I am a citizen of America and Nigeria. My American passport allows me to travel abroad with ease, though I've remained in the United States since I flew back from Lagos at the beginning of the year. It also attaches me to ideals that America is yet to realize for the descendants of Africans who were brought here against their will. I write about this in my forthcoming novel, *The Bad Immigrant*, and if there was ever any doubt as to the gravity of the situation, the police killings that gave rise to the Black Lives Matter marches have exposed just how far America needs to go.

My Nigerian passport guarantees my entry to Nigeria alone, but it connects me to my history, culture, family and primary audience. When I am there, I don't have to explain to anyone who I am or where I am from. I am considering this when Baseball Guy announces that if applicants don't have a certain form, they will not be seen to.

He holds up the form and Gboyega turns to me and says, 'That doesn't look like the one we have.'

He retrieves ours from a yellow A4 envelope under his arm and walks up to Baseball Guy, who appears dismissive during their brief exchange, which I'm unable to catch.

Gboyega comes back and says, 'We're okay.'

'Are you sure?' I ask.

He says he is, but he doesn't appear to be.

I am wondering how a doctor who is as self-assured as Gboyega is during medical emergencies can be this tentative queuing outside the Nigerian Consulate when he gets a call notifying him that a nurse at his clinic has tested positive for Covid-19. I say I'm sorry to hear the news and head back to our car to check on Temi.

All the windows of the car are rolled up and Temi is inside, lounging in the back and swiping her iPhone. She is off work today.

I open the passenger-seat door and say, 'It's hot in here, baby.'

She continues her task with a 'hm'.

I leave the door open, but within minutes get so sweaty I have to step out of the car, not without asking Temi to roll down the windows behind.

'I don't need to,' she says.

I panic. 'You can die, you know.'

'Mom,' she says, 'only kids die that way.'

'Adults, too,' I insist. 'If their blood pressure drops and they pass out.'

I have a memory bank of dubious medical facts I've read or heard, which her father often disputes.

She says she's not that dumb and I return to him and report her.

'Hun,' I begin, 'hear what your daughter is telling me . . .'

'Sef,' he says, when I finish, 'she's 26.'

I can accept that the risk of getting heatstroke and contracting Covid-19 are different, but I get petty whenever they side with each other. He was the one who told me I should avoid going grocery shopping during peak hours because people in Meridian used their masks incorrectly, and she was the one who said, 'Mom, you can't be travelling all over the globe at a time like this,' because I said I wished I could go off to the Bahamas.

Texas Man is still ahead of us. The local woman was apparently called into the Consulate in my absence. She comes out fairly soon and I ask her, 'Did you get it?'

She says 'Yes,' with a smile.

We exchange waves and I turn to Texas Man and ask, 'When are they going to call us, eh?'

He, too, smiles, but with a shrug.

Gboyega says the process can't be that bad if the woman was attended to that quickly. I tell him his standards are low. Texas Man says his wife would agree with me. She hasn't bothered to renew her passport in fifteen years.

They get into a discussion about the process we will go through inside the Consulate, the details of which don't interest me, so I again head back to the car to check on Temi.

When I get there, I tell her I'm fed up of standing around, which is true, but I say that so she won't think I'm being overprotective. I sit in the passenger seat and roll down the front windows and open both doors. This time, I wait with her until 11 a.m., when Gboyega rings me.

'They've called us,' he says.

Temi and I reach the gates as he is passing our papers through the fence. I notice a cut on his forefinger, which has bled on his shirt. I dig into my handbag and bring out my travel pack of Wet Ones wipes and a mini bottle of Purell hand sanitiser. The Wet Ones are hypoallergenic with a Tropical Splash scent – they were all I could find. The Purell is clear, as opposed to the aloe vera kind that's tinted green. They both kill 99.99 per cent of germs. He goes for the Purell.

With the gates now open, we are walking through them when he unknowingly drops a form on the ground. Temi picks it up as Baseball Guy, on the other side, tells him our forms are incomplete.

I turn to Temi instinctively. 'Maybe you should give that to Dad.'

'Hey, Dad,' she says. 'Are you missing this?'

Gboyega realizes he is and hands the form to Baseball Guy. Temi, meanwhile, has forgotten her KN95 mask in the car and hurries back to the parking lot. We wait for her to return and that is when I observe that Texas Man is no longer around.

The main room in the Consulate has green carpeting and tape markings for social distancing purposes. Its windows are indeed fixed.

There are photos of Nigeria's past and present leaders on a wall, next to a framed print of Nigeria's coat of arms, with the red eagle on top, the two white horses on either side of a black shield and underneath, our national motto: 'Unity and faith, peace and progress'.

We sit in chairs appropriately spaced. In front of us is a large screen which runs adverts featuring Burna Boy, Teni the Entertainer and trailers for Nollywood movies. The trailers grab my attention because I've been working on a Netflix adaptation of my novel *Swallow* with Kunle Afolayan, a Nigerian film director.

A tall man comes out of one of the small rooms. He is the same man who processed our passports five years ago. I recognize him under his mask because he is still just as rude.

'Move up, move up,' he orders, motioning us as a teacher would naughty schoolkids who stay behind in class. Then he demands, 'Where are your forms? Where are your forms?'

He strides around collecting them and practically snatches mine after taking Gboyega's, and I wonder if this is because my expression always reveals what I'm thinking.

He summons Gboyega first and they go into his room. Gboyega comes out about five minutes later and I look at him expectantly. He is stone-faced, which is a good sign. He can ignore bad behaviour so long as he gets what he wants. Before he heads outside, he stops at a shelf, on top of which is a tub of sanitiser designated for public use. He pumps it several times and rubs his hands together.

Temi is next, and she comes out shaking her head to warn me. She inherited her father's ability to disregard rudeness if needs be, and knows I lack it. She, too, disinfects her hands and leaves.

I follow the man, who proceeds at a swift pace. In his room, he sits behind a desk, which is cluttered with files, a computer and related equipment. I sit across from him as he prepares to take a digital photo of me. For a second, I feel sorry for him because whatever happened to diminish his humanity to the extent that he is hostile to strangers must have been terrible. Then I feel sorry for myself, because I might remember him every time I look at my passport photo. I narrow my eyes and thin my lips as he raises an ID camera and clicks.

At the fingerprinting stage, I immediately notice the machine is unclean and regret not listening to the details of the process. There are greasy fingerprints on the screen and nothing to sanitise my hands with. I want to tell the man that this makes no sense, after the effort I've made to wear a mask and observe the Consulate's social distancing guidelines, but I fear my new and old passports may go missing. I am debating whether to clean the screen with a sheet of Wet Ones when he tells me to make sure my fingers are firmly pressed.

I do as he instructs, one hand after the other, as I imagine Gboyega, Temi and other applicants have done all morning, without resisting. I even thank him afterwards. Yet, on my way out, I walk past the sanitiser for public use and opt for my Purell.

You Are Not Going Back

Abi Daré

Two decades ago my life changed with those five words.

The words were my mother's response to my query about my return flight to Nigeria after a four-week summer holiday in England.

'You are not going back,' she repeated, sitting on top of an over-stuffed suitcase and trying in vain to yank the zip closed. Sensing my despair in my shocked silence, she glanced at me with a mildly triumphant smile, 'This is your home now. You are going to study law! Here in England!'

I did not want to 'study law here in England', at least not at that precise moment. I wanted to go back. London had emptied of its tourists and the weather had turned, become colder. The wind blew with a ferocious wrath, a blast of cold breath that ached my thirty-degree-heat-weathered bones and screamed: *Go back to Lagos!*

I missed Lagos. The sporadic electricity: this constant and stable supply was not the kind of luxury I was used to. I missed screaming 'Up NEPA'* in jubilation, as the light flickered on after long nights without electricity; our generator was only reserved for daytime and dependent on fuel availability. I was not used to the silence on the streets of London; where was the chaos that was the asphalt on the streets of Lagos? Where were

* NEPA – National Electric Power Authority.

255

the tight woven threads of vehicles that clogged the streets so that the lanes were barely visible as each driver deftly manoeuvred between a snake of cars and okadas, armed with curses and maniacal horning? I couldn't understand how the drivers in the red double-decker buses in London drove with such calmness and serenity, the doors hissing open as it dutifully, and consistently, stopped at every stop. It was in stark contrast to the black and yellow danfo and molue buses that swarmed the third mainland bridge in Lagos, a metallic contraption with the door barely held in place by the strong arms of a drunk or crazy-looking conductor.

I missed the rain pummelling windowpanes and zinc roofs with a sound that lulled my tired body to sleep after a long day. I missed eating Ghana High jollof rice at the buka, going to parties on Saturdays, but most of all, I missed life as a student, living on campus at the University of Lagos, where, just a few months earlier, I had started to study French.

The year before, my application to study law at the same university was rejected and instead, my offer letter arrived with the words 'BA French' printed in tiny font at the top right. I was distraught, not because I had particularly strong feelings about studying law, but because I felt as though I had failed my mother.

Like many Nigerians in my generation, my brother and I were lavished with lofty academic expectations: I was to be a lawyer and my brother an accountant. Law, like Accounting, Engineering and Medicine, were deemed to be choice courses by Nigerian parents. This offer to study French felt an apology, a badly applied bandage on a sore, festering wound. A trio of influence, power and connections have a major role to play in the advancement of the average Nigerian, but for certain 'choice' courses in top academic establishments, stiff competition for a limited number of spaces means that thousands of students, despite influence or economic power are offered alternatives.

I was discouraged. I had zero interest in studying *any* language, but I dragged myself out of bed each morning and lumbered to class because I was wired to be resilient, to never give up. This desire to succeed, in spite of circumstances, is deeply ingrained, woven into the fabric of every Nigerian's DNA. I attended a primary school where we were ranked from first to last on our termly report cards, and I strived hard to attain and retain a top position. In secondary school, high-performing students were collectively put into an A class, and then the next in line in B class and so on. This was not without its drawbacks; it encouraged an intensely competitive nature and a disregard for students in the lowest-performing class.

Academic pursuits, once complete, are often put on a pedestal. I have seen some email signatures (of Nigerians) read like a mini-CV, complete with noteworthy lines of achievement typed in bold, italicised font. Call it self-aggrandisement, the Nigerian would tell you it is 'packaging'. Qualifications, titles, achievements, statuses – achieved or imagined – are 'packaged' and used as a weapon to club doors open.

It is not unusual to be chastised for not addressing people with the right title, and sometimes, the very ambitious and proud to show it would insist on being addressed by a combination of titles: Chief-Engineer-Dr-Mrs Thomas, or something along those lines. My friend Tinuke was introduced as 'Baby-Lawyer Tinuke' by her father, shortly after she was offered a place to study law at university.

While at university in Lagos, I shared a room in the Halls of Residence with six women by day and twenty-three women by night (the women who turned up at night had mastered the art of disappearing before dawn and so I never met them). A semester or two after my course, I decided it might make sense to rent a flat outside the university grounds. I had discussed this with my mother before we left for England that summer. My mother, her head bent over a thick, padded exercise book, had agreed with my proposal without looking up. She had been furiously transcribing notes from a board meeting she'd recorded earlier that day.

I asked her again because I needed to be certain that she had heard me correctly. I was barely 18 years old and I was proposing to live outside of university grounds with three other girls whose parents she had never met.

My mother paused her cassette tape recorder, a trusty Sony she'd been using for years, and looked me in the eye. 'Yes, I heard you the first time. You can rent a flat, buy a car, do whatever. Just write me a list and we'll sort it out after our summer holidays.'

Four weeks later, those five words punctured my dreams. I stared at her with tears burning the inside of my eyelids, my heart curling with pain at the optimism in her eyes. She wanted much more than Nigeria could offer me, and because she knew I would refuse if she'd gently presented the idea before leaving Lagos, decided to 'surprise' me with the news. It couldn't have come at a worse time. I had tasted the sweetness of freedom and was on the cusp of new beginnings. My life was pulsing with the possibilities of a future as a multilingual jet-setting human (even though I still could not grasp simple basics of the language after nearly a year studying it), and I had imagined myself cruising around campus, showing off in my red Toyota Corolla.

Afterwards, there were many moments of excruciating desperation to return home, of unflinching resolution to remain while struggling to fit in, to succeed. It has now been over two decades since those five words were uttered, and I have learnt to love, learn and take ownership of my dual national identities.

*

Explaining what it means to be Nigerian often feels like a private but difficult thing to do, an innate, instinctive knowledge reserved for Nigerians alone. I sometimes imagine the country as a toddler who was given this burden, this gift of extreme wealth and opportunities and who, without understanding the gravity and potential in such a gift, invited a bunch of insane teenagers to help manage it. There are times I want to curl up in frustration and scream into a void at the political leadership shepherding the nation, a vicious circle of clueless and corrupt leaders who are running a joke of a political relay race around a track constructed on the rotten foundations of selfishness, nepotism and tribalism while we, the citizens, continue to cheer on each leader with hope and expectations that would never manifest. As our voices grow raspy from screaming, the standard of living for the average Nigerian continues to plummet.

There are moments I wonder if our drive to remain optimistic, to succeed in spite of deprivation and adversity is an inherent response to years of shattered expectations and broken promises swathed around a denial of our rights.

We are a resiliently happy bunch, we deeply value and celebrate relationships and family, and one way of showing this is by regularly throwing garish, colourful and for the few who can afford to, opulent parties. Our weddings, funerals and birthdays are an experience. My wedding, a considerably humble affair, had over 500 guests. My mother and her friends arrived from Lagos, their suitcases filled with beautiful aso-ebi (a Yoruba word for the matching fabric worn by friends and family to identify with, or to support each other); burgundy patterned Ankara dresses for the ladies, gold embroidered aso-oke caps for the men. During the wedding reception, a woman, slim and forlorn-looking, was leaning on a mop stick, staring at the wedding display, clearly baffled. She was watching us, watching the elegantly constructed geles on the heads of the women – my mother's had a giant banana-leaf-like shape to hers, the tip curling gracefully towards her forehead – as they danced into the hall, the stones in their lace materials blinking under the spotlights of the Essex town hall that was probably more used to quiet council meetings and yoga classes than a boisterous Nigerian wedding.

At times, her eyes would flick to the gently warming chafing dishes filled with spicy jollof rice, pounded yam and efo, beef and chicken stew, Nigerian salad (a merging of an obscene amount of baked beans, corned beef, sliced boiled eggs, diced tomatoes, kidney beans, sweetcorn, sliced spring onions, peppers and carrots on a bedding of lettuce and cooked pasta, buried beneath an avalanche of Maggi-seasoned Heinz Salad Cream).

It wasn't until my mother's friends started to distribute souvenirs: burgundy and gold hardcover notebooks, mine and my husband's grinning faces printed on vinyl stickers on the cover with the words, *Congratulations to the latest couple from the Bride's mother & friends*, that the woman at the reception gave her first and only reaction. She shook her head slowly, as though she was both deeply sorry for and irritated by what she'd witnessed. How to explain to this woman that personalised souvenirs, a staple of Nigerian parties, are a thank-you gift of some sort? That our love for parties is part of the fabric that weaves us together, along with pride and an uncanny ability to find humour in everything? I recently read that a Nigerian grandmother named her grandson Degree because her daughter had left home for her education and returned home pregnant. Since a university degree was what her parents expected, and their daughter brought home a baby, they simply named him Degree.

Our pride and relentless optimism remain a national characteristic we all share in the face of our disparate ethnicities and religions. A Nigerian would relish the opportunity to criticise Nigeria with little restraint, but will be first to condemn outsiders of doing the same.

A few years ago, while standing in the queue at the Nigerian High Commission in London, a man in front of me, dressed in black corduroy trousers, was yelling at the security guard manning the entrance. 'I came all the way from Manchester,' he screamed, sweat dripping from his brows on that cold winter morning. 'And you are telling me I cannot enter? I booked my appointment online!' He waved his phone in the air. 'I will record you! I will put you people on the YouTube of the internet. Yes! The whole world will see what a mess this place is. God will judge you!'

Later, in the waiting room, I sat clutching my ticket in my hand, waiting to be called to submit my passport for renewal. The man was now sitting beside me, still clearly irritated. We all were, but his was characterized by a particularly loud and aggressive chewing of his fingernails and tapping of his feet. I ignored him. I was tired, hungry and desperate to get back to work.

'I swear,' the man said, slapping his green passport against the empty seat of a plastic chair, 'if my mother wasn't sick, I wouldn't have come to renew my passport. I would have burnt it.' I had heard variations of similar statements in the past. Frustrated Nigerians swear to *de-Nigerianise* themselves on a daily basis. I had been there, had felt the frustration rattle every bone in my body every time I had to renew my passport. The lengthy delays, the rude staff, the cramped-out basement waiting room filled with equally frustrated applicants, some with screaming babies or upset toddlers, the area filled with sweat-infused moist air. It was all too familiar.

'My children will never have a Nigerian passport,' he uncrossed his legs, slapped his feet on the floor. 'In fact, they will never have anything to do with Nigeria.'

'Fair point, sir,' I said, turning to him, 'but you cannot make a sour fruit sweet by yanking the tree that bore it out of its roots.'

He stared at me for a moment before he gently put his passport down and began to passionately explain the pains and pleasures of being Nigerian to me. Somewhere in the middle of his speech, somebody else, from somewhere at the back of the room, interjected:

'Gentleman, with all due respect, Babangida is not the root cause of our predicament.' He had that crisp voice of an overeducated Nigerian man who was eager to show off his ability to speak 'big English'. 'The problem, distinguished ladies and gentlemen,' he said, 'lies in the fundamental fallacy that is colonisation. It ravaged us. Ransacked us! Pillaged us! The nation is nothing but a hollow coconut shell, ladies and gentlemen, the kind irresponsible touts pass around on parched land in the name of playing professional football.'

I had opened a can of worms by publicly reacting to the frustration voiced by another Nigerian, knowing that the fastest way to unite a group of Nigerians in conversation is to spark a discussion about the state of affairs of the nation.

'If Babangida had not stolen billions from the nation's coffers, we would not be here,' someone else added. I did not turn to look, but he sounded elderly, tired, his voice stretched thin by the pressures of life or by illness or both.

'Nigeria *is* a very useless country,' another man added. He sounded distinctly non-Nigerian. A tourist or businessman waiting for a visa?

'Terribly useless,' he said again, his *terribly useless* sounding like *terri-bry use-ress.*

Silence.

I turned around.

He had rich, dark skin that shone under the bright fluorescent bulb and exceptionally bright and large eyeballs that gave him a startled look. He was holding a thick book, his palm pressed into the middle as a bookmark. He nodded at me, at the woman sitting beside him, who was patting a hiccupping infant on her back, at the man from Manchester, who was now rolling up a newspaper and slapping his thigh with it.

The non-Nigerian smiled again, nodded again, as if to ask, *Isn't it? Isn't it a useless country? Weren't you all just discussing how bad things are?*

No one smiled back. The man beside me was glaring at the non-Nigerian, his fingers twitching. It was as though he wanted to pounce on something.

'If the country is useless,' the woman with the hiccupping child said slowly, her gaze travelling all over the non-Nigerian as though searching for the best spot to detonate her bomb, 'Why are you here to collect our visa – *ehn?* Is it not because you want to come and do business in our country that you are here? Go to your own country now, since our own is so useless. See his mouth like useless,' she hissed, patted her baby's back. 'With your frog eyes like this fluorescent bulb on half-current. Nonsense!'

The man appeared to want to respond, but instead turned to his book and began to read. I imagined that he was wondering where he went wrong.

'What it is yeah, is basically yeah,' a young man from behind me added, his words faltering as he struggled to unravel the false British accent from the rope his thick Yoruba accent had tied it with. 'Our problem yeah,' he said, 'is the *bree-ish*, who basically took over us yeah, messed us up like so bad, and basically like, left us with these clueless leaders. You get me?'

We had put the meddling non-Nigerian in his place and were ready to move on with our banter. That the guy with the quasi-British accent was sounding this way was not surprising. Many Nigerians are inclined to put on a concoction of accents, a transatlantic blend of British/American/(insert the ethnic tribe of the individual) accent garnished with an elaborate elongation of *R*s, a twisting and lifting and dipping of vowels and consonants. My mother's cousin, a wonderful woman who had never travelled abroad, surprised me when, on my first visit back to Nigeria after many years, asked me in that strange accent that was not her usual Ibadan accent, how *Londin* (London) was, and if I brought back some *brees-kreets* (biscuits). Sometimes I wonder if this sorcery of accents – we call it 'speaking-*phoneh*' (for phonetics) – is a cloak of pretension sewn with threads of colonialism. I have heard it in movies, on the radio, from the mouth of an overly excited Uber driver as he ferried me away from the airport on arrival from England.

As I exited the High Commission that day, I left with two things: laughter in my mouth – someone had cracked a joke about the *phoneh*-speaking individual, which had elicited collective laughter, and the solemn realization that the cord that ties us is thick and tight and reserved for us only.

*

Nigerians wade through affliction, bad governance and corruption and emerge on the other side, fuelled by humour and resilience. Even though the other side is another long, uncertain road, filled with the same corruption, affliction and bad governance, we keep going. But resilience, hard work and eternal optimism cannot make up for unity and a house divided against itself cannot stand. There is a considerable amount of distrust between the over-250 ethnic groups and diverse religions. As a result, the majority of Nigerians see things from their perspective (tribal or otherwise) rather than from a collective point of view. People have been killed, denied marriage, refused job opportunities for belonging to another tribe or religion. The Nigerian society is steeped in patriarchy and women's voices are often the last to be heard, if heard at all. There is a great deal of class division as the widening gap between the poor and the rich continues to expand. We are hurting each other and causing pain to each other by allowing this to continue.

I think back to that day at the Nigerian High Commission, and as I recall the shared desire and fervent burning in our eyes and in our voices as we argued for the possibility of a better Nigeria, I am filled with hope that a new and urgent generation of Nigerians is emerging. An impassioned group of people who have been set on fire by the determinate and incessant demand for change. A people who will not be silenced.

And as the wind of change blows, the tide is beginning to turn. In it, I see a future where the patriarchy pyramid is dismantled, where accountability is demanded and given by those in leadership positions, where there is equitable distribution of wealth, and where our voices are not allowed to be silenced by threats of citizen arrest and violence. I look forward to constant and stable electricity, to swift justice for perpetrators of crime and corruption, to affordable education for all.

This wind, fuelled by the power of social media, is quickly becoming a tornado. It is whipping up a storm and sweeping across the nation, and bringing along with it, the possibility of a revived and reconstructed Nigeria, one which a mother, full of the promise of a bright future, can someday tell her child with confidence: '*This is home now. You are not going back.*'

About the Authors

Nels Abbey is a British Nigerian (Itsekiri) writer, satirist and media executive based in London. He is the author of *Think Like a White Man* (Canongate, 2018), a satirical self-help book on being Black in corporate spaces. He is the co-founder of The Black Writers' Guild. He is also a former banker.

Ayọ̀bámi Adébáyọ̀ is the author of *Stay with Me* which won the 9mobile Prize for Literature and Prix Le Afriques. It was shortlisted for the Baileys Women's Prize for Fiction and the Wellcome Book Prize. Her new novel, *A Spell of Good Things*, will be published by Canongate and Knopf in 2022.

Yomi Adegoke is a multi-award winning journalist who is a columnist at *British Vogue*, the *i* paper, and the *Guardian*. She is also co-author of the bestselling book *Slay In Your Lane: The Black Girl Bible*, co-editor of the *Loud Black Girls* anthology and working on her first fiction novel.

Chimamanda Ngozi Adichie is an author whose works include *Purple Hibiscus, Americanah, We Should All Be Feminists, The Thing Around Your Neck* and *Half of a Yellow Sun*. She has won the Women's

Prize 'Winner of Winners', National Books Critics' Circle Award and Orange Prize. She divides her time between Nigeria and the United States.

Oyinkan Akande is a Nigerian-born writer currently living in London. She frequently writes on topics to do with art, design, pop culture and identity. Working as a copywriter at Christie's, she also contributes on a freelance basis to several different publications, including *Wallpaper**, *Elephant Magazine*, *gal-dem* and *Roundtable Journal*.

Ike Anya: Public health physician, Co-founder: Abuja Literary Society, TEDxEuston, Nigeria Health Watch; EpiAfric, TED Global Fellow. Advisory Council, Caine. Co-editor Weaverbird Collection of New Nigerian Fiction. Granta (*People Don't Get Depressed in Nigeria*) & Catapult (*Poison*). Recently completed memoir on becoming a doctor. Working on stories of grandparents & stories from life in public health.

Born in Lagos, Nigeria, in 1964, **Sefi Atta** is an award-winning Nigerian American novelist, short-story writer, playwright and screen-writer. She is the author of *Everything Good Will Come, Swallow, News from Home, A Bit of Difference, The Bead Collector, Sefi Atta: Selected Plays, Drama Queen* and forthcoming *The Bad Immigrant*.

A writer of books, scripts, culture pieces and retorts, a lover of love and self-coined 'romcomoisseur', **Bolu Babalola** writes stories of dynamic women with distinct voices who love and are loved auda-ciously, stories that centre hope, joy and human connection.

J K Chukwu is a writer and visual artist from the Midwest. Her debut novel, *The Unfortunates*, will be published in Spring 2022 by

Houghton Mifflin Harcourt (US) and The Borough Press (UK). She was a 2019 Lambda Fellow, and her work has appeared in *Black Warrior Review*, *DIAGRAM*, *TAYO*, and elsewhere.

Abi Daré is the author of *The Girl with the Louding Voice*, a *New York Times* bestseller which was shortlisted for the Desmond Elliot Prize and the British Book Awards for debut of the year. She grew up in Lagos, Nigeria and now lives in Essex, UK with her family.

Born in Nigeria, **Inua Ellams** is an award-winning poet, playwright & curator. Identity, Displacement & Destiny are reoccurring themes in his work in which he mixes the old with the new, traditional with the contemporary. His books are published by Flipped Eye, Akashic, Nine Arches, Penned In The Margins, Oberon & Methuen.

Chịkọdịlị Emelụmadụ was born in Nottinghamshire and raised in Nigeria. Her work has been shortlisted for the Shirley Jackson Awards, the Caine Prize for African Literature and won a Nommo award. Her debut novel *Dazzling*, which won the inaugural Curtis Brown First Novel Prize in 2019, will be published by Wildfire in 2023.

Caleb Femi is a writer and filmmaker born in Kano and raised in South London. From 2016 to 2018, he served as the Young People's Laureate for London. His debut poetry collection, *POOR*, was published in November 2020.

Helon Habila is the author of *Oil on Water*, *Measuring Time*, *Waiting for an Angel*, and *The Chibok Girls*. He is professor of creative writing at George Mason University and lives in Virginia with his wife and three children.

Abubakar Adam Ibrahim is the author of *Season of Crimson Blossoms* (Nigerian Prize for Literature winner) and two story collections, *The Whispering Tree* (shortlisted for the Caine Prize for African Writing and Etisalat Prize for Literature), and *Dreams and Assorted Nightmares*. He is a recipient of the BBC African Performance Prize.

Anietie Isong has worked as a writer for many brands in the UK and Nigeria. His first novel, *Radio Sunrise*, won the McKitterick Prize. His collection, *Someone Like Me*, won Kennesaw State University's Headlight Review Chapbook Prize for Prose Fiction. His second novel, *News at Noon* is forthcoming from Jacaranda Books in 2022.

Okey Ndibe's books include the novels *Arrows of Rain* and *Foreign Gods, Inc*, and a memoir, *Never Look an American in the Eye*. After a remarkable career as a journalist in Nigeria, he relocated to the US to edit an international magazine co-founded by novelist Chinua Achebe.

Chigozie Obioma is a writer and associate professor of Creative Writing. His novels, *The Fishermen* (2015) and *An Orchestra of Minorities* (2019) which were shortlisted for the Booker Prize and have won awards including the NAACP Image Award, have been translated into more than 30 languages. He divides his time between the US and Nigeria.

Irenosen Okojie is a Nigerian British author whose experimental works and vivid narratives play with form and language. Her debut novel *Butterfly Fish* and story collections *Speak Gigantular* and *Nudibranch* have won and been shortlisted for multiple awards. A fellow of the RSL, in 2020 she won the AKO Caine Prize for her story, *Grace Jones*.

Cheluchi Onyemelukwe is a lawyer, academic and writer. She works extensively on health, gender and other social policy. Her novel, *The Son of the House*, variously called' intimate,' 'powerful,' and 'masterful storytelling' won the Best International Fiction Book Prize, at the Sharjah International Book Festival and the SprinNG Women Author's Prize.

Lola Shoneyin has written three books of poems and three children's books. Her debut novel, *The Secret Lives of Baba Segi's Wives* was nominated for the Orange Prize for Fiction and won the PEN Oakland 2011 Josephine Miles Literary Award. Shoneyin is the director of Ake Arts and Book Festival, and publisher at Ouida Books, Nigeria.

Umar Turaki is a writer and filmmaker from Jos, Nigeria. His debut novel, *Such A Beautiful Thing to Behold*, is forthcoming from Little A and Farafina in 2022.

Chika Unigwe was born in Enugu, Nigeria. She was educated at UNN and KUL (Belgium) and earned her PhD from Leiden University, Holland. Widely translated, she has won awards for her writing. Her books include *On Black Sisters Street* and *Better Never than Late*. She teaches at Georgia College, Milledgeville.

Hafsa Zayyan is half-Nigerian, half-Pakistani and was born and raised (mostly) in the UK. She is a dispute resolution lawyer working in the City of London, and is also the author of *We Are All Birds of Uganda*, the winner of #MerkyBooks' inaugural New Writer's Prize.

Acknowledgements

Of This Our Country would never have existed without the incredible work and talent of the writers within it. Thank you so much for sharing your experiences, time, and words with us and with readers. Making yourselves vulnerable to so many in such a public way is no mean feat, and each of your contributions is invaluable.

It takes a village (and them some) to create a book, and this was no different, so thank you to those who have worked behind the scenes, in both big and small ways, to make it a reality: Laura Amos, Alice Gomer, Ben Wright, Mary Thompson, Robyn Watts, Charles Light, Suzie Dooré, Margot Gray, Fionnuala Barrett, Charlotte Brown, Ammara Isa, Bengono Bessala Nyada De Besbeck, Sabah Khan, Georgina Ugen, Melissa Okusanya, Hannah Stamp, Claire Ward, Kate Elton, Kim Young, Roger Cazalet, Abbie Salter, Sarah Munro, Caroline Bovey, Gemma Rayner, Isabel Coburn, Katrina Troy, Lydia Logan, Jane Donovan, Mayada Ibrahim, Sade Omeje, Alexis Adimora, Uche Ume, Abimbola Agbaje-Williams and Grace Shutti.

Specific thank yous are due to Jeannelle Brew, Ann Bissell, Holly Macdonald, Diana Ejaita and Lola Shoneyin. This book and campaign could not have been as outstanding as it is without each of you.

Lola, thank you to you and your incredible team for partnering with us on this very special project. To make this book available in the very place it is about is a dream come true, as has been working with you, and we're so proud to have been able to do so.

Diana, thank you for a cover that is beyond beautiful. It was an easy decision to work with you, and the best decision to work with you too. Thank you for creating something memorable, bespoke and absolutely perfect – your work has captured in its entirety the essence of this book and we could not be prouder to have been able to work with someone as talented as you.

Holly, thank you first and foremost for being *so* easy and *enjoyable* to work with. Thank you for the perfect layout, the research, genuine passion and time you've put into this project. A particular thank you for listening to our every concern and helping us to put together a package that we cannot imagine looking any other way. Your support on this project will never be forgotten and is hugely appreciated.

Ann, Queen of Publicity! Thank you for loving this project from the get-go, for your ideas, enthusiasm and belief that there's no limit to what this book, and we as a team can achieve. Having you on our team has been one of highlights of this project, and to have your golden touch on the publicity campaign has been a gift. Thank you for your patience, your time, your positivity and your brilliance. We couldn't have done it without you.

Jeannelle 'this is my passion project' Brew. This book would not have been the same without your blue-sky thinking that you turned into reality. Your genuine love for this book and its purpose has been clear in everything you've done, and it has been such a joy and a privilege to work with you. Your innovation and dedication to this project has helped to make it as brilliant and beautiful as it is, and readers who might never have picked it up owe their knowledge of it to you. Thank you.

Finally, thank you to those who have tweeted, instagrammed, texted a friend or relative, or done anything at all to spread the word about *Of This Our Country*. Our collective knowledge of what Nigeria looks like to Nigerians has grown because of people like you.